The First Colonists

The First Colonists

Documents on the Planting of the First English Settlements in North America
1584–1590

Edited with an Introduction by
David B. Quinn
and
Alison M. Quinn

Raleigh
North Carolina Department of Cultural Resources
Division of Archives and History
1982
Publication of this volume was made possible by funds provided by
America's Four Hundredth Anniversary Committee

Foreword

In 1948 the State Department of Archives and History published a pamphlet entitled *Explorations, Descriptions, and Attempted Settlements of Carolina, 1584–1590*. Editor David Leroy Corbitt selected material taken from *The Third and Last Volume of the Voyages, Navigations, Traffiques, and Discoveries of the English Nation . . .*, collected by Richard Hakluyt and printed in London in 1600. Additional material was incorporated into a revised and enlarged edition in 1953. That publication has been out of print for several years.

With the approach of the quadricentennial of the 1584 adventure, it seemed appropriate to issue a revised edition of *Explorations*. Because much of the documentary material included in the Archives and History publication had later been published in David B. and Alison M. Quinn's *Virginia Voyages from Hakluyt*, issued by the Oxford University Press in 1973, it seemed logical to approach that press and seek an arrangement for publication of a paperback edition of the book. The Oxford press graciously transferred rights for such an edition to the Division of Archives and History, North Carolina Department of Cultural Resources, and agreed to a new preface by the Quinns and a change in title for the North Carolina publication. Appreciation is hereby expressed to the press and to Dr. and Mrs. Quinn for making possible *The First Colonists: Documents on the Planting of the First English Settlements in North America, 1584–1590*.

Gratitude is also due America's Four Hundredth Anniversary Committee for its subsidy for printing. Without this financial aid *The First Colonists* could not have been published this year.

The member of the Historical Publications Section's staff who ably saw the book through the press was Dr. Jeffrey J. Crow, historical publications editor and head of the General Publications Branch. It was he who located a printer with type to match that used by the Oxford University Press for the original edition of the book, who worked with the Quinns, and who expedited the project in ways too many to enumerate.

Memory F. Mitchell

February, 1982   *Historical Publications Administrator*

Preface

The Roanoke Voyages and Colonies in Perspective

I

The Roanoke voyages and colonizing experiments of the years 1584 to 1590 were the first to bring English men, women, and children to settle in any part of North America. Although these attempts failed, they lie at the very roots of English experience in North America and the beginnings of what was to become the thirteen colonies and the United States. For this reason they have attracted and will continue to attract much more attention from both historians and ordinary people than the small number of individuals actually involved in the ventures might seem to justify. But there is another reason too. We are extremely fortunate to have so much firsthand evidence about these colonizing attempts, both in the narratives that Richard Hakluyt collected and in the drawings of John White.[1] These sources allow us to follow the colonists' progress, put ourselves into the minds and actions of those who took part, see what they saw, and yet have to fill many gaps with our imaginations where documents fail us. The exact way of life that the settlers of the first colony of 1585–1586 followed and even precisely where they lived offer us many problems that have yet to be solved. The mystery of the Lost Colony, the band of family groups that disappeared in 1587 and were never seen again by any white man so far as we can tell, has led to many conjectures and will continue to do so. The figures of the first English family to be constituted on American soil, Ananias and Elynor Dare and their daughter Virginia, stand out as elements in an American myth that has clung to them since the early days when colonial Americans began to look back on their own past.

This popular appeal is important. It means that the Roanoke colonists symbolize a beginning, a brave, tragic, mysterious beginning that rises out of the mists before the concrete, specific history of the Chesapeake and the New England colonies can be grasped and understood. But this mythical aspect of the colonies ought not to be exaggerated or overemphasized. It can grip the imagination, but it should not lead thoughtful people of our own day into a sentimental attachment to largely mythical concepts about the first colonists. Those hardy folk who came in the years between 1585 and 1587 were men (mainly) and women who had difficult, pioneering tasks to perform, and the serious study of the colonies must begin with what those labors were and how successfully the colonists accomplished them. We must use all the evidence we have to make this story as sharp and clear as possible, and where we have to use our historical imagination to fill in the inevitable gaps, we must control and direct our speculations to fit, as best we can, the positive evidence at our disposal.

II

Earlier writers of North Carolina and colonial American history have tended to put the peoples who inhabited the areas first touched by the settlers into the background as if they were part of the landscape. We must now bring them into the foreground with all the skills with which the archaeologist and ethnologist can supply us.[2] The Indians were the occupiers and owners of the land into which the English intruded. They had a highly developed society going far back in time and developing over long periods before the European discovery of America. The inroads that they had made into the wilderness that was America enabled the Europeans to follow in their tracks, to learn their ways of growing crops, which were new to the settlers, to discover new ways of catching fish and game, and above all to confront new concepts of belief and of the relationship between man and his environment. Their languages too were very different from anything existing in Europe, and the knowledge and concepts conveyed in them were hard to learn and difficult to understand. It was consequently easy to establish short-term relationships based on the mutual curiosity of two such different culture groups and the natural desire to learn by the exchange of gifts and by the admiration conveyed in simple, nonlinguistic terms. But long-term contacts, the continued occupation of parts of the Indians' land by English people—even though they had been accepted—inevitably brought tensions, while the assumption by the settlers that they could go anywhere and pass from tribe to tribe whether friendly or not imposed strains on accustomed patterns of life and thought.

Each society expected too much from the other. The English anticipated at first that the Native Americans could go on producing food—corn, fish, and game—throughout the year for their support without any deep understanding of the fragile and cyclical nature of the native economy. From the Indians' perspective a glut of copper, of glittering ornaments, even the much more important iron tools and weapons did not in the long run compensate for the demands of the strangers for continuous supplies of food. The first colony on Roanoke Island was to find that, whatever its attempts to remain on reasonably good terms with the native people, these deteriorated almost inevitably in face of the demands that the settlers made; and hostility, the use of force on both sides, soured a relationship between the settlers and many, though not all, of the peoples among whom they had come to dwell. Thus, in June, 1586, when Sir Francis Drake removed the settlers who had arrived with such optimistic hopes the previous July, much of the mutual goodwill and cooperation between the two peoples had been used up, and it was time for the settlers to leave as most of them wished to do.

The colonists of 1587 arrived under very different premises. They desired to make their own life near Indian friends but as far as possible to be self-supporting in their family units and not to impose themselves economically on their Indian hosts. Their leader John White had friends both on the island of Croatoan and also in the area well to the north near the southern shores of Chesapeake Bay. The attitudes of the peoples who lived in the near vicinity of Roanoke Island, however, were potentially hostile rather than friendly, and so another resting place had to be found. The majority of the settlers found their new homeland to the north in southern Virginia, alongside or mingled with the Chesapeake tribe, but it is likely that they did so with the loss of a number of their young, single men who went south to Croatoan and from there to an unknown and probably unknowable destination, for reasons, to be discussed below, partly recorded and partly guessed.

III

The travels of John White and Thomas Harriot, made between July, 1585, and June, 1586, provide us with the first and most important view of North America before European occupation took place. These two men must have been almost constantly on the move, recording Indian individuals, places, and practices, drawing and annotating birds, fish, and animals, and gradually surveying the area on the ground. Along with Joachim Ganz, the mineral expert, they searched for metals and minerals, bringing back specimens to be tested at the colony. Their initial sketches and notes must have been closely coordinated and afterward copied out and put into coherent form. They began their survey of the resources of the area, human and material, during Sir Richard Grenville's reconnaissance of Pamlico Sound in July, 1585, and it is probable that from that occasion we derive two of White's revealing and sympathetic paintings, those of the villages of Secotan and Pomeioc, together with a number of individual figure studies of local personalities in both settlements. The careful and immensely detailed record of these villages, their setting, their buildings, their ceremonial structures (the ring of posts in the Secotan picture, for example), their crops growing in garden fields, and the pleasant, lively, detailed figures of individuals are something quite new in European observation of the peoples of America.

The main body of White's surviving drawings of people and of their social and economic activity derives from his residence on Roanoke Island, and from them we learn to know women and children, men such as Wingina (Pemisapan), the "conjuror" or shaman, the old man in his winter garment, and others. We see the Indians spearfishing and net fishing in the sounds, and we have a striking picture of their elaborate fish weir. We watch them eating, listening to tales told by a shaman around the fire; we can follow in part the intricate dance pattern of the green-corn festival. We do not see Indians as savages but as recognizable and knowable human beings.

As Harriot and White moved about the sounds and the Outer Banks, they slowly mapped the area, making for the first time a detailed cartographical survey of the coastland between the Neuse River and the James River and inland to the head of Albemarle Sound and beyond. Perhaps even more significant their completed map provides our only evidence that they were among those who spent the winter with the Chesapeake Indians. They located the principal village, Skicóak, well inland from where the waterfront of Norfolk now lies and another, Chesepiuc, not far from Lynnhaven Bay; they also outlined clearly Cape Henry as a guide into Chesapeake Bay. All the time they moved about they asked questions. Harriot had mastered spoken Algonquian, and so they inquired about the natural habitat of crops, plants, birds, fish, turtles, and animals. White drew them, from life if possible, or else from freshly caught specimens. Names by which the native people called them were recorded. A body of information in notes and pictures grew over the eleven months of their stay. It included data on building materials and on the chances of obtaining minerals and metals. Much of it was lost when papers fell into the water as they were leaving with Drake. Much remained in Harriot's possession that has not survived, though he was able to preserve the basic elements of it in *A briefe and true report of the new found land of Virginia*, published in 1588 as the first English book wholly about North America.[3]

In that short book Harriot gave us some insights into the discontents of the soldiers and gentlemen in the colony. Their profession of arms—with the additional prospect of hunting for gold—alone attracted them. Only a handful of men besides Harriot and White played an active part in observing and planning what should come next. Harriot too examined the inner life and beliefs of the native people. He was interested in their animistic concepts and practices, but he was something of a missionary too, expounding the Bible to them in their own language. The Indians thought that the power of the Englishmen's religion lay in the book itself. Additionally, he recorded that mysterious epidemics marked the travel of himself and his companions through Indian villages and thus informed us of one of the earliest of the dire results of European contact—epidemic diseases that were soon to decimate aboriginal populations.

Harriot believed Indians to be skilled, intelligent, and teachable. Europeans indeed learned from them, and they learned from Europeans. Manteo was an example. His stay in England from September, 1584, to April, 1585, had begun to familiarize him with Englishmen in their own strangely complex society. He insisted on going back to

England in 1586 and returned to Roanoke Island in August, 1587, where White appointed him the queen's deputy in Roanoke Island and Croatoan and baptized him a Christian. His investiture, in the eyes of the English, nominally gave him supreme authority over Indian matters in the area. We cannot tell how he exercised this charge. Wanchese, the other visitor to England in 1584–1585, reacted against English mastery, returned to the body of his own people, and may well have contributed to the increasingly strained relations between Wingina's people and the colonists. To fervent revivalists of Native American culture Wanchese is the hero; Manteo the one who sold out to the foreign invaders' ways. But to most historians Manteo will remain the more interesting personality, the Native American who assimilated European culture and yet returned to take up a position of leadership among his own people.

Harriot's objective account of Indian life and White's even more sympathetic depictions of it make the later unhappy relations of Lane and the Indians seem even sadder than they were to be. But the Indians in the notebooks and portfolios were almost overshadowed by the mass of data collected on the natural history of the region. Moreover, Harriot's tract was to circulate in four languages throughout Europe along with engraved pictures of his Indians (somewhat Europeanized) for the next century or more.[4] The Roanoke Island area, with its inhabitants and produce, was the best-known part of North America long before its permanent occupation began in the 1650s.

There are many facets of the first colony that can engage our interest and attention. Perhaps the least fruitful is that it was partly designed for purposes that were not directly concerned with colonization. The 1585–1586 colony was to act as an English military outpost in the maritime and colonial struggle with Spain, which was entering an acute stage, and as a maritime supply base for the ships plundering Spanish vessels in the Caribbean and along the Gulf Stream, which was the homeward route of the great annual fleets and to which the Carolina Outer Banks were conveniently near. Consequently, most of the members of the colony were soldiers—many of them gentlemen—and its governor, Ralph Lane, was an experienced military man and an expert in planning fortifications. The colonists' job was to look out for, prepare for, and repel Spanish invaders. The Spanish were no empty threat, since from late in 1585 their vessels were indeed searching for the English base. In the Englishmen's view Indians were there to provide food as needed; if they refused or ambushed settlers or resisted, they would be repressed as a matter of course, not with any deep-seated hostility but as a recurrent nuisance that must be kept in check. In June, 1586, Lane sought out Wingina as the leading impediment to his settlers and killed him, but his men did not attempt to destroy the tribe as they could easily have done at that particular moment. Inaction, for soldiers and particularly for the gentlemen, was sterile; civilian pursuits were beneath them, and so they formed a restless element in the colony over the winter and through the spring to early summer.

IV

The turbulent seas of the Outer Banks also exacted a price from the first colonists. Philip Amadas and Arthur Barlowe, whom Walter Ralegh, upon receiving a royal patent, dispatched in 1584 to find a suitable site for settlement, had quite unaccountably failed to provide indications of the depths of the sounds into which at least one of Ralegh's two small vessels could apparently penetrate. The 1585 expedition expected a harbor and did not find it. Having sounded their way round Cape Fear, Sir Richard Grenville's ships passed out of the eastward flowing current into a calm sea, but the first attempt to bring a large vessel into a promising inlet (at Ocracoke) brought about the grounding of the *Tiger* and a new caution about the waters off the Banks. Off Port Ferdinando or Hatarask (near present Oregon Inlet), however, a pinnace could enter, a landing stage could be built, and vessels could ride well off the Banks as in a roadstead with gentle winds and a slow countercurrent. From July to September this condition prevailed. The larger vessels (all except a pinnace) returned home with news that though (disappointingly) a deepwater harbor was not to be had, fairly good anchorage could be found not too far from land. It was not until June, 1586, when Drake's large fleet was there that the roadstead proved a deathtrap; a northeaster struck and wrecked many ships and damaged others.

Thereafter, for those who planned in England, the anchorage off the Banks and with it Roanoke Island were considered an unsafe base from which to plunder Spanish ships or territories. The new objective, Chesapeake Bay, discovered by the colonists, was in their minds from then on. But chance prevented it from being used until another twenty years had passed. The landing of Grenville's men on the Banks in 1586 (after Drake had gone home with the Lane colony) was done in ignorance of the experience of the storm Drake had met. The landing of White's new colony in 1587 was intended as a mere call on the way to Chesapeake Bay, but it became (through the greed and malice of the sailors) the first home of the new colonists. When White came back at last in 1590 to find them gone, autumnal storms wrecked a ship's boat and drowned its crew, while the roadstead was too rough for the ships to await a long boat haul down the sound to see which of the colonists (if any) were still with Manteo at Croatoan. There proved no way by which White could get the seamen to winter in the western Atlantic. The colonists remained lost, with the uncertain shoals, the waters and winds outside, on, and inside the Banks contributing their toll to the colony's disappearance.

V

When White left Roanoke Island so reluctantly in August, 1587, he said that the colony was about to move "50 miles into the maine,"[5] and yet he clearly expected even as late as August, 1590, a whole three years later, that someone would be there on Roanoke Island to receive him. This paradox has puzzled many commentators and can be resolved in only one way. The main body of the colonists, all family groups, children, and most of the single men must undoubtedly have gone north to the area where White had wintered with the Chesapeake Indians in 1585–1586. We are obliged to assume that a party of single men, with the pinnace, after it had been used several times to transport the colonists to the head of Currituck Inlet, then penetrating perhaps much farther north than now, settled on Roanoke Island to await White. They took down the flimsy cottages of 1585 that had been briefly renovated by the larger group, dismantled the remains within the old fort perimeter, and nearby (the site never found) built themselves a stout palisade enclosure inside which they constructed temporary dwellings for themselves. They were standing guard over White's personal possessions as well as some cannon and bars of iron too heavy to go with the main body.

White did not come in the spring or summer of 1588, but in July, 1588, a Spanish ship put into Port Ferdinando and men came ashore on the Banks to find the slipway and the barrels placed in the sand to catch water.[6] They saw no Englishmen, but we can be almost certain that the English were aware of the Spanish visit. The small group would feel threatened: the Spanish having found traces of them would come back. Consequently, we can envisage a hurried evacuation of Roanoke Island, the burying of White's baggage, the abandonment of the heavy goods, and the inscribing of "Croatoan" on a tree to indicate their destination. The absence of any crosses with the inscription showed they were not in distress when they left. That they came to and were welcomed at one of Manteo's villages on Croatoan near modern Cape Hatteras we can have little doubt. But after the first winter what would they do? Certainly in 1589 they would go, or some of them, to camp inside their enclosure to await White, but when he had not come what then? Would or could Manteo maintain them? Should they not go to Chesapeake Bay to join the rest? We cannot even guess what they would have done or did. Perhaps some had already found women with whom they wished to stay on Croatoan. Perhaps some tried to go north and lost their pinnace in a gale and were shipwrecked somewhere on the sounds. Possibly some met Negroes, whites, or South American Indians, shipwrecked remnants from Drake's storm, and joined them.[7] Most likely a majority died in some way, and a few were incorporated into the Croatoan tribe. But, if not, did some find a means of establishing themselves on the mainland and, reinforced by later outcasts, become the ancestors of the Lumbee? From the evidence that remains that seems very unlikely to have happened.

VI

The documents that Hakluyt preserved for us and that are printed below are complete in themselves and are well known to all students of North Carolina and early American history. A brief attempt only can be made here to summarize information that has come to hand to supplement what Hakluyt provided.

Spanish reports on the 1584 voyage make it clear that a call was made at Chesapeake Bay and that there the Indians showed some hostility to the English.[8] If they were Indians of Powhatan's tribal group, this is not surprising. The ship is likely to have been that commanded by Philip Amadas, which arrived home later than that of Barlowe.

After Barlowe's return we learn much about the plans of 1584–1585 for developing the resources of North America by English colonies from Hakluyt's unpublished *Discourse of Western Planting* ("a particuler discourse").[9] We know also that the knighting of Ralegh, the naming of Virginia, and the authorizing of Ralegh's seal as lord and governor of Virginia were all the help, apart from the charter of a ship and a gift of gunpowder, that Queen Elizabeth would give toward the foundation of a colony.[10] If we know more detail about the 1585 preparations,[11] we also learn that the colonizing objectives of the expedition became known to the Spanish when the ships were in the Caribbean, which explains why, as early as December, 1585, a Spanish ship attempted without success to locate the colony.[12] Correspondence tells us something about the founding of the colony, but we learn little fresh about the events there.[13] The restoration of the earthworks at Fort Raleigh and the recovery of some of the possessions of the colonists tell us something, but far from enough, of their life there from July, 1585, to June, 1586.[14] The reconstruction itself is a masterpiece. We now find too a major reason for Drake's visit to the colony, after destroying Saint Augustine, was that he had learned of Spanish preparations to search out the colonists and annihilate them.[15] His first hope was to reinforce them with materials and with released slaves and others taken from the Spanish, but the colonists wished to come home after exploring Chesapeake Bay, which a party had visited and enjoyed in the winter of 1585–1586. The storm that scattered some of Drake's ships and wrecked others forced him to take the colonists home, but did he leave Negroes, South American Indians, or even some shipwrecked men behind to become the first Lost Colonists? We cannot tell. Grenville's leaving of a handful of men to hold Roanoke Island later in 1586 is better known from a Spanish source, but their ultimate fate is unknown.[16]

We are still uncertain how the 1587 colonial project was begun and financed. Clearly, Thomas Harriot and John White had very different ideas from the soldiers and gentlemen about the viability of the country, especially the area near Chesapeake Bay, to support an English colony. The humble artist, John White, had learned from experience and from association with his intellectual partner, Thomas Harriot, to assert himself. Clearly, again, he and his friends from among the minor City of London guilds (like his own, the Painter Stainers, and that of his son-in-law Ananias Dare, the Tilers) provided the core of the expedition. Others came from rural Essex. How many educated men from middle-class backgrounds joined the farmers and craftsmen we still cannot tell.[17] Nor can we say what bound them together, unless it was the promise of 500 acres of land (uncleared land, though they could not know it) contained evidently in the document that incorporated the city of Ralegh in Virginia under the terms of Ralegh's trust. Ralegh himself was to take no direct part in this plantation. His obtaining of grants of arms for the city, John White, and the Assistants (i.e., counselors to the colony's governor) was evidently an attempt to give them status.[18] They must have sold their own possessions to finance their venture, but we can still only assume that it was Ralegh's merchant friends, William Sanderson and Thomas Smith among them, who found some additional capital for them to complete their equipment for the voyage. The fact that there were only eighteen women in the party left behind in America explains the stress the settlers placed on the essential need for White's return with more colonists as well as with further stores.

The threat from the Spanish was a real one. The 1588 expedition had called at Hatarask Inlet in the summer about the time White would have arrived if his pinnaces had succeeded in crossing the Atlantic. At the time White made his unavailing attempt to reestablish contact with the colonists in 1590 further major plans were being made for a Spanish colony on Chesapeake Bay after the English had been dealt with. The Spanish continued to believe the English were still established on Chesapeake Bay a decade later and again proposed to establish themselves there. They appear to have been right, if for the wrong reasons.[19]

The plan by the 1587 colonists to plant a living English community of men, women, and children, concentrating on subsistence farming rather than on exploitation of resources for export, and living in harmony with Indian neighbors, was potentially a fruitful one. Only mischance prevented it from being developed and perhaps being made the basis for a more humane and limited type of colonization than was later attempted on the Chesapeake and on the Carolina sounds. But if the Lost Colonists, cut off from England, continued to live and even prosper for nearly twenty years, as William Strachey in 1610–1611 believed that they had, then they were the first enduring colony of English people on North American soil.[20]

On his forced return to England to obtain supplies for the colonists, White evidently convinced Ralegh and Grenville that the colonists would settle on or near Chesapeake Bay. The decision to prepare a large expedition in 1588 to take advantage of the deepwater harbor at Chesapeake Bay for further attacks on Spanish ships and bases was thus governed by the belief that the colonists would be there. The incorporation of this expedition in March, 1588, into the force assembled to resist the Spanish Armada forced White to struggle bravely but ineffectively in the pinnaces *Brave* and *Roe* to bring out more colonists and some stores. After he returned, robbed and wounded, he was compelled to remain in England. By 1589 the company of supporters and merchants that had been formed to back up the colony failed to get a ship to sea, and we hear no more of a naval expedition. White obtained passage on a privateer, the *Hopewell*, which was to call at Roanoke Island on its way home. What he does not tell us is that William Sanderson's ship, *Moonlight*, which joined him in the Caribbean, was stored with equipment for the colonists.[21] But there was no one on Roanoke Island in 1590. The party that had awaited White's coming in 1588 was presumed to be still on Croatoan Island. Misfortunes to the crew of the *Moonlight* and unwillingness on the part of *Hopewell*'s men to stay over the winter led to White's sad return to England, leaving the fate of the colonists, the smaller party and the larger settlement alike, besides the Chesapeake tribe farther north, to remain a mystery.

Ralegh, until the Spanish War should end and the seas be reopened to peaceful traffic, was unwilling to make any further moves to aid the colonists, since the assumption that the Lost Colonists still survived allowed him to retain his rights under his 1584 grant. Ironically, it appears that some indication of the survival of the Lost Colonists may have been brought to England by Indians captured from the Chesapeake late in 1603, but by this time Ralegh had been accused of treason and had lost his rights to American land.[22] By the time Christopher Newport was established at Jamestown in 1607, the surviving members of the colony had been killed by Powhatan. All attempts to find traces of any members of the smaller group or of survivors of the massacre were to fail; indeed all certain traces of Lost Colonists had disappeared, and none has yet been found.

As we remember and honor the Lost Colonists, we should not forget that it was the work of John White in drawing Indian scenes on the Carolina sounds and islands and the description by Thomas Harriot of the resources, natural and human, of the area that first of all gave Europeans some real insight into North American life and resources and that still provide much of what we value about these subjects today.

Notes

¹ See Paul H. Hulton and David B. Quinn (eds.), *The American Drawings of John White, 1577-1590* (London: Trustees of the British Museum; Chapel Hill: University of North Carolina Press, 1964). Examples are given opposite pp. 85, 100, 101, 116, and 117 below.

² Both general and specific information on the Indians of eastern North America may be found in Bruce G. Trigger (ed.), *The Northeast*, Volume XV of *Handbook of North American Indians*, edited by William C. Sturtevant (Washington, D.C.: Smithsonian Institution, 1978).

³ The first edition of Harriot's book, of which only six copies survive, is reprinted with notes in David B. Quinn (ed.), *The Roanoke Voyages* (Cambridge, Eng.: Hakluyt Society, 2 volumes, 1955), I, 317–387, hereinafter cited as Quinn, *Roanoke Voyages*. The second edition is given below, pp. 46–76, with notes on pp. 150–157.

⁴ Theodor de Bry, *America* (Frankfurt-am-Main, 1590), Part I, hereinafter cited as Bry, *America*, contains Harriot's text (the third edition), engravings of Indians and of ancient inhabitants of the British Isles, and notes on the Indian engravings. The languages in which Harriot's account appeared were Latin, English, French, and German.

⁵ Bry, *America*, 126.

⁶ Quinn, *Roanoke Voyages*, II, 811–812. The ship was commanded by Captain Vicente González.

⁷ Quinn, *Roanoke Voyages*, I, 251–252; II, 722.

⁸ Deposition of Richard Butler, ca. 1594, in David B. Quinn (ed.), *New American World: A Documentary History of North America to 1612* (New York: Arno Press, 5 volumes, 1979), III, 329–330, hereinafter cited as Quinn, *New American World*, and an earlier deposition by an unknown man cited in Quinn, *Roanoke Voyages*, I, 80–81.

⁹ Quinn, *New American World*, III, 71–123.

¹⁰ Quinn, *Roanoke Voyages*, I, 144–145, 147–150, 156–157.

¹¹ Quinn, *Roanoke Voyages*, I, 118–157; Tom Glasgow, Jr., "H.M.S. *Tiger*," *North Carolina Historical Review*, XLIII (April, 1966), 115–121.

¹² Quinn, *Roanoke Voyages*, II, 733–748.

¹³ Quinn, *Roanoke Voyages*, I, 197–221; Quinn, *New American World*, III, 288–294.

¹⁴ Jean C. Harrington, in *The Cittie of Ralegh in Virginia* (Washington, D.C.: National Park Service, 1972), discusses the excavations and reconstruction of Fort Raleigh. See also Quinn, *Roanoke Voyages*, II, 901–910.

[15] Letter, dated August 1, 1586, by an unknown correspondent at the English court, Quinn, *New American World*, III, 307–310.

[16] The Relation of Pedro Diaz, made on March 11/21, 1589, is valuable for the period from late 1585 to May, 1588, but especially so for the events of 1586. See Quinn, *Roanoke Voyages*, II, 786–795; also I, 465–496.

[17] William S. Powell, in "Roanoke Colonists and Explorers: An Attempt at Identification," *North Carolina Historical Review*, XXXIV (April, 1957), 202–226, provides many clues, of mixed value, on the identity of some of these colonists. Professor Powell's information is by now much more extensive than that published in 1957, but there is little hope of identifying everyone. See also Quinn, *Roanoke Voyages*, II, 539–543.

[18] Quinn, *Roanoke Voyages*, II, 506–512.

[19] Quinn, *Roanoke Voyages*, II, 772–838; David B. Quinn, *England and the Discovery of America, 1481–1620* (New York: Alfred A. Knopf, 1974), 265–282, 450–451, hereinafter cited as Quinn, *England and the Discovery of America*.

[20] The indications of the colonists' survival are fully examined in Quinn, *England and the Discovery of America*, 432–481. William Strachey provided the crucial piece of evidence: "his Majestie [James I] hath bene acquainted, that the men, women and Children of the first plantation at Roanoak were by practize and Commaundement of Powhatan (he himself perswaded thereunto by his Priests) miserably slaughtered without any offence given him . . . by the first planted (who 20. and od years had peacably lyved and intermixed with thos Savadges, and were out of his Territory." See William Strachey, *The Historie of Travell into Virginia Britania* (*1612*), edited by Louis B. Wright and Virginia Freund (London: Hakluyt Society, 1953), 44. This view has been reiterated by David N. Durant, *Ralegh's Lost Colony* (New York: Atheneum, 1981), 154–164.

[21] All the extant materials are printed in Quinn, *Roanoke Voyages*, II, 579–716.

[22] See the possible indications in Quinn, *England and the Discovery of America*, 414–416, 419–431, 445–448, 450–452.

Introduction

Richard Hakluyt led a relatively long, assured, and peaceful life from 1552 to 1616. He studied, taught, and lectured at Christ Church from 1570 to 1583: he acted as chaplain to the English ambassador in Paris from 1583 to 1588, though with long home leaves, and enjoyed thereafter a pleasing plurality of benefices, canonries at Westminster and Bristol, livings at Wetheringsett and Gedney, a chaplaincy at the Savoy. Once he had passed through the discipline of his university training and had reinforced it with a wide range of modern languages, he devoted himself almost wholly to geographical and historical studies. These were not confined to libraries and to correspondence or personal contacts with English and continental scholars, but involved a considerable amount of research and fieldwork of a less conventional sort.

In 1568 when he was still a schoolboy at Westminster School, he was inspired by a visit to his elder cousin, Richard Hakluyt of the Inner Temple, to take up the study of geography and, in particular, that of the new discoveries outside Europe which had taken place in the previous century. His cousin, giving more time to this, one feels, than to law, had built up an impressive range of correspondence with men as far afield as Mexico and Goa, was busy assembling documents on economic and trading conditions outside Europe and was exploiting his knowledge by placing it at the disposal of merchants who were interested in opening up new channels of trade. The younger Hakluyt, during the next ten years, while he was completing his formal education (he graduated B.A. in 1573 and M.A. in 1577), followed his cousin's example in the study of the expanded world picture which presented itself at this time to young Englishmen (as it had earlier to Europeans), but gradually developed a personal approach or rather a series of personal approaches to its problems.

He was keenly interested in descriptions of foreign lands and of travel to and in them by sea and land: he rapidly appreciated that a great deal of the attraction in the literature of discovery lay in being able to capture the authentic voice of the traveller. The traveller's descriptions of what he saw, experienced, of what he felt even, formed a vital part in the understanding which the scholar and the reader could gain from sharing, through him, in the process of discovery. This led Hakluyt to despise the historical compendia, such as those of Sebastian Münster and André Thevet, into which the records of the discoveries and the new empires were being assimilated. His first and inevitable approach to the narratives of overseas exploration was, not surprisingly for one of his academic training, a literary one. He looked for effective narratives which were already in print. He found a great variety in Ramusio's *Navigationi et viaggi*, arranged in order on a regional basis, and as he learnt Italian and got his friend (and probably tutor) John Florio to translate some of them, he gradually established his own criteria as a collector and interpreter of travel materials. Though he remained willing to read and collect records of travel by anyone at any time or place he came to concentrate on two reasonably distinguishable categories of material. His first was that by non-English writers on areas which he thought Englishmen ought to travel to, trade with, perhaps even settle in; his second was that written by Englishmen in any circumstances involving travel outside the British Isles. These were categories at once shifting and didactic, shifting because the grounds on which such actions might appear advisable changed as the result of external forces and the expanding range of his own interests; didactic because it assumed that Hakluyt knew or thought he knew what English travellers, merchants, would-be colonists should do. This latter confidence sprang initially from his cousin's expertise in advising merchants on possible channels of trade; it was fostered and canalized by meeting men who had firm beliefs, even obsessions, about their own objectives as explorers or settlers and who proved willing to consult and employ him to further their particular ends. Hakluyt thus found himself not only collecting but selecting travel literature, picking out those narratives which would best illustrate the region which interested him or which those who consulted him wished at once to promote, explore, and exploit.

Precisely what fixed his attention so particularly on North America is not wholly clear: it may partly have been the result of his own selective intelligence working on the available material: it was largely the effect of being involved in a small but expanding group of persons, centring on his cousin and on John Dee, who had begun seriously to discuss prospects of North American exploration and who were being stirred into action by the restless insistence of Sir Humphrey Gilbert.

England's earliest continuous interest in North America was in the Newfoundland inshore fishery. This had grown up without corporate or governmental sponsorship but as an economic asset it was vulnerable to international pressures and so was bound, as tension with Spain grew, to involve at least the concern of government. A more temporary interest had been Florida (then understood as the coastline of the three most southerly states in the present-day southeastern United States). Aroused by French activity shortly after 1560, it had faded out, it seemed, in the early 1570s. It had subsequently been replaced by much higher latitudes, in the North-west Passage speculations and adventures between 1574 and 1578, culminating when the Baffin Island gold-search, into which it had been diverted, was proved a fiasco and brought discredit on north-west venturing. Before this lost its glamour, a new phase of interest developed farther south, in the mainland to the south of Newfoundland and to the north of whatever posts the Spaniards had been able to maintain in Florida. Gilbert's patent of June 1578 gave him potential authority in an undefined area, which his supporters knew to be this part of North America. The elder Hakluyt wrote notes to show how the more northerly parts of it might be both exploited commercially and settled; John Dee presented a map to the Queen and attempted to convince her that England had good prior title by discovery to North America. It was into this activity that the younger Richard Hakluyt was drawn. The precise date is not known. It is most likely to have been in 1579, after Gilbert returned unsuccessful from his first poorly planned and executed voyage of reconnaissance. His function was to add both propaganda and information to the publicity for the western ventures. It is characteristic of him that he should have done so by presenting documents of travel, carefully translated, edited from manuscript or reprinted, rather than lengthy appeals to national pride or even to commercial cupidity: narrative as specific as possible, and hard facts as reliable as he could find them, were his stock in trade. Thus he set John Florio to work to translate Cartier texts from Ramusio in support of a detached (and unsuccessful) branch of the Gilbert enterprises and these duly appeared in 1580 as *A shorte and briefe narration of the two nauigations and discoueries to the Northweast partes called Newe Fraunce*. His next was a more ambitious one in which he (with some help from a young Hungarian scholar, Stephen Parmenius) put together a collection of English, French, and Spanish documents on what was known of eastern North America and which could prove at the same time useful to English explorers and also informative and stimulating to readers who were potential investors in the enterprises. *Diuers voyages touching the discouerie of America, and the ilands adiacent vnto the same, made first of all by our Englishmen, and afterwards by the Frenchmen and Britons* appeared in May 1582, and played its part in getting Gilbert on his way, though not until June 1583. Hakluyt was now launched as an adviser, as an editor, and as a man who had lent a somewhat new note to the publication of English travel collections (though it had already been sounded rather mutely by Richard Eden and Richard Willes), that of the forceful direct narrative by a leading participant in an exploring voyage, even if his leading narrative (Verrazzano's) had come to him from Ramusio and the other, Ribault's, had already been printed in 1563 but forgotten.

The years 1583 to 1588 were the busiest in Hakluyt's quiet life. In Paris between September 1583 and July 1584, he read and digested a large number of Spanish and Italian works on the New World, sought out manuscripts of French American ventures, talked to the royal cosmographer André Thevet and the botanist Pierre Pena, visited merchants and pilots in Paris, Rouen, and elsewhere. The main focus of his activity was directed to eastern North America. Successively, Gilbert, Sir George Peckham, and Christopher Carleill during this period of time failed to mount any effective expedition to explore the North American coastline, to find new trades in its waters and amongst its indigenous peoples, or to lay any foundations for English transatlantic settlement. This last had come to Hakluyt to represent the greatest good; Englishmen still had a chance to step in and conquer where Spaniards and French hesitated. There was, moreover, one last leader left in the field, Walter Ralegh. Gaining in March 1584 the patent relinquished by his dead half-brother, he had sent out in April a reconnaissance under Amadas and Barlowe, on the long route by way of the West Indies, to find a harbour and a possible place for settlement to the north of Spanish Florida, whose northernmost outpost was in modern South Carolina. Apprised of this voyage by Sir Francis Walsingham (who was himself deeply interested in the venture) and by Ralegh, Hakluyt was brought back to England by July to give his advice on both broader and narrower implications of the American enterprise. Between July and early October Hakluyt completed his longest sustained piece of argument, 'The particuler discourse'—labelled by successive editors as 'Discourse on Western Planting' and 'Discourse of Western Planting'. Its purpose was to spell out why and how England should establish herself in North America. It appeals to history, to rivalry with imperial and Catholic Spain, to geography (climate and ease of access), to commerce at sea, on land, and by means of English colonies, to settlement for English men and women who might be regarded as surplus to the needs of their own land. North America could make England rich; could make her powerful as well. The discourse was basically an appeal to Queen Elizabeth to lend at least some of the resources of the state to the American enterprise. Both Walsingham and Ralegh hoped for something from the Queen when Hakluyt laid it in her hands on 3 October 1584, before he went back to his Paris post. The Queen in the end provided a few crumbs, but little comfort for the 1585 venture. But the discourse was intended as ammunition for the promoters of further expeditions as well. Though confidential and unpublished, a few copies were circulated in influential hands, and much detailed advice was culled from it for the planning of the next American voyage.

Though Hakluyt stayed long enough in England to hear of the discovery by Amadas and Barlowe of the Carolina Outer Banks and the forest-ringed sounds which lay behind them, he was nevertheless away from England during the preparations for the voyage which was to plant the first tentative English colony on American soil and which represented thus the coming to fruition of his fondest hopes. The Queen agreed that the new land called, it was thought, Wingandacoia should be named for her hardest-held attribute, Virginia. She knighted Walter Ralegh, made him governor of Virginia with a seal of his own but without permission himself to attend the establishment of the settlement. The last honour was reserved for Sir Richard Grenville;

but the Queen gave the expedition powder, a ship and loaned some of her soldiers, including Ralph Lane, who was at this time serving in Ireland but was now to be first commander of the small colonial garrison in Virginia. A garrison was duly placed on Roanoke Island, inside the Outer Banks, in July. Exploration was to be undertaken inland and to the north; Thomas Harriot was to survey and John White to record graphically the resources, human, animal, and vegetable, of the hot summery coastlands. Grenville came back in triumph in October, having taken a rich Spanish prize on his return voyage— an action which was now the highest patriotism since a sea war between England and Spain had begun in May while he was absent. Hakluyt was in England in the early summer of 1585 and again in 1586, hanging on there into July and possibly August. He thus learnt both of the establishment of the first colony and of its end. For Lane, lacking supplies and reinforcements, came back with Drake, who had called in at the Outer Banks after his successful raid on the West Indies. He was thus primed on the resources of North America and on the problems which its indigenous peoples and its character presented. He stressed that the colonizing programme should be renewed, but farther north on Chesapeake Bay where an exploring party had reported more fertile land and deeper harbours and channels accessible from the ocean. He also interviewed with Harriot a rescued Frenchman and a Spanish prisoner on the geography of the American coastland and hinterland to the south of Virginia.

Hitherto Ralegh's ventures had been given no direct printed publicity; now it was decided that Hakluyt should publish all the contingent materials he could in order to provide some comparison between what the English were doing and the French and Spaniards had done. Ralegh commissioned Harriot and White to prepare the notes and drawings they had as the basis for a comprehensive report on the area explored 1585–6 (though some had been lost and they were consequently not fully comprehensive). Harriot was also given the task of compiling a chronicle of successive voyages and would therefore have been entrusted with a growing body of documentary material. Hakluyt, once back in Paris, employed a young friend Martin Basanier to put in print the manuscript of René de Laudonnière's *L'histoire notable de la Floride*, which he had obtained from Thevet, with a flattering dedication to Ralegh for emulating and surpassing the

French Florida ventures. He himself obtained a copy of Mendoza's *China* (Madrid, 1586) which had an interesting narrative of the expedition of Antonio de Espejo in western North America in 1583, which he excerpted and published immediately in Paris, following it up by Basanier's French translation. Preparations were made to have both Laudonnière and Mendoza translated into English and published in London later.

Meantime, Sir Richard Grenville, who had gone out too late with supplies and reinforcements for the first Virginia colony, had left only a handful of men to maintain an English presence on Roanoke Island, and came home in December not unduly optimistic. Many of the settlers of 1585–6 had also given Virginia a bad press; not only were there no gold, jewels, or exotic commodities, but the Indians had been hostile, and there seemed little hope of establishing a flourishing colony.

Hakluyt's intensive publicity in Paris was not seconded in England. It would appear that Harriot's report on the resources of Virginia was ready in February 1587 but was held back. Laudonnière, it is true, appeared in translation and with a propagandist dedication to Ralegh which provided an advertisement for future Virginia voyages. Ralegh, deprived of subscribers by the tales Lane's men told, held back any major venture in 1587. Instead he sponsored an autonomous venture under John White, this time as governor and not simply artist, to establish the City of Ralegh on the shore of Chesapeake Bay. White's colonists were mainly persons and families of small resources who backed his beliefs and those of Harriot and some others of the first colonists, that Virginia was indeed a place for farmers to prosper, even if there was no Peru or Mexico to open up its mines for them.

White sailed in April: his colonists established themselves not on Chesapeake Bay but on the old site at Roanoke Island—from which the 1586 party left by Grenville had disappeared—but they sent him back to England to make sure that their location was known and that supplies were rapidly sent. As his daughter, son-in-law, and granddaughter were among those left behind he was not likely to relax his efforts to return. He did not get back until November, by which time Hakluyt had returned to Paris. During what was probably a short visit to England in October he had had news from an earlier vessel of the safe arrival of the colonists. He incorporated this good news in his dedication to his translation of Laudonnière. But this was the last good news that was to be received from Virginia for a considerable time.

Though he did not send White away at once with aid, Ralegh changed his mind again about Virginia. He decided to launch with sufficient backing a new large Virginia venture to be under the command of Sir Richard Grenville. The squadron was preparing early in 1588 at Bideford when Harriot's *A briefe and true report* was at last released as publicity for Virginia and for a further enterprise. But fate—or Spain—intervened. The departure of the Spanish Armada was now believed to be imminent. Every ship was needed in the Channel and so the Virginia venture was called off. Grenville's squadron was incorporated in Drake's fleet at Plymouth. After hard pressing White got two small vessels in which to go, with a few planters and supplies, to the aid of the Virginia settlers. He set out in May but the piratical activity of his seamen and of the other ships they met drove them home, robbed and helpless, so that contact with the Roanoke Island settlement was lost. Hakluyt had been in England between January and March while prospects still were bright. During a further visit from May to July he learnt of the severe setback which first Ralegh and then White had suffered. There was little he, in Paris, or anyone in England could do until the clash with Spain was over. Already, too, his activities had turned in another direction: in Paris in 1587 he had edited his first scholarly work—a Latin edition, the first since 1530, of all eight decades of the new world by Peter Martyr (*De orbe novo . . . decades octo*). On his visit to England he had met Theodor de Bry, the Frankfurt entrepreneur, to whom he had conveyed the news of the existence, first, of a series of fine Indian drawings by John White (to which Harriot was compiling what was in effect a commentary), and second, a second series of drawings of Florida Indian scenes made by Jacques le Moyne de Morgues in 1564–5 and now recopied at Ralegh's instance and expense. De Bry went back with a collection of White drawings, doubtless to White's financial benefit, and so the germ was planted of the great project to publish an illustrated series of volumes, with texts in various languages, on America.

Hakluyt's tour of duty in France ended in 1588. Later in the year he conveyed the ambassador's wife to London and settled there. Early in 1589 he was engaged in trying to see what could be salvaged from the Virginia venture. Ralegh encouraged the formation of a sort of holding company of London merchants and interested persons who would try to find backing for a further attempt to supply or rescue the Roanoke colonists. Hakluyt was named as one of nineteen grantees on 7 March 1589. But nothing was done: shipping was still held back from all but damaging anti-Spanish ventures: money too must have been short: for the time being Virginia like its settlers was in limbo.

It was in this period of inaction so far as North America was concerned that Hakluyt's major work which had been claiming his attention for many years, finally took shape. It appears probable that, at the time (1581–2) he was completing *Divers voyages*, he was struck by how little was known or was available about English enterprises to North America or indeed about English travel, discovery, and commerce outside the rather narrow bounds of European trade and journeyings. His elder cousin had much interest of his own on conditions in India, Mexico, and elsewhere. Thus the younger man obtained, possibly before he went to France in 1583, more probably on one or more of his visits in later years, information on these areas. Moreover, Hakluyt had many personal contacts with leading members of the Muscovy and Levant Companies who let him see and probably lent him records of their ventures. He had the assistance of Sir Francis Walsingham and Lord Burghley in getting access to government papers. He worked through many older chronicles and books on Portuguese and Spanish overseas enterprises for gleanings on English activity overseas. He gathered up what had already appeared in print in English. He requested journals and documents from captains and seamen returned from overseas voyages—he was, for example, on close terms, with Hawkins, Frobisher, Drake, and Cavendish, all of whom gave him materials. Gradually, a body of narrative material, with linking documents, began to take shape in his hands as the first framework of a general collection on the English voyages. What we cannot assess is how rapidly the collection grew, though each of his visits from Paris must have been occupied, partly, in assembling its constituents. By the time of his final return in 1588 the bulk of the materials was already in his possession.

He wished above all else to present as much as possible on North America. To the few items he had in 1582 he added only rather garbled accounts of voyages by John and Sebastian Cabot, by John Rut in 1527, and by Richard Hore in 1536. From Hawkins he got John

Sparke's account of the English visit to Florida in 1565. From Edward Hayes and Richard Clarke he obtained full accounts of Sir Humphrey Gilbert's last voyage, to which he added various propagandist tracts of the years 1582–4; but he was determined to bring together as much as he could on the recent Virginia voyages.

In the end he did well so far as bulk is concerned, and also in the quality of the material; but it is highly probable that what he was to print on the ventures of 1584–6 came to him from Ralegh by way of Thomas Harriot and that it had been to some extent predigested while in their hands. Arthur Barlowe's narrative of the 1584 voyage was not a simple journal but a journal rewritten, perhaps by Ralegh, possibly by Harriot, to fit the propaganda needs of the last months of 1584 and the first of 1585. The journal of the 1585 voyage was similarly trimmed to highlight some and to suppress other episodes in the voyage. Lane's narrative of the 1585 colony, too, had almost certainly had some passages deleted or pruned. Moreover, Walsingham had received letters from the participants in the 1585 voyages, Lane and Grenville among them, which he did not pass on to Hakluyt to print, perhaps because there were in them reflections on certain persons engaged on the voyage. There was certainly some suppression and some consequent distortion in the picture which these narratives presented of the two expeditions and the first settlement, but there is no reason to consider that everything, or almost everything, contained in them was not first hand and authentic. There was gain too in their pruning: Ralegh certainly had a better ear for a good phrase, for a vivid paragraph, for the contrast between significant detail and stark outline, which gives, for example, the so-called *Tiger* journal of the 1585 voyage so much of its effect. We cannot be sure that the subeditor was Ralegh rather than Harriot, but it was certainly one or the other. To balance narrative with analysis Hakluyt had permission to reprint Harriot's *A briefe and true report*, with its discussion of settlement problems and analysis of natural resources and aboriginal society. There is no reason to consider that Hakluyt was in any way dissatisfied with what he obtained.

For Grenville's 1586 voyage Hakluyt was unlucky. There is reason to think Grenville kept his own journal of the 1585 voyage, though this did not reach Hakluyt. It is highly probable that he kept one also in 1586 and that others were kept as well, but Hakluyt could not lay hands on any and so he collected such scanty information as he could and wrote his own brief secondhand narrative. John White kept journals of the 1587 and 1588 voyages and these he passed on, probably directly, to Hakluyt. Hakluyt seems to have presented them in full with the possible excision of entries where little took place on the long transatlantic passages. They were plain and unadorned but effective, even poignant, documents of a lost colony. Later in the production of the book Hakluyt added the grant of 7 March 1589 to which he was a party to signify that all intention of relieving the Roanoke settlers had not been given up. The voyage collection, now at last given the title *The principall navigations voiages and discoueries of the English nation*, was put through the press efficiently, though with some signs of pressure towards the end, in the closing months of 1589. Whether it appeared in December 1589 or in January (or even February) 1590 we cannot tell.

To Hakluyt the narratives of the Virginia voyages from 1584 onwards represented a vital element in his record of English enterprise in North America. He considered them as historical documents, no doubt, but he also thought of them as guides and an inspiration to future transatlantic explorers and planters. When he came in the 1590s to assemble his voyage collections on a much larger scale there was not much he could add to what had been already published. He suppressed White's narration of the abortive voyage in 1588, cut the almost equally abortive assignment of 1589, as both had been wholly superseded. He added another, characteristic, narrative by John White of the voyage to Roanoke Island which he had eventually been able to make in 1590. Though in this White told much less than the full story of the outward voyage, his picture of the search on Roanoke Island for the lost colonists is an intricate and effective one. The latest document was a covering letter sent with the 1590 narrative from Ireland, to which White had retired, discouraged, unable to find either the backers or the will to cross the Atlantic to Roanoke Island for a sixth time. In the collections which Hakluyt made towards a final edition in the years after 1600 there was apparently nothing more on the Virginia voyages—at least Samuel Purchas makes no mention of any in his *Pilgrimes*, for which he used so much of Hakluyt's later collections, and which had come to him in Hakluyt's last years and after his death in 1616.

Note on the Text

Of the fifteen items which follow, nine are taken from Richard Hakluyt, *The principall navigations . . . of the English nation* (1589), where eight of them were published for the first time. The ninth, Thomas Harriot's *A briefe and true report of the new found land of Virginia*, had already appeared separately in 1588; Hakluyt in his second edition gave a careful reprint with a few verbal changes only. Eight of them were reprinted (all except the narrative of the 1588 voyage) by Hakluyt in his second edition, *The principal nauigations . . . of the English nation* (3 vols., 1598–1600), iii (1600), together with the other seven items in this collection. Of these two were reprinted, one from Hakluyt's epistle dedicatory to Sir Walter Ralegh of his translation of René de Laudonnière, *A notable historie containing foure voyages made by certayne French captaynes vnto Florida* (1587), in which he made a few changes, and Walter Bigges (etc.), *A summarie and true discourse of Sir Frances Drakes West India voyage*, of which there had been three printings in English in 1589 and one in 1596 (it would appear that Hakluyt's was that published by Roger Ward in 1589), and of which only the relevant extract is given below.

The earlier text printed by Hakluyt has been used for the copy in each case and collation has been confined to corrections and substantive changes where there are two printings. In the case of reprinted matter the original editions have been checked against Hakluyt's texts but few divergences have been noted. Hakluyt altered his sidenotes a good deal as between his two editions of the same document, but as they are mostly explanatory, they have been ignored in respect to his second printing though those appearing in the first printing have been retained but set as footnotes.

In the texts 'u' and 'v', 'i' and 'j' have been normalized.

A Select Bibliography

The principall navigations . . . of the English nation, by Richard Hakluyt, first appeared in one volume in 1589, and is most conveniently consulted in the facsimile (2 vols., with an introduction by D. B. Quinn and R. A. Skelton) published by the Hakluyt Society in 1965 (Extra Series, 38–9). The second edition, *The principal nauigations . . . of the English nation*, was published in 3 vols., 1589–1600, the American material being in volume iii (1600). This was reprinted in 12 vols., with an introduction by Professor Sir Walter Raleigh, in 1903–5, by MacLehose at Glasgow University Press (The Hakluyt Society's part of the edition being ranked as Extra Series 1–12). The texts derived from English sources were afterwards reprinted in Everyman's Library.

The texts included in this volume, with others, were edited with extensive annotations by D. B. Quinn as *The Roanoke voyages, 1584–90*, 2 vols., 1955 (Hakluyt Society, Second Series, 104–5). P. H. Hulton and D. B. Quinn, *The American drawings of John White*, one volume of introduction and one of plates (British Museum and University of North Carolina Press, 1964), can be considered as a graphic supplement to the printed texts.

BIBLIOGRAPHY. The lists of Hakluyt's publications and associated literature will be found in G. B. Parks, *Richard Hakluyt and the English voyages* (New York, 1928; corrected reprint 1961), and more fully in *The Hakluyt handbook*, ed. D. B. Quinn, 2 vols., 1973 (Hakluyt Society, Second Series, 144–5). There is an extensive bibliography in Quinn, *Roanoke voyages*.

ENGLISH AND AMERICAN BACKGROUND. A brief introduction will be found in D. B. Quinn, *Raleigh and the British Empire* (1947; latest edition, Penguin Books, 1973); A. L. Rowse, *The expansion of Elizabethan England* (1955); and S. E. Morison, *The discovery of America: the northern voyages* (1971).

Chronology of the Virginia Voyages

25 March   Walter Ralegh obtains a patent entitling him to occupy such lands as he may discover in the name of the crown of England (North America is implied but not mentioned)

27 April   Two barks, commanded by Philip Amadas and Arthur Barlowe, respectively, set out on a reconnaissance to North America. Sailing by way of the West Indies, they reached the North American coast early in July

13 July   On what are now the Carolina Outer Banks (apparently at what they called Port Ferdinando, near the entry leading to Roanoke Island) they took formal possession for Queen Elizabeth of the land (and by implication of all that lay to the north or south for 600 miles in each direction, which was not already in European possession)

July   Having made friendly contact with the local Carolina Algonkian Indians, the Englishmen were taken to their village at the north-west end of Roanoke Island, inside the Outer Banks, and learnt something of the country and of Indian ways of life

August   They left the coast (making their way apparently to the mouth of Chesapeake Bay where they were met with some hostility) and made their way homewards, taking with them from the North Carolina coast two Indians, Manteo and Wanchese, who soon became interpreters

September   About the middle of the month they returned to England

December   By this time the Indians were said to be able to speak some English; Ralegh promoted a bill to confirm the discoveries to him, but it did not pass the House of Lords

1585

6 January   Ralegh was knighted; the Queen allowed him to use the name Virginia (instead of Wingandacoa) for the land recently discovered, and named him governor

19 April   After extensive preparations, seven ships, with about 600 men, including more than 100 would-be colonists, left Plymouth under Sir Richard Grenville for Virginia

15 May   Grenville's ship, later joined by another, put in at Guayanilla Bay, Puerto Rico, where a temporary camp was established and occupied until 29 May

1 June   Grenville put in at Isabela, Española, and visited other parts of the north coast, leaving on 7 June

26 June   After sailing through the Florida channel and examining the coast as they went they put into Wococon Island in the Carolina Outer Banks, part of their Virginia, on 26 June

11 July   After making contact with other ships and crews and sending messages to Roanoke Island, Grenville, between 11 and 17 July, made an expedition round the shores of Pamlico Sound, inside the Outer Banks (and now part of North Carolina)

27 July   The fleet anchored off Port Ferdinando and after receiving an invitation from the Indians, planned to establish a settlement on Roanoke Island, while preparations were made to build a fort and houses there

17 August   The fort was roughly completed; Ralph Lane took over command as governor over a colony of 107 men (no women being left)

25 August   Grenville, in the *Tiger* left for England, arriving 18 October

circa October   A party under a colonel (who may just possibly have been Thomas Harriot) was detached to settle over the winter near the southern shore of Chesapeake Bay, in modern Virginia. They may have stayed until February 1586

1586

March   Lane carried out expeditions up Albemarle Sound, the Chowan River, and the Moratuc (now Roanoke) River. He was forced to turn back before locating the Mangoak (Tuscarora) tribe, who were said to have much copper (or gold). He returned safely on 4 April, where he sowed corn on Roanoke Island

Late April (or early May) Grenville left Bideford with 7 or 8 ships for Virginia

10 June Learning of an Indian conspiracy against him, Lane struck at the village of Dasemunkepeuc, on the mainland, killed the ringleader, the chief Wingina, and, according to him, cowed the Indians

June John White and Thomas Harriot, the one making notes, the other sketches, had almost finished their map, scenes, and notes of Indian life, pictures of birds, fishes, plants, and animals, with notes and specimens, for their survey report. Lane was forced to disperse his men to collect seafood on the Outer Banks as he was short before the corn harvest.

8 June Captain Edward Stafford sighted a northward bound fleet approaching the islands. It proved to be Sir Francis Drake, who had raided the Spanish Caribbean possessions and Florida. He was bringing supplies, equipment, and liberated Negroes and South American Indians for the settlement

10 June Drake landed at Port Ferdinando and offered Lane a ship with which to reconnoitre Chesapeake Bay for a better site for a settlement. The transfer was almost complete when a hurricane developed on 13 June

16 June Assembling his fleet after the storm, Drake found many of the smaller ships had sunk, others had left for home (including that intended for Lane and with some of his men on her), and he could offer only too large a vessel for Lane's purposes, so Lane decided to bring the colonists home, reinforcements and supplies being overdue

18 or 19 June The first colonists left Roanoke Island and the Carolina Outer Banks for England

June About the end of the month a supply ship arrived to find the colony deserted: it returned to England

July–August In late July or early August Grenville arrived with about seven ships. Finding the settlement deserted, he put a small, well-supplied party of 15 (or 18) men in the fort, did some exploration and left before the end of August

September (or later) The Roanoke Island garrison was attacked by

Indians; two were killed, but thirteen escaped in their boats, leaving no trace of their destination or fate.

1587

7 January   The incorporation of the City of Ralegh in Virginia was established in London, under licence from Sir Walter Ralegh. It had John White as governor, and 13 assistants, and was to establish a settlement on Chesapeake Bay

8 May   Three ships, with 115 members of the company (though 150 had been expected to sail) left Plymouth; they included 17 women (two of them pregnant) and 11 children. John White as governor commanded the flagship; Simon Fernandes (as assistant) was chief pilot

28 June   The expedition put in at Puerto Rico and later visited several islands for water and supplies

7 July   The vessels sailed for Virginia

22 July   The ships anchored at Port Ferdinando, intending to supply the 1586 settlers on Roanoke Island, find out whether they wished to stay, and then move on to Chesapeake Bay. When White had a party ready to visit Roanoke Island Fernandes ordered them to stay there (he wished to leave quickly to pick up prizes on the way home), and White acquiesced. He later learnt the 1586 party had departed after the Indian attack. His colonists were disembarked and installed over the next few weeks

13 August   White after visiting Croatoan, Manteo's home, had this Indian baptised and invested as Lord of Roanoke, under Sir Walter Ralegh

18 August   Virginia, daughter of White's daughter Elenor and Ananias Dare, was christened on Roanoke Island

22 August   The settlers insisted that White should go to England to obtain supplies

27 August   John White left for England on the flyboat, the colonists intending 'to remove 50 miles further up into the maine presently'

16 October   After a difficult voyage White reached Ireland, and took ship from Dingle for England

8 November   White reached Southampton

20 November   White met Ralegh and urged him to send instant relief to the colonists, which was put in hand, but the vessel failed to depart

1588

February   Thomas Harriot's *A briefe and true report*, appeared (having been held over from February 1587): it gave a full account of Virginia's resources and potentiality

31 March   Ralegh had prepared a new colonizing expedition to Virginia, Grenville agreeing to command seven (or eight) ships, and having them almost ready at Bideford

31 March–9 April   The Privy Council countermanded the sailing and instructed Grenville to join Drake with his squadron at Plymouth

22 April   John White, with 7 men and 4 women for the settlement, was allowed to leave Bideford, in the *Brave* and the *Roe*, specially detached from Grenville's fleet. The *Brave* attacked and was attacked by several vessels, being finally looted off Madeira on 6 May

22 May   The *Brave* returned and the *Roe* followed, White having to give up his plan to go to Virginia

1589

7 March   What may be described as a holding company for the City of Ralegh colony venture was set up in London, with co-operation from Ralegh. It included White and Richard Hakluyt, a number of London merchants, who were to finance the relief and development of the Roanoke colony. But shipping was still under an embargo and no expedition could leave England

December 1589 (or possibly January 1590)   Richard Hakluyt's *Principall navigations* was published giving full account of the Virginia voyages, 1584–8

1590

20 March   John White took passage on the *Hopewell* which, with two other vessels, undertook to bring him to Roanoke Island on their return from a privateering expedition in the West Indies

May   The *Moonlight*, a ship belonging to William Sanderson a member of the 1589 syndicate, set out for Virginia with stores for the colony

May   Through Hakluyt's influence, Theodor de Bry brought out (in

Latin, English, French, and German) at Frankfurt, his *America*, Part I, containing a full account of the Virginia colony of 1585–6, with Harriot's *Briefe and true report*, engravings after John White's Indian drawings, and notes on Indian life

26 May The *Hopewell* and her consorts began their attacks on Spanish ships off Hispaniola

2 July They were joined by the *Moonlight*

31 July The *Hopewell* and the *Moonlight* sailed through the Florida Channel for Virginia

15 August They anchored off Port Ferdinando

18 August John White, with a party of sailors, reached Roanoke Island. The settlement was deserted, much of its heavy gear left behind, and White's own possessions (left buried) spoiled by Indians. A cross and the letters CRO cut on a tree, convinced White the settlers were well when they left and that they (or some of them) had gone south to Manteo on Croatoan Island (near modern Cape Hatteras)

About 20 August After urging the sailors to remain, or to go to the West Indies to winter, White was forced (in the face of bad weather) to return to England

24 October White in the *Hopewell* reached Plymouth

1591 (or later)

After 1591 John White went to settle in Munster as a planter, at Newtown, Kilmore, Co. Cork

1593

4 February White wrote to Hakluyt from Newtown, enclosing a copy of his narrative of the 1590 voyage, and expressing his sorrow at not being able to do any more to locate and supply the Roanoke settlers, who eventually become 'the Lost Colonists' of modern American legend

1600

Richard Hakluyt published the third volume of his revised *Principal nauigations*, containing a reprint of most of the material on Virginia formerly printed in 1589, with a few additional items on the earlier voyages, and White's narrative of the 1590 voyage and his 1593 letter

The First Colonists

I

Arthur Barlowe's
Narrative of the 1584 Voyage[1]

THE first voyage made to the coastes of America, with two barkes,[2] wherein were Captaines Master Philip Amadas,[3] and Master Arthur Barlowe,[4] who discovered part of the Countrey, now called Virginia, Anno 1584: Written by one of the said Captaines, and sent to sir Walter Raleigh, knight, at whose charge, and direction, the said voyage was set foorth.

The 27. day of Aprill, in the yeere of our redemption, 1584. we departed the west of England,[5] with two barkes, well furnished with men and victuals, having receyved our last, and perfect directions by your letters, confirming the former instructions, and commande-ments delivered by your selfe at our leaving the river of Thames. And I thinke it a matter both unnecessarie, for the manifest discoverie of the Countrey, as also for tediousnes sake, to remember unto you the diurnall of our course, sailing thither, and returning: onely I have pre-sumed to present unto you this briefe discourse, by which you may judge how profitable this land is likely to succeede, as well to your selfe, (by whose direction and charge, and by whose servants this our discoverie hath beene performed) as also to her Highnes, and the Common wealth, in which we hope your wisedome will be satisfied, considering, that as much by us hath bene brought to light, as by those small meanes, and number of men we had, could any way have bene expected, or hoped for.

The tenth of May, we arrived at the Canaries, and the tenth of June in this present yeere, we were fallen with the Islands of the West Indies, keeping a more southeasterly course then was needefull,[6] be-cause we doubted that the current of the Baye of Mexico, disbogging[7] betweene the Cape of Florida, and the Havana, had bene of greater

1

force then afterwardes we found it to be. At which Islands[1] we found the aire very unwholsome, and our men grewe for the most part ill disposed: so that having refreshed our selves with sweete water, and fresh victuall, we departed the twelfth daye after our arrivall there. These Islands, with the rest adjoyning, are so well knowen to your selfe, and to many others, as I will not trouble you, with the remembrance of them.

The second of July, we found shole water, which smelt so sweetely, and was so strong a smell, as if we had bene in the midst of some delicate garden, abounding with all kind of odoriferous flowers, by which we were assured, that the land could not be farre distant: and keeping good watch, and bearing but slacke saile, the fourth of the same moneth, we arrived upon the coast, which we supposed to be a continent, and firme lande, and wee sailed along the same, a hundred and twentie English miles, before we could finde any entrance, or river,[2] issuing into the Sea. The first that appeared unto us, we entred,[3] though not without some difficultie, and cast anker about three harquebushot within the havens mouth, on the left hande of the same: and after thankes given to God for our safe arrival thither, we manned our boates, and went to viewe the lande next adjoyning, and to "take possession of the same,* in the right of the Queenes most excellent Majestie, as rightfull Queene, and Princesse of the same, and after delivered the same over to your use, according to her Majesties grant, and letters patents, under her Highnes great Seale. Which being performed, according to the ceremonies used in such enterprises,[4] wee viewed the lande about us, being whereas we first landed,[5] very sandie, and lowe towards the water side,[6] but so full of grapes, as the very beating, and surge of the Sea overflowed them, of which we founde such plentie, as well there, as in all places else, both on the sande, and on the greene soile on the hils, as in the plaines, as well on every little shrubbe, as also climing towardes the toppes of the high Cedars,[7] that I thinke in all the world the like aboundance is not to be founde: and my selfe having seene those partes of Europe[8] that most abound, finde such difference, as were incredible to be written.

We passed from the Sea side,[9] towardes the toppes of those hils next adjoyning, being but of meane heighth,[10] and from thence wee behelde the Sea on both sides to the North, and to the South, finding no

* "July 13. possessions taken.

ende any of both waies. This lande laye stretching it selfe to the West, which after wee founde to be but an Island of twentie leagues[1] long, and not above sixe miles broade. Under the banke or hill, whereon we stoode, we behelde the vallies replenished with goodly Cedar trees, and having discharged our harquebushot, such a flocke of Cranes (the most part white) arose under us, with such a crye redoubled by many Ecchoes, as if an armie of men had showted all together.

This Island had many goodly woods, and full of Deere, Conies, Hares, and Fowle, even in the middest of Summer, in incredible aboundance. The woodes are not such as you finde in Bohemia, Moscovia, or Hyrcania, barren and fruitlesse, but the highest, and reddest Cedars of the world, farre bettering the Cedars of the Açores, of the Indias, or of Lybanus, Pynes, Cypres, Sassaphras, the Lentisk, or the tree that beareth the Masticke, the tree that beareth the rinde of blacke Sinamon,[2] of which Master Winter brought from the Streights of Magellane, and many other of excellent smell, and qualitie. We remained by the side of this Island two whole daies, before we sawe any people of the Countrey: the third daye we espied one small boate rowing towards us, having in it three persons: this boate came to the landes side,[3] foure harquebushot from our shippes, and there two of the people remaining, the thirde came along the shoare side towards us, and we being then all within boord, he walked up and downe uppon the point of the lande next unto us: then the Master, and the Pilot of the Admirall, Simon Ferdinando,[4] and the Captaine Philip Amadas, my selfe, and others, rowed to the lande, whose comming this fellowe attended, never making any shewe of feare, or doubt. And after he had spoken of many things not understoode by us, we brought him with his owne good liking, aboord the shippes, and gave him a shirt, a hatte, and some other things, and made him taste of our wine, and our meate, which he liked very well: and after having viewed both barkes, he departed, and went to his owne boate againe, which hee had left in a little Cove, or Creeke adjoyning: assoone as hee was two bowe shoote into the water, hee fell to fishing, and in lesse then halfe an howre, hee had laden his boate as deepe, as it could swimme, with which he came againe to the point of the lande, and there he devided his fishe into two partes, pointing one part to the shippe, and the other to the Pinnesse: which after he had (as much as he might,) requited the former benefits receaved, he departed out of our sight.

The next day there came unto us divers boates, and in one of them the Kings brother, accompanied with fortie or fiftie men, very handsome, and goodly people, and in their behaviour as mannerly, and civill, as any of Europe. His name was Granganimeo, and the King is called Wingina,[1] the countrey Wingandacoa, (and nowe by her Majestie, Virginia,[2]) the manner of his comming was in this sorte: hee left his boates altogether, as the first man did a little from the shippes by the shoare, and came along to the place over against the shippes, followed with fortie men. When hee came to the place, his servants spread a long matte uppon the grounde, on which he sate downe, and at the other ende of the matte, foure others of his companie did the like: the rest of his men stoode round about him, somewhat a farre off: when wee came to the shoare to him with our weapons, he never mooved from his place, nor any of the other foure, nor never mistrusted any harme to be offered from us, but sitting still, he beckoned us to come, and sitte by him, which wee perfourmed: and beeing sette, hee makes all signes of joy, and welcome, striking on his head, and his breast, and afterwardes on ours, to shewe we were all one, smiling, and making shewe the best hee could, of all love, and familiaritie. After hee had made a long speech unto us, wee presented him with divers thinges, which hee receaved very joyfully, and thankefully. None of his companye durst to speake one worde all the tyme: onely the foure which were at the other ende, spake one in the others eare very softly.

The King is greatly obeyed, and his brothers, and children reverenced: the King himselfe in person was at our beeing there sore wounded, in a fight which he had with the King of the next Countrey, called Wingina,[3] and was shotte in two places through the bodye, and once cleane thorough the thigh, but yet he recovered: by reason whereof, and for that hee laye at the chiefe Towne of the Countrey, beeing six dayes journeye off, wee sawe him not at all.

After wee had presented this his brother, with such things as we thought he liked, we likewise gave somewhat to the other[4] that sate with him on the matte: but presently he arose, and tooke all from them, and put it into his owne basket, making signes and tokens, that all things ought to be delivered unto him, and the rest were but his servants, and followers. A daye or two after this, we fell to trading with them, exchanging some thinges that we had for Chammoys,[1] Buffe,[2] and Deere skinnes: when we shewed him all our packet of merchandize, of all things that he saw, a bright tinne dishe most pleased him, which he presently tooke up, & clapt it before his breast, & after made a hole in the brimme thereof, & hung it about his necke, making signes, that it would defende him against his enemies arrowes: for those people maintaine a deadlie and terrible warre, with the people and King adjoyning. We exchanged our tinne dishe for twentie skinnes, woorth twentie Crownes, or twentie Nobles: and a copper kettle for fiftie skinnes woorth fiftie Crownes. They offered us very good exchange for our hatchets, and axes, and for knives, and would have given any thing for swordes:[3] but we would not depart with any. After two or three daies, the Kings brother came aboord the shippes, and dranke wine, and ate of our meate, and of our bread, and liked exceedingly thereof: and after a few daies overpassed, he brought his wife with him to the shippes, his daughter, and two or three little children: his wife was very well favored, of meane stature, and very bashfull: she had on her backe a long cloke of leather, with the furre side next to her bodie, and before her a peece of the same[4]: about her forehead, she had a broad bande of white Corrall,[5] and so had her husband many times: in her eares she had bracelets of pearles, hanging downe to her middle,[6] (whereof we delivered your Worship a litle bracelet) and those were of the bignes of good pease. The rest of her women of the better sorte, had pendants of copper, hanging in every eare, and some of the children of the Kings brother, and other Noble men, have five or sixe in every eare:[7] he himselfe had upon his head, a broad plate of golde, or copper, for being unpolished we knew not what metall it should be, neither would he by any meanes suffer us to take it off his head, but feeling it, it would bowe very easily.[8] His apparell was as his wives, onely the women weare their haire long on both sides, and the men but on one.[9] They are of colour yellowish,[10] and their haire blacke for the most, and yet we sawe children that had very fine aburne, and chestnut colour haire.[11]

After that these women had bene there, there came downe from all parts great store of people, bringing with them leather, corrall,[12] divers kindes of dies very excellent, and exchanged with us: but when Granganimeo, the kings brother was present, none durst to trade but himselfe, except such as weare redde peeces of copper on their

5

heades,[1] like himselfe: for that is the difference betweene the Noble men, and Governours of Countries, and the meaner sort. And we both noted there, and you have understood since by these men, which we brought home,[2] that no people in the worlde carry more respect to their King, Nobilitie, and Governours, then these doe. The Kings brothers wife, when she came to us, as she did many times, shee was followed with fortie or fiftie women[3] alwaies: and when she came into the shippe, she left them all on lande, saving her two daughters, her nurce, and one or two more. The Kings brother alwaies kept this order, as many boates as he would come withall to the shippes, so many fires would he make on the shoare a farre off, to the ende wee might understand with what strength, and companie he approched.[4] Their boates are made of one tree, either of Pine, or of Pitch trees: a wood not commonly knowen to our people, nor found growing in England. They have no edge tooles to make them withall: if they have any, they are very fewe, and those it seemes they had twentie yeeres since, which as those two men declared, was out of a wracke[5] which happened upon their coast of some Christian shippe, being beaten that way by some storme, and outragious weather, whereof none of the people were saved, but onely the shippe, or some part of her, being cast upon the sande, out of whose sides they drewe the nailes, and spikes,[6] and with those they made their best instruments. Their manner of making their boates, is this: they burne downe some great tree, or take such as are winde fallen, and putting myrrhe, and rosen[7] upon one side thereof, they sette fire into it, and when it hath burnt it hollowe, they cutte out the coale with their shells, and ever where they would burne it deeper or wider, they laye on their gummes, which burneth away the timber, and by this meanes they fashion very fine boates, and such as will transport twentie men. Their oares are like scoopes, and many times they sette with long poles, as the depth serveth.

The Kings brother had great liking of our armour, a sworde, and divers other things, which we had: and offered to laye a great boxe of pearle in gage for them: but wee refused it for this time, because we would not make them knowe, that wee esteemed thereof, untill we had understoode in what places of the Countrey the pearle grewe: which nowe your Worshippe doth very well understand.[8]

He was very just of his promise: for many times wee delivered him merchandize uppon his worde, but ever he came within the daye, and performed his promise. Hee sent us every daye a brase or two of fatte Buckes, Conies, Hares, Fishe, the best of the worlde. Hee sent us divers kindes of fruites, Melons, Walnuts, Cucumbers, Gourdes, Pease, and divers rootes, and fruites very excellent good, and of their Countrey corne,[1] which is very white, faire, and well tasted, and groweth three times in five moneths: in Maye they sowe, in July they reape: in June they sowe, in August they reape: in July they sowe, in September they reape: onely they cast the corne into the ground, breaking a little of the soft turfe with a woodden mattocke, or pickeaxe:[2] our selves prooved the soile, and put some of our Pease into the ground,[3] and in tenne daies they were of foureteene ynches high: they have also Beanes very faire, of divers colours, and wonderfull plentie: some growing naturally, and some in their gardens, and so have they both wheat and oates.[4]

The soile[5] is the most plentifull, sweete, fruitfull, and wholsome of all the world: there are above foureteene severall sweete smelling timber trees,[6] and the most part of their underwoods are Bayes, and such like: they have those Okes that we have, but farre greater and better. After they had bene divers times aboord our shippes, my selfe, with seven more, went twentie mile into the River,[7] that runneth toward the Citie of Skicoake, which River they call Occam: and the evening following, we came to an Island, which they call Roanoak, distant from the harbour by which we entred, seven leagues: and at the North ende thereof, was a village[8] of nine houses, built of Cedar, and fortified round about with sharpe trees, to keepe out their enemies, and the entrance into it made it like a turne pike very artificially:[9] when we came towards it, standing neere unto the waters side,[10] the wife of Grangyno, the Kings brother, came running out to meete us very cheerefully, and friendly, her husband was not then in the village: some of her people she commanded to drawe our boate on the shoare, for the beating of the billoe:[11] others shee appointed to carry us on their backes to the dry ground, and others to bring our oares into the house, for feare of stealing. When we were come into the utter roome, having five roomes[12] in her house, she caused us to sitte downe by a great fire,[13] and after tooke off our clothes, and washed them, and dried them againe: some of the women pulled off our stockings, and washed them, some washed our feete in warme water, and shee her selfe tooke great paines to see all thinges ordered in the best manner shee coulde, making great haste to dresse some meate for us to eate.

After we had thus dried our selves, shee brought us into the inner roome, where shee set on the boord[1] standing along the house, some wheate like furmentie,[2] sodden Venison, and roasted, fishe sodden,[3] boyled, and roasted, Melons rawe, and sodden, rootes of divers kindes, and divers fruites: their drinke is commonly water, but while the grape lasteth, they drinke wine,[4] and for want of caskes to keepe it all the yeere after, they drinke water, but it is sodden with Ginger in it, and blacke Sinamon, and sometimes Sassaphras, and divers other wholesome, and medicinable hearbes[5] and trees. We were entertained with all love, and kindnes, and with as much bountie, after their manner, as they could possibly devise. Wee found the people most gentle, loving, and faithfull, void of all guile, and treason, and such as lived after the manner of the golden age. The earth bringeth foorth all things in aboundance, as in the first creation, without toile or labour. The people onely care to defend them selves from the cold, in their short winter, and to feede themselves with such meate as the soile affoordeth: their meate is very well sodden, and they make broth very sweete, and savorie: their vessels[6] are earthen pots, very large, white, and sweete: their dishes are woodden platters[7] of sweete timber: within the place where they feede, was their lodging, and within that their Idoll,[8] which they worship, of which they speake uncredible things. While we were at meate, there came in at the gates, two or three men with their bowes, and arrowes, from hunting, whome when we espied, we beganne to looke one towardes another, and offered to reach our weapons: but assoone as she espied our mistrust, she was very much mooved, and caused some of her men to runne out, and take away their bowes, and arrowes, and breake them, and withall beate the poore fellowes out of the gate againe. When we departed in the evening, and would not tarry all night, she was very sorie, and gave us into our boate our supper halfe dressed, pots, and all, and brought us to our boates side, in which wee laye all night, remooving the same a pretie distance from the shoare: shee perceiving our jealousie, was much grieved, and sent divers men, and thirtie women, to sitte all night on the bankes side by us, and sent us into our boates five mattes to cover us from the rayne, using very many wordes to intreate us to rest in their houses: but because wee were fewe men, and if wee had miscarried, the voyage had beene in very great daunger, wee durst not adventure any thing, although there was no cause of doubt: for a more kinde, and loving people, there can not be found in the world, as farre as we have hitherto had triall.

Beyonde this Islande, there is the maine lande, and over against this Islande falleth into this spatious water, the great river called Occam,[1] by the Inhabitants, on which standeth a Towne called Pemeoke, and sixe daies journey further upon the same is situate their greatest citie, called Schycoake,[2] which this people affirme to be very great: but the Savages were never at it, onely they speake of it, by the report of their Fathers, and other men, whome they have heard affirme it, to be above one daies journey[3] about.

Into this river falleth another great river, called Cipo, in which there is found great store of the Muscels, in which there are pearles: likewise there descendeth into this Occam, another river, called Nomopana,[4] on the one side whereof standeth a great Towne, called Chowanoake,[5] and the Lord of that Towne and Countrey, is called Pooneno: this Pooneno is not subject to the King of Wingandacoa, but is a free Lorde. Beyonde this Countrey, is there another King, whome they call Menatoan,[6] and these three Kinges are in league with eache other. Towards the Sunne set, foure daies journey, is situate a Towne called Sequotan, which is the Westermost Towne of Wingandacoa, neere unto which, sixe and twentie yeeres past, there was a shippe cast away,[7] whereof some of the people were saved, and those were white people, whom the Countrey people preserved.

And after ten daies, remaining in an out Island unhabited, called Wococan,[8] they with the helpe of some of the dwellers of Sequotan, fastened two boates of the Countrey together, and made mastes unto them, and sailes of their shirtes, and having taken into them such victuals as the Countrey yeelded, they departed after they had remained in this out Island three weekes: but shortly after, it seemed they were cast away, for the boates were found uppon the coast, cast aland in another Island adjoyning:[9] other then these, there was never any people apparelled, or white of colour, either seene, or heard of amongst these people, and these aforesaide were seene onely of the Inhabitants of Sequotan: which appeared to be very true, for they wondred mervelously when we were amongest them, at the whitenes of our skinnes, ever coveting to touch our breastes, and to view the same: besides they had our shippes in marvelous admiration, and all things els was so strange unto them, as it appeared that none of them had ever seene the like. When we discharged any peece, were it but a harquebush, they would tremble thereat for very feare, and for the strangenes of the same: for the weapons which themselves use, are bowes and arrowes: the arrowes are but of small canes, headed with a sharpe shell, or tooth of a fishe sufficient enough to kill a naked man. Their swordes are of wood hardened: likewise they use wooddin breastplates[1] for their defense. They have besides a kinde of clubbe, in the ende whereof they fasten the sharpe hornes of a stagge, or other beast. When they goe to warres, they carry with them their Idoll,[2] of whome they aske counsell, as the Romanes were woont of the Oracle of Apollo. They sing songs as they march towardes the battell, in steede of drummes, and trumpets: their warres are very cruell, and bloodie, by reason whereof, and of their civill dissentions, which have happened of late yeeres amongst them, the people are marvelously wasted, and in some places, the Countrey left desolate.[3]

Adjoyning unto this Towne aforesaide, called Sequotan, beginneth a Countrey called Ponouike[4] belonging to another King, whom they call Piemacum, and this King is in league with the next King, adjoyning towardes the setting of the Sunne, and the Countrey Neiosioke, situate uppon the side of a goodly River, called Neus: these Kings have mortall warre with Wingina, King of Wingandacoa, but about two yeeres past, there was a peace made betweene the King Piemacum, and the Lorde of Sequotan,[5] as these men which we have brought with us into England, have made us understande: but there remaineth a mortall malice in the Sequotanes, for many injuries and slaughters done uppon them by this Piemacum. They invited divers men, and thirtie women, of the best of his Countrey, to their Towne[6] to a feast: and when they were altogether merrie, and praying before their Idoll, which is nothing else, but a meere illusion of the Devill: the Captaine or Lorde of the Towne came suddenly upon them, and slewe them every one, reserving the women, and children: and these two have oftentimes since perswaded us to surprise Piemacum his Towne, having promised, and assured us, that there will be founde in it great store of commodities. But whether their perswasion be to the ende they may be revenged of their enemies, or for the love they beare to us, we leave that to the triall hereafter.

Beyond this Island, called Croonoake, are many Islands, very plenti-full of fruites and other naturall increases, together with many Townes, and villages, along the side of the continent, some bounding upon the Islands, and some stretching up further into the land.

When we first had sight of this Countrey, some thought the first lande we sawe, to be the continent: but after wee entred into the Haven, wee sawe before us another mightie long Sea: for there lieth along the coast a tracte of Islands, two hundreth miles in length, adjoyning to the Ocean sea, and betweene the Islands, two or three entrances: when you are entred betweene them (these Islands being very narrowe, for the most part, as in most places sixe miles broad, in some places lesse, in fewe more,) then there appeareth another great Sea, containing in bredth in some places, fortie, and in some fiftie, in some twentie miles over, before you come unto the continent: and in this inclosed Sea, there are about a hundreth Islands of divers bignesses, whereof one is sixteene miles long, at which we were, finding it to be a most pleasant, and fertile ground, replenished with goodly Cedars, and divers other sweete woods, full of Currans, of flaxe, and many other notable commodities, which we at that time had no leasure to view. Besides this Island, there are many, as I have saide, some of two, of three, of foure, of five miles, some more, some lesse, most beautifull, and pleasant to behold, replenished with Deere, Conies, Hares, and divers beastes, and about them the goodli-est and best fishe in the world, and in greatest aboundance.

Thus Sir, we have acquainted you with the particulars of our dis-coverie, made this present voyage, as farre foorth, as the shortnes of the time we there continued, would affoord us to take viewe of: and so contenting our selves with this service at this time, which we hope hereafter to inlarge, as occasion and assistance shall be given, we resolved to leave the Countrey,[1] and to apply our selves to returne for England, which we did accordingly, and arrived safely in the West of England, about the middest of September.

And whereas we have above certified you of the Countrey, taken in possession by us, to her Majesties use, and so to yours, by her Majes-ties grant, wee thought good for the better assurance thereof to re-corde some of the particular Gentlemen, and men of accompt, who then were present, as witnesses of the same, that thereby all occasion of cavill to the title of the Countrey, in her Majesties behalfe, may be prevented, which other wise, such as like not the action may use, and pretend, whose names are:

Master Philip Amadas,	} Captaines.
Master Arthur Barlowe,	
William Greeneville,	
John Wood,	
James Browewich,	
Henrie Greene,	} Of the companie.
Benjamin Wood,	
Simon Ferdinando,	
Nicholas Petman,	
John Hewes,	

We brought home also two of the Savages being lustie men, whose names were Wanchese and Manteo.[1]

II

Anonymous
Journal of the 1585 Virginia Voyage[1]

THE voyage made by Sir Richard Greenvile, for Sir Walter Ralegh, to Virginia, in the yeere, 1585.

The 19. day of Maye,[2] in the yeere above saide, wee departed from Plymmouth, our fleete consisting of the number of seven sailes, to wit, the Tyger,[3] of the burden of seven score tunnes: a Flie boate called the Roe Bucke, of the like burden: the Lyon of a hundred tunnes, or thereabouts: the Elizabeth, of fiftie tunnes, and the Dorothie, a small barke, whereunto were also adjoyned for speedie services, 2. small Pinnesses.[4] The principall Gentlemen of our companie, were, Master Ralfe Lane, Master Thomas Candishe, Master John Arundell, Master Raimund, Master Stukely, Master Bremige, Master Vincent, and Master John Clarke, and divers others, whereof some were Captaines, and other some Assistants for counsell,[5] and good directions in the voyage.

The 14. day of Aprill, we fell with Lançacota, and Forte Ventura, Isles of the Canaries, and from thence we continued our course for Dominica, one of the Antiles, of the West India, wherewith we fell the 7. day of Maye, and the 10. day following, we came to an anker at Cotesa, a little Island situate neere to the Island of S. John, where wee landed, and refreshed our selves all that day.

The 15. day[6] of Maye, we came to an anker, in the Baye of Mus-kito,[7] in the Island of S. John, within a Fawlcon shot of the shoare: where our Generall Sir Richard Greenvill, and the most part of our companie landed, and began to fortifie, very neere to the sea side: the river ranne by the one side of our forte,[8] and the other two sides were environed with woods.

The 13. day we began to builde a new pinnesse[9] within the Fort, with the timber that we then felled in the countrey, some part whereof we fet[1] three myle up in the land, and brought it to our Fort upon trucks, the Spaniards not daring to make or offer resistance.

The 16. day, there appeared unto us out of the woods 8. horsemen[2] of the Spaniards, about a quarter of a myle from our Fort, staying about halfe an hower in viewing our forces: but as soone as they saw x. of our shot marching towards them, they presently retyred into the woodes.

The 19. day, Master Candish, who had bene seperated from our fleete in a storme in the Bay of Portingal arrived at Cotesa, within the sight of the Tiger: we thinking him a farre off to have ben either a Spaniard or French man of warre thought it good to waigh ankers, and to goe roome with him, which the Tyger did, and discerned him at last to be one of our Consorts, for joy of whose comming our ships discharged their ordinance, and saluted him, according to the manner of the Seas.

The 22. day, 20. other Spanishe horsemen shewed them selves to us upon the other side of the river: who being seene, our General dispatched 20. footemen towards them, and two horsemen of ours, mounted upon Spanish horses, which wee before had taken in the time of our being on the Iland: they shewed to our men a flagge of truce, and made signes to have a parle with us: whereupon two of our men went halfe of the way upon the sands, and two of theirs came and met them: the two Spaniards offred very great salutations to our men, but began according to their Spanish proud humors, to expostulate with them, about their arrival, and fortifying in their countrie, who notwithstanding by our mens discrete answers were so cooled, that whereas they were told, that our principal intention was onely to furnish our selves with water, and victuals, and other necessaries whereof we stood in neede, which we craved might be yelded us with faire, and friendly means, otherwise our resolution was to practise force, and to releeve our selves by the sworde: the Spaniards in conclusion, seeing our men so resolute, yelded to our requestes with large promises of all curtesie, and great favor, and so our men and theirs departed.[3]

The 23. day our pinnesse was finished, and lanched, which being done, our Generall with his Captaines, and Gentlemen, marched up into the Country about the space of 4. myles, where in a plaine marsh, they stayed expecting the comming of the Spanyards according to their promise, to furnish us with victuals: who keeping their old custome for perjurie and breache of promise came not, whereupon our General fired the woods thereabout, and so retired to our Fort, which the same day was fired[1] also, and each man came aboord to be ready to set saile the next morning.

The 29. day[2] we set saile from Saint Johns, being many of us stoong before upon shoare with the Muskitoes: but the same night we tooke a Spanish Frigat, which was forsaken by the Spanyards upon the sight of us,[3] and the next day in the morning very early, wee tooke another Frigat,[4] with good and rich fraight, and divers Spaniards of accompt in her, which afterwards we ransomed for good round summes, and landed them in Saint Johns.

The 26. day our Lieutenant Master Ralfe Lane, went in one of the Frigats which we had taken, to Roxo bay[5] upon the Southwest side of Saint Johns, to fetch salt, being thither conducted by a Spanish Pilot:[6] as soone as he arrived there, he landed with his men, to the number of 20. and intrenched him selfe upon the sandes immediatly, compassing one of their salt hils within the trench:[7] who being seene of the Spanyards, there came downe towards him two or three troopes of horsemen, and footemen, who gave him the looking, and gazing on, but durst not come neere him to offer any resistance, so that Master Lane mauger[8] their troopes, caried their salt aboord and laded his Frigat, and so returned againe to our fleete the 29. day, which road at Saint Germans Bay. The same day we all departed, and the next day arrived in the Iland of Hispaniola.

June.

The 1. day of June we ankered at Isabella,[9] in the North side of Hispaniola.

The 3. day of June, the Governor of Isabella, and Captaine of the Port de Plata, beeing certifyed by the reports of sundry Spanyards, who had bene wel intertained aboord our shippes by our General, that in our fleete were many brave, and gallant Gentlemen, who greatly desired to see the Governor aforesaid, he thereupon sent gentle commendations to our Generall, promising within few daies to come to him in person, which he performed accordingly.

The 5. day the foresaid governor, accompanied with a lusty Frier,

& xx. other Spaniards, with their servants, & Negroes, came downe to the sea side, where our ships road at anker, who being seene, our General manned immediatly the most part of his boats with the chiefe men of our fleete, every man appointed, and furnished in the best sort: at the landing of our Generall, the Spanishe Governor[1] received him very curteously, and the Spanish Gentlemen saluted our English Gentlemen, and their inferior sort did also salute our Souldiers and Sea men, liking our men, and likewise their qualities, although at the first, they seemed to stand in feare of us, and of so many of our boats, whereof they desired that all might not land their men, yet in the end, the curtesies that passed on both sides were so great, that all feare and mistrust on the Spanyardes part was abandoned.

In the meane time while our English Generall and the Spanish Governor discoursed betwixt them of divers matters, as of the state of the Country, the multitude of the Townes and people, and the commodities of the Iland, our men provided two banquetting houses covered with greene boughs, the one for the gentlemen, the other for the servants, and a sumptuous banquet was brought in served by us all in Plate, with the sound of trumpets, and consort of musick, wherewith the Spanyards were more than delighted. Which banquet being ended, the Spanyardes in recompense of our curtesie, caused a great heard of white buls, and kyne, to be brought together from the Mounteines, and appointed for every Gentlemen and Captaine that would ride, a horse ready sadled, and then singled out three of the best of them to be hunted by horsemen after their manner, so that the pastime grew very plesant for the space of three houres, wherein all three of the beasts were killed, whereof one tooke the sea, and there was slaine with a musket. After this sport, many rare presents and gifts were given and bestowed on both partes, and the next day wee plaied the Marchants in bargaining with them by way of trucke and exchange for divers of their commodities, as horses, mares, kyne, buls, goates, swine, sheepe, bul hydes, sugar, ginger, pearle, tabacco, and such like commodities of the Iland.[2]

The 7. day we departed with great good will from the Spanyardes from the Island of Hispaniola: but the wiser sort do impute this greate shew of friendship, and curtesie used towardes us by the Spanyards rather to the force that we were of, and the vigilancie, and watchfulnes that was amongst us, then to any harty good will, or sure freindly intertainment: for doubtlesse if they had bene stronger then wee, we might have looked for no better curtesie at their handes, then Master John Hawkins received at saint John de Ullua, or John Oxnam neere the streights of Dariene, and divers others of our Countrymen in other places.

The 8. day we ankred at a small Iland to take Seales which in that place wee understood to have bene in great quantitie, where the Generall and certaine others with him in the pinnesse, were in very great danger to have bene all cast away, but by the helpe of God they escaped the hazard, and returned aboord the Admirall[1] in safetie.

The 9. day we arrived and landed in the Isle of Caycos, in which Islande we searched for salt pondes, upon the advertisement, and information of a Portingall:[2] who in deede abused our General and us, deserving a halter for his hire, if it had so pleased us.

The 12. we ankered at Guanema, and landed.

The 15. and 16. we ankered and landed at Sygateo.

The 20. we fell with the mayne of Florida.

The 23. wee were in great danger of a Wracke on a breache called the Cape of Feare.[3]

The 24. we came to anker in a harbor where we caught in one tyde so much fishe as woulde have yelded us xx. pounds in London: this was our first landing in Florida.

The 26. we came to anker at Wocokon.[4]

The 29. wee waighed anker to bring the Tyger into the harbour, where through the unskilfulnesse of the Master whose name was Fernando, the Admirall strooke on grounde, and sunke.[5]

July.

The 3. we sent word of our ariving at Wococon, to Wingino at Roanocke.

The 6. Master John Arundell was sent to the mayne, and Manteio with him: and Captayne Aubry[6] and Captaine Boniten the same day were sent to Croatoan, where they found two of our men left there, with 30. other by Captaine Reymond, some 20. daies before.

The 8. Captaine Aubry, and Captaine Boniten returned with two of our men found by them to us at Wocokon.[7]

The 11. day the Generall accompanied in his Tilt boate[8] with

Master John Arundell, Master Stukelye, and divers other Gentel-men, Master Lane, Master Candish, Master Harriot, and 20. others in the new pinnesse, Captaine Amadas, Captaine Clarke,[1] with tenne others in a ship boate, Francis Brooke, and John White[2] in another ship boate passed over the water from Ococon to the mayne land victualled for eight dayes, in which voyage we first discovered the townes of Pomioke, Aquascogoc and Secota, and also the great lake called by the Savages Paquype, with divers other places, and so returned with that discovery to our Fleete.

The 12. we came to the Towne of Pomeioke.[3]

The 13. we passed by water to Aquascococke.

The 15. we came to Secotan[4] and were well intertayned there of the Savages.

The 16. we returned thence, and one of our boates with the Admirall was sent to Aquascococke to demaund a silver cup which one of the Savages had stolen from us, and not receiving it according to his promise, we burnt, and spoyled their corne, and Towne,[5] all the people beeing fledde.

The 18. we returned from the discovery of Secotan, and the same day came aboord our fleete[6] ryding at Wocokon.

The 21. our fleete ankering at Wokocon, we wayed anker for Hatoraske.

The 27. our fleete ankered at Hatoraske,[7] and there we rested.

The 29. Grangino,[8] brother to King Wingino, came aboord the Admirall, and Manteo with him.

August.

The 2. The Admirall[9] was sent to Weapemeoke.

The 5. Master John Arundell[10] was sent for England.

The 25. our Generall wayed anker, and set saile for England.[11]

About the 31. he tooke a Spanish ship of 300. tunne richly loaden, boording her with a boate made with boards of chests, which fell a sunder, and sunke at the shippes side, assoone as ever hee and his men were out of it.

September.

The 10. of September, by foule weather the Generall then shipped in the prise lost sight of the Tyger.[12]

October.

The sixt the Tyger fell with the landes ende, and the same day came to an anker at Falmouth.

The 18. the Generall came with the prise to Plymmouth, and was courteously received by diverse of his worshipfull friends.[1]

III

The Names of Lane's Colonists[1]

THE names of all those as well Gentlemen as others, that remained one whole yeere in Virginia, under the Governement of Master Ralfe Lane.

Master Philip Amades,
    Admirall of the countrie.
Master Hariot.
Master Acton.
Master Edward Stafford.
Thomas Luddington.
Master Marvyn.
Master Gardyner.
Captaine Vaughan.
Master Kendall.
Master Prideox.
Robert Holecroft.
Rise Courtney.
Master Hugh Rogers.
Thomas Foxe.
Edward Nugen.
Darby Glande.
Edward Kelle.
John Gostigo.
Erasmus Clefs.
Edward Ketcheman.
John Linsey.
Thomas Rottenbury.
Roger Deane.
John Harris.

Master Thomas Harvie.
Master Snelling.
Master Anthony Russe.
Master Allyne.
Master Michel Polyson.
John Cage.
Thomas Parre.
William Randes.
Geffrey Churchman.
William Farthowe.
John Taylor.
Philppe Robyns.
Thomas Phillippes.
Valentine Beale.
James Skinner.
George Eseven.
John Chaundeler.
Philip Blunt.
Richard Poore.
Robert Yong.
Marmaduke Constable.[2]
Thomas Hesket.
William Wasse.
John Fever.
Daniel.

Frauncis Norris.
Mathewe Lyne.
Edward Kettell.
Thomas Wisse.
Robert Biscombe.
William Backhouse.
William White.
Henry Potkin.
Dennis Barnes.
Joseph Borges.
Doughan Gannes.[1]
William Tenche.
Randall Latham.
Thomas Hulme.
Walter Myll.
Richard Gilbert.
Steven Pomarie.
John Brocke.
Bennet Harrye.
James Stevenson.
Charles Stevenson.
Christopher Lowde.
Jeremie Man.
James Mason.
David Salter.
Richard Ireland.
Thomas Bookener.
William Philippes.
Randall Mayne.

Thomas Taylor.
Richard Humfrey.
John Wright.
Gabriell North.
Bennet Chappell.
Richard Sare.
James Lasie.
Smolkin.
Thomas Smart.
Robert.
John Evans.
Roger Large.
Humfrey Garden.
Frauncis Whitton.
Rowland Griffyn.
William Millard.
John Twyt.[2]
Edwarde Seklemore.
John Anwike.
Christopher Marshall.
David Williams.
Nicholas Swabber.
Edward Chipping.
Sylvester Beching.
Vincent Cheyne.
Haunce Walters.[3]
Edward Barecombe.
Thomas Skevelabs.
William Walters.

IV

Ralph Lane to Richard Hakluyt the Elder[1]
and Master H—— of the Middle Temple
3 September 1585

AN extract of Master Lanes letter, to Master Richard Hakluyt Esquire, and another gentleman of the middle Temple, from Virginia:

In the meane while you shall understand that since sir Richard Greenvils departure from us, as also before, we have discovered the maine[2] to bee the goodliest soile under the cope of heaven, so abounding with sweete trees, that bring such sundry rich and most pleasant gummes, grapes of such greatnes, yet wild, as France, Spaine nor Italy hath no greater, so many sortes of Apothecarie drugs, such severall kindes of flaxe, and one kind like silke, the same gathered of a grasse, as common there as grasse is here. And now within these few dayes we have found here a Guinie wheate,[3] whose eare yeeldeth corne for bread, 400. upon one eare, and the Cane maketh very good and perfect suger, also Terra Samia, otherwise Terra sigillata. Besides that, it is the goodliest and most pleasing territorie of the world (for the soile is of an huge unknowen greatnesse, and very wel peopled and towned, though savagelie) and the climate so wholesome, that we have not had one sicke, since we touched land here. To conclude, if Virginia had but Horses and Kine in some reasonable proportion, I dare assure my selfe being inhabited with English, no realme in Christendome were comparable to it. For this alreadie we find, that what commodities soever Spaine, France, Italy, or the East parts do yeeld unto us in wines of all sortes, in oiles, in flaxe, in rosens, pitch, frankenscence, currans, sugers, & such like,[4] these parts do abound with y[e] growth of them all, but being Savages that possesse the land, they know no use of the same. And sundry other rich commodities, that no parts of the world, be they West or East Indies, have, here we finde great abundance of. The people naturally most curteous,

& very desirous to have clothes, but especially of course cloth rather than silke, course canvas they also like wel of,[1] but copper carieth ye price of all, so it be made red.[2] Thus good Master Hakluyt and master H. I have joyned you both in one letter of remembrance, as two that I love dearely well, and commending me most hartily to you both, I commit you to ye tuition of the almighty. From the new Fort[3] in Virginia, this 3 September[4] 1585.

Your most assured friend, Rafe Lane.

V

Ralph Lane's
Narrative of the Settlement of Roanoke Island
1585–1586[1]

AN account of the particularities of the imployments of the English men left in Virginia by Sir Richard Greenevill under the charge of Master Ralfe Lane Generall of the same, from the 17. of August, 1585. untill the 18. of June 1586.[2] at which time they departed the Countrie: sent, and directed to Sir Walter Ralegh.[3]

That I may proceed with order in this discourse, I thinke it requisite to devide it into two partes. The first shall declare the particularities of such partes of the Country within the mayne, as our weake number, and supply of things necessary did inable us to enter into the discovery thereof.

The second part,* shall set downe the reasons generally moving us to resolve on our departure at the instant with the General Sir Frauncis Drake, and our common request for passage with him, when the barkes, pinnesses, and boates with the Masters and Mariners ment by him to bee left in the Countrie for the supply of such, as for a further time ment to have stayed there were caried away with tempest, and foule weather: In the beginning whereof shalbe declared the conspiracie of Pemisapan, with the Savages of the mayne to have cutt us off, &c.

The first part declaring the particularities of the Countrey of Virginia.

First therefore touching the particularities of the Countrey, you shall understand our discovery of the same hath bene extended from the Iland of Roanoak, (the same having bene the place of our settlement or inhabitation) into the South, into the North, into the Northwest, and into the West.

The uttermost place to the Southward of any discoverie was

* 2 Parts of this discourse.

Secotan, being by estimation foure score miles[1] distant from Roanoak. The passage from thence was thorowe a broad sound within the mayne, the same being without kenning of land, and yet full of flats and shoales: we had but one boate with foure oares to passe through the same, which boat could not carry above fifteene men with their furniture, baggage, and victuall for seven dayes at the most: and as for our Pinnesse, besides that she drewe too deepe water for that shalow sound, she would not stirre for an oare:[2] for these and other reasons (winter also being at hand) we thought good wholy to leave the discovery of those partes[3] untill our stronger supplie.

To the Northwarde our furthest discoverie was to the Chesepians,[4] distant from Roanoak about 130. miles, the passage to it was very shalow and most dangerous, by reason of the breadth of the sound, and the litle succour that upon any flawe was there to be had.

But the Territorie and soyle of the Chesepians (being distant fifteene miles from the shoare) was for pleasantnes of seate,* for temperature of Climate, for fertilitie of soyle, and for the commoditie of the Sea, besides multitude of beares (being an excellent good victuall, with great woods of Sassafras, and Wall nut trees) is not to be excelled by any other whatsoever.

There be sundry Kings, whom they call Weroances,[5] and Countries of great fertilitie adjoyning to the same, as the Mandoages, Tripanicks, and Opossians, which all came to visit the Colonie of the English, which I had for a time appointed to be resident there.[6]

To the Northwest the farthest place of our discoverie was to Choanoke distant from Roanoak about 130. miles. Our passage thither lyeth through a broad sound, but all fresh water, and the chanell of great depth, navigable for good shipping,[7] but out of the chanell full of shoales.

The Townes[8] about the water side situated by the way, are these following: Pysshokonnok, The womans Towne, Chipanum, Weopomiok, Muscamunge, and Mattaquen: all these being under the jurisdiction of the king of Weopomiok, called Okisco: from Muscamunge we enter into the River, and jurisdiction of Choanoke: There the River beginneth to straighten untill it comes to Choanoke, and then groweth to be as narrowe as the Thames betweene Westminster, and Lambeth.

* The excellency of the seate of Chesepiok.[9]

Betweene Muscamunge and Choanoke upon the left hand as we passe thither, is a goodly high land, and there is a Towne which we called the blinde Towne, but the Savages called it Ooanoke, and hath a very goodly corne field belonging unto it: it is subject to Choanoke.

Choanoke* it selfe is the greatest Province and Seigniorie lying upon that River, and the very Towne it selfe is able to put 700. fighting men[1] into the fielde, besides the forces of the Province it selfe.

The King of the sayd Province is called Menatonon, a man impotent in his lims, but otherwise for a Savage, a very grave and wise man, and of very singular good discourse in matters concerning the state, not onely of his owne Countrey, and the disposition of his owne men, but also of his neighbours round about him as wel farre as neere, and of the commodities that eche Countrey yeeldeth. When I had him prisoner with me, for two dayes that we were together, he gave me more understanding and light of the Countrey then I had received by all the searches and salvages that before I or any of my companie had had conference with: it was in March last past 1586. Amongst other things he tolde me, that going three dayes journey in a canoa up his River of Choanoke, and then descending to the land, you are within foure dayes journey to passe over land Northeast to a certaine Kings countrey,[2] whose Province lyeth upon the Sea, but his place of greatest strength is an Iland† situate as he described unto me in a Bay, the water round about the Iland very deepe.

Out of this Bay hee signified unto mee, that this King had so great quantitie of Pearle,‡ and doeth so ordinarily take the same, as that not onely his owne skins that he weareth, and the better sort of his gentlemen and followers, are full set with the sayd Pearle, but also his beds, and houses are garnished with them, and that hee hath such quantitie of them, that it is a wonder to see.

He shewed me that the sayd King was with him at Choanoak two yeeres before, and brought him certaine Pearle, but the same of the worst sort, yet was he faine to buy them of him for copper at a deere rate, as he thought: He gave me a rope of the same Pearle, but they were blacke, and naught, yet many of them were very great, and a fewe amongst a number very orient and round, all which I lost with

* The Towne of Choanoak able to make 700. men of warre.
† An Iland in a Bay.　　‡ Pearles in exceeding quantitie.

other things of mine, comming aborde Sir Francis Drake his Fleete: yet he tolde me that the sayd King had great store of Pearle that were white, great, and round, and that his blacke Pearle his men did take out of shalowe water, but the white Pearle[1] his men fished for in very deepe water.

It seemed to mee by his speech, that the sayde king had traffike with white men that had clothes as we have for these white Pearle, and that was the reason that he would not depart with other then with blacke Pearles,[2] to those of the same Countrey.

The king of Choanoak promised to give me guides to goe over land into that kings Countrey whensoever I would: but he advised me to take good store of men with mee, and good store of victuall, for he sayd, that king would be loth to suffer any strangers to enter into his Countrey, and especially to meddle with the fishing for any Pearle there, and that hee was able to make a great many of men into the fielde, which he sayd would fight very well.[3]

Hereupon I resolved with my selfe, that if your supplie had come before the end of April, and that you had sent any store of boats, or men, to have had them made in any reasonable time, with a sufficient number of men, and victuals to have found us untill the new corne were come in, I woulde have sent a small Barke with two Pinnesses about by Sea to the Northwarde to have found out the Bay he spake of, and to have sounded the barre if there were any, which shoulde have ridden there in the sayd Bay about that Iland, while I with all the small boats I could make, and with two hundreth men[4] would have gone up to the head of the River of Choanoak, with the guides that Menatonon would have given, which I would have bene assured should have bene of his best men, (for I had his best beloved sonne prisoner with me) who also should have kept me companie in an handlocke with the rest foote by foote all the voyage over land.

My meaning was further at the head of the River in the place of my descent where I would have left my boates to have raysed a sconse with a small trench, and a pallisado upon the top of it, in the which, and in the garde of my boates I would have left five and twentie, or thirtie men, with the rest would I have marched with as much victuall as every man could have carried, with their furniture, mattocks, spades and axes, two dayes journey. In the ende of my marche upon some convenient plot would I have raysed another sconse according to the former, where I would have left 15. or 20. And if it would have fallen out conveniently, in the way I woulde have raised my sayd sconse[1] upon some corne fielde, that my companie might have lived upon it.

And so I would have holden this course of insconsing every two dayes march, untill I had bene arrived at the Bay or Porte he spake of:* which finding to be worth the possession, I would there have raised a mayne forte, both for the defence of the harboroughs, and our shipping also, and would have reduced our whole habitation from Roanoak and from the harborough and port there (which by proofe is very naught) unto this other[2] before mentioned, from whence, in the foure dayes march before specified could I at all times returne with my companie backe unto my boats ryding under my sconse, very neere whereunto directly from the West runneth a most notable River, and in all those partes most famous, called the River of Morotico.[3] This River openeth into the broad sound of Weopomiok: And whereas the River of Choanoak, and all the other sounds, and Bayes, salt and fresh, shewe no currant in the world in calme weather, but are mooved altogether with the winde: This River of Morotico hath so violent a currant from the West and Southwest, that it made me almost of opinion that with oares it would scarse be navigable: it passeth with many creeks and turnings, and for the space of thirtie miles rowing, and more, it is as broad as the Thames betwixt Greenwich, and the Ile of dogges, in some place more, and in some lesse: the currant runneth as strong being entred so high into the River, as at London bridge upon a vale water.[4]

And for that not onely Menatonon, but also the Savages of Morotico themselves doe report strange things of the head of that River, and that from Morotico it selfe, which is a principall Towne upon that River, it is thirtie dayes as some of them say, and some say fourtie dayes voyage to the head thereof, which head they say springeth out of a maine rocke in that abundance, that forthwith it maketh a most violent streame: and further, that this huge rocke standeth nere unto a Sea, that many times in stormes (the winde comming outwardly from ye Sea) the waves thereof are beaten into the said fresh streame, so that the fresh water for a certaine space, groweth salt and brackish:[5]

* Whether Master Ralph Lane meant to remoove.

28

I tooke a resolution with my selfe, having dismissed Menatonon upon a ransome agreed for, and sent his sonne into the Pinnesse to Roanoak, to enter presently so farre into that River with two double whirries,[1] and fourtie persons one or other, as I could have victuall to carrie us, untill we could meete with more either of the Moratiks, or of the Mangoaks[2] which is another kinde of Savages, dwelling more to the Westwarde of the sayd River: but the hope of recovering more victuall from the Savages made me and my company as narowly to escape starving in that discoverie before our returne, as ever men did that missed the same.

For Pemisapan, who had changed his name[3] of Wingina* upon the death of his brother Granganimo, had given both the Choanists, & Mangoaks word of my purpose touching them, I having bin inforced to make him privie to ye same, to be served by him of a guide to the Mangoaks, and yet he did never rest to solicite continually my going upon them, certifying me of a generall assembly even at that time made by Menatonon at Choanoak of all his Weroances, & allyes to the number of 3000.[4] bowes preparing to come upon us at Roanoak, and that the Mangoaks also were joyned in the same confederacie, who were able of themselves to bring as many more to the enterprise: And true it was, that at that time the assembly was holden at Choanoak about us, as I found at my comming thither, which being unlooked for did so dismay them, as it made us have the better hand at them. But this confederacie against us of the Choanists and Mangoaks was altogether and wholly procured by Pemisapan himselfe, as Menatonon confessed unto me, who sent them continuall worde that our purpose was fully bent to destroy them: on the other side he tolde me that they had the like meaning towards us.[5]

Hee in like sort having sent worde to the Mangoaks of mine intention to passe up into their River, and to kill them (as he sayd) both they and the Moratiks, with whome before we were entred into a league, and they had ever dealt kindely with us, abandoned their Townes along the River, and retyred themselves with their Crenepoes,† and their corne within the mayne: insomuch as having passed three dayes voyage up the River, we could not meete a man, nor find a graine of corne in any their Townes: whereupon considering with my selfe, that wee had but two dayes victuall left, and that wee

* Wingina changeth his name.   † Their women.

29

were then 160. miles from home,[1] besides casualtie of contrarie windes or stormes, and suspecting treason of our owne Savages in the discoverie of our voyage intended, though we had no intention to be hurtfull to any of them, otherwise then for our copper to have had corne of them: I at night upon the corps of garde, before the putting foorth of centinels, advertised the whole companie of the case wee stoode in for victuall, and of mine opinion that we were betrayed by our owne Savages, and of purpose drawen foorth by them, upon vaine hope to be in the ende starved, seeing all the Countrey fledde before us, and therefore while we had those two dayes victuall left, I thought it good for us to make our returne homewarde, and that it were necessarie for us to get the other side of the sound of Weopo-miok in time, where we might be relieved upon the weares of Chypanum, and the womans Towne, although the people were fled.

Thus much I signified unto them, as the safest way: neverthelesse, I did referre it to the greatest number of voyces, whether we should adventure the spending of our whole victuall in some further viewe of that most goodly River in hope to meete with some better hap, or otherwise to retyre our selves backe againe.: And for that they might be the better advised, I willed them to deliberate all night upon the matter, and in the morning at our going aborde to set our course according to the desires of the greatest part. Their resolution fully and wholly was (and not three found to be of the contrary opinion) that whiles there was left one halfe pinte of corne for a man, that we should not leave the search of that River, and that there were in the companie two mastives, upon the pottage of which with sassafras leaves (if the worst fell out) the companie would make shift to live two dayes, which time would bring them downe the currant to the mouth of the River, and to the entrie of the sound, and in two dayes more at the farthest they hoped to crosse the sounde and to bee relieved by the weares, which two dayes they would fast rather then be drawen backe a foote till they had seene the Mangoaks, either as friends or foes. This resolution of theirs did not a little please mee; since it came of themselves, although for mistrust of that which afterwards did happen, I pretended to have bene rather of the contrary opinion.

And that which made me most desirous to have some doings with the Mangoaks either in friendship or otherwise to have had one or two of them prisoners,[2] was, for y^t it is a thing most notorious to all ye countrey, that there is a Province to the which the sayd Mangoaks have recourse and traffike up that River of Morattico, which hath a marveilous and most strange Minerall.* This Mine is so notorious amongst them, as not onely to the Savages dwelling up the sayde river, and also to the Savages of Choanoke, and all them to the westward, but also to all them of the mayne: the countries name is of fame, and is called Chaunis Temoatan.[1]

The mineral they say is Wassador, which is copper, but they call by the name of Wassador every mettall whatsoever: they say it is of the couler of our copper, but our copper is better then theirs: and the reason is for that it is redder and harder, whereas that of Chaunis Temoatan is very soft, and pale: they say that they take the sayd mettall out of a river that falleth very swift from hie rocks, and hyls, and they take it in shallowe water: the manner is this. They take a great bowle by their discription as great as one of our targets, and wrap a skinne over the hollowe part thereof, leaving one part open to receive in the minerall: that done, they watch the comming downe of the currant, and the change of the couler of the water, and then suddenly chop downe the said bowle with the skin, and receive into the same as much oare as will come in, which is ever as much as their bowle wil hold, which presently they cast into a fire, and forthwith it melteth, and doeth yeelde in 5. partes, at the first melting, two parts of metall for three partes of oare.[2] Of this metall the Mangoaks have so great store, by report of all the savages adjoyning, that they beautifie their houses with great plates of the same: and this to be true, I received by report of all the country, and particularly by yong Skiko, the King of Choanokes sonne my prisoner, who also himselfe had bene prisoner with the Mangoaks, and set downe all the particularities to mee before mentioned: but hee had not bene at Chawnis Temoatan himselfe: for he sayd, it was twentie dayes journey overlande from the Mangoaks, to the saide minerall country, and that they passed through certaine other territories betweene them and the Mangoaks, before they came to the said country.

Upon reporte of the premisses, which I was very inquisitive in all places where I came to take very particular information of, by all the savages that dwelt towards those parts, and especially of Menatonon himselfe, who in every thing did very particularly informe mee, and

* A marvellous Minerall in the countrey of Chaunis Temoatan.

promised mee guides of his owne men, who shoulde pass over with mee, even to the sayde country of Chaunis Temoatan, (for over lande from Choanok to the Mangoaks is but one dayes journey from sunne rysing to sunne setting, whereas by water it is 7. daies[1] with the soonest:) These things I say, made me verie desirous by all meanes possible to recover the Mangoaks & to get some of that their copper for an assay, and therefore I willingly yeelded to their resolution: But it fell out very contrarie to all expectation, and likelyhood: for after two dayes travell, and our whole victual spent, lying on shoare all night, wee could never see man, onely fires wee might perceive made alongst the shoare where we were to passe, and up into the countrie untill the very last day. In the evening whereof, about three of the clocke we heard certaine savages call as we thought, Manteo, who was also at that time with mee in boate, whereof we all being verie glad, hoping of some friendly conference with them, and making him to answere them, they presently began a song, as we thought in token of our welcome to them: but Manteo presently betooke him to his peece, and tolde mee that they ment to fight with us:* which word was not so soone spoken by him, and the light horseman ready to put to shoare, but there lighted a vollie of their arrowes amongst them in the boate, but did no hurt God be thanked to any man. Immediatly, the other boate lying ready with their shot to skoure the place for our hand weapons to land upon, which was presently done, although the lande was very high and steepe, the Savages forthwith quitted the shoare, and betooke themselves to flight: we landed, and having fayre and easily followed for a smal time after them, who had wooded themselves we know not where: the sunne drawing then towards the setting, and being then assured that the next day, if wee would pursue them, though wee might happen to meete with them, yet we should bee assured to meete with none of their victuall, which we then had good cause to thinke of, therefore choosing for the companie a convenient grounde in safetie to lodge in for the night, making a strong corps of garde, and putting out good centinels, I determined the next morning before the rising of the sunne to be going backe againe, if possibly wee might recover the mouth of the river into the broade sownde, which at my first motion I found my whole companie ready to assent unto: for they were nowe come to their dogs porredge,

* A conflict begun by ye Savages.

that they had bespoken for themselves, if that befell them which did, and I before did mistrust we should hardly escape. The ende was, we came the next day by night to the rivers mouth within 4. or 5. miles of the same, having rowed in one day downe the currant,* as much as in 4. dayes we had done against the same: we lodged upon an Islande,[1] where wee had nothing in the worlde to eate but pottage of sassafras leaves, the like whereof for a meate was never used before as I thinke. The broad sownde wee had to passe, the next day all fresh and fasting: that day the winde blewe so strongly,[2] and the billow so great, that there was no possibilitie of passage without sinking of our boates. This was upon Easter eve,[3] which was fasted very trulie. Upon Easter day in the morning the wind comming very calme, wee entred the sownde, and by 4. of the clocke we were at Chipanum, where all the Savages that wee had left there were fled, but their wears did yeelde us some fish, as God was pleased not utterly to suffer us to be lost: for some of our companie of the light horsemen[4] were far spent. The next morning we arrived at our home Roanoake.

I have set downe this voyage somewhat particularly, to the ende it may appeare unto you (as true it is) that there wanted no great good will from the most to the least amongst us, to have perfited this discoverie of the mine: for that the discovery of a good mine, by the goodnesse of God, or a passage to the Southsea, or someway to it, and nothing els can bring this country in request to be inhabited by our nation. And with the discovery of any of the two above shewed, it wilbe the most sweete, and healthfullest climate, and therewithall the most fertile soyle, being manured in the world: and then will Sassafras, and many other rootes & gummes there found make good Marchandise[5] and lading for shipping, which otherwise of themselves will not bee worth the fetching.

Provided also, that there be found out a better harborough then yet there is, which must bee to the Northward, if any there be, which was mine intention to have spent this summer in the search of, and of the mine of Chawnis Temoatan: the one I would have done, if the barks that I should have had of Sir Francis Drake, by his honorable curtesie, had not bene driven away by storme: the other if your supply of more men, and some other necessaries had come to us in any convenient sufficiencie. For this river of Moratico promiseth great

* The great currant of the River of Morottico.

things, and by the opinion of Master Harriots[1] the heade of it by the description of the country, either riseth from the bay of Mexico, or els from very neere unto the same, that openeth out into the South sea.

And touching the Minerall, thus doth Master Yougham affirme, that though it be but copper,[2] seeing the Savages are able to melt it, it is one of the richest Minerals in the worlde.

Wherefore a good harborough founde to the Northward, as before is sayd, and from thence foure dayes overland, to the river of Choanoak sconses being raysed, from whence againe overlande through the province of Choanoak one dayes voyage to the first towne of the Mangoaks up the river of Moratico by the way, as also upon the sayd river for the defence of our boats like sconses being set, in this course of proceeding you shall cleare your selfe from all those dangers and broad shallowe sownds before mentioned, and gayne within foure dayes travell into the heart of the mayne 200. myles[3] at the least, and so passe your discoverie into that most notable, and to the likeliest partes of the mayne, with farre greater felicitie then otherwise can bee performed.

Thus sir, I have though simply, yet truely set downe unto you, what my labour with the rest of the gentlemen, and poore men of our company, (not without both payne, and perill which the lorde in his mercy many wayes delivered us from) could yeelde unto you, which might have bene performed in some more perfection, if the lorde had bene pleased that onely that which you had provided for us had at the first bene left with us, or that he had not in his eternall providence now at the last set some other course in these things, then the wisedome of man could looke into, which truely the carying away, by a most strange, & unlooked for storme all our provision, with barks, master, Marryners, and sundrie also of mine owne company, all having bene so curteously supplyed by the Generall Sir Francis Drake, the same having bene most sufficient to have performed the greatest part of the premisses, must ever make me to thinke, the hand of God only, (for some his good purpose to my selfe yet unknowne), to have bene in the matter.

The second part[4] touching the conspiracy of Pemisapan, the discoverie of the same, and at the last, of our request to depart with Sir Francis Drake for England.

Ensenore a savage father[1] to Pemisapan being the only frend to our nation that we had amongst them, and about the king, dyed the 20. of April, 1586. hee alone, had before opposed himselfe in their consultations against al matters proposed against us, which both the king, and all the rest of them after Grangemoes death, were very willing to have preferred. And he was not onely by the meere providence of God during his life, a meane to save us from hurt,[2] as poysonings and such like, but also to doe us very great good, and singulerly in this.

The king was advised and of himselfe disposed, as a ready meane to have assuredly brought us to ruine in the moneth of March, 1586, himselfe also with all his Savages to have runne away from us, and to have left his ground in the Island unsowed, which if he had done, there had bene no possibilitie in common reason, (but by the immediate hand of God) that we could have bene preserved from starving[3] out of hand. For at that time wee had no weares for fishe,[4] neither could our men skill of the making of them, neither had wee one grayne of corne for seede to put into the ground.

In mine absence on my voyage that I had made against the Chaonists, and Mangoaks, they had raised a bruite among themselves, that I and my company were part slayne, and part starved by the Chaonists, and Mangoaks. One part of this tale was too true, that I and mine were like to be starved, but the other false.

Neverthelesse untill my returne, it tooke such effect in Pemisapans breast, and in those against us, that they grew not onely into contempt of us, but also (contrary to their former reverend opinion in shew, of the almightie God of heaven, and Jesus Christ, whome wee serve and worship, whome before they woulde acknowledge and confesse the onely God[5]:) nowe they began to blaspheme, and flatly to say, that our Lord God was not God, since hee suffered us to sustaine much hunger, and also to be killed of the Renapoaks,[6] for so they call by that generall name, all the inhabitants of the whole mayne, of what province soever. Insomuch as olde Ensenore, neither any of his fellowes, coulde for his sake have no more credite for us: and it came so farre that the King was resolved to have presently gone away as is aforesaid.

But even in the beginning of this bruite I returned, which when hee sawe contrarie to his expectation, and the advertisement that he had received: that not only my selfe, and my company were al safe, but also by report of his owne 3. savages, which had bene with mee besides Manteo in that voyage, that is to say, Tetepano, his sisters husband[1] Eracano, and Cossine, that the Chaonists, and Mangoaks, (whose name, and multitude besides their valour is terrible to al the rest of the provinces) durst not for the most part of them abide us, and that those that did abide us were killed, and that we had taken Menatonon prisoner, and brought his sonne[2] that he best loved to Roanoak with me, it did not a little asswage all devises against us: on the other side, it made Ensenors opinions to be received againe with greater respects. For hee had often before tolde them, and then renewed those his former speeches, both to the king and the rest, that wee were the servants of God, and that wee were not subject to be destroyed by them: but contrariwise, that they amongst them that sought our destruction, should finde their owne, and not be able to worke ours, and that we being dead men were able to doe them more hurt, then now we coulde do being alive: an opinion very confidently at this day holden by the wisest amongst them, and of their olde men, as also, that they have bene in the night, beeing 100. myles from any of us in the ayre shot at, and stroken by some men of ours, that by sicknesse had dyed among them: and many of them holde opinion, that wee be dead men returned into the worlde againe, and that we doe not remayne dead but for a certaine time, and that then we returne againe.

All these speeches then againe grew in ful credite with them, the King and all touching us, when hee saw the small troupe returned againe, and in that sort from those whose very names were terrible[3] unto them: but that which made up the matter on our side for that time, was an accident, yea rather, (as all the rest was) the good providence of the Almightie for the saving of us, which was this.

Within certaine dayes after my returne from the said journey, Menatonon sent a messengere to visite his sonne the prisoner with me, and sent me certaine pearle for a present, or rather as Pemisapan told me, for the ransome of his sonne, and therefore I refused them: but the greatest cause of his sending then, was to signifie unto me, that hee had commaunded Okisko king of Weopomiok, to yelde him-selfe servant, and homager, to the great Weroanza of England,[4] and after her to Sir Walter Ralegh: to perfourme which commandement received from Menatonon, the sayd Okisko joyntly with this Mena-

Sir Walter Ralegh: from the miniature by Nicholas Hilliard, now in the National Portrait Gallery

An · DNI · 1571
ÆTATIS · SVÆ
·29·

r Richard Granville, killed
a sea-fight near the Azores
1591

Sir Richard Grenville, from a painting in the National Portrait Gallery:
artist not known

tonons messenger, sent foure and twentie of his principallest men to Roanoak to Pemisapan, to signifie that they were readie to perfourme the same, and so had sent those his men to let me knowe, that from that time forwarde hee, and his successours were to acknowledge her Majestie their onely Soveraigne,[1] and next unto her, as is aforesayde.

All which being done, and acknowledged by them all, in the presence of Pemisapan his father, and all his Savages in counsel then with him, it did for the time, thorowly (as it seemed) change him in disposition towards us: Insomuch as forthwith Ensenore wan this resolution of him, that out of hand he should goe about, & withall, to cause his men to set up weares forthwith for us: both which he, at that present went in hand withal & did so labour the expedition of it, that in the end of April, he had sowed a good quantitie of ground, so much as had bene sufficient, to have fed our whole company (God blessing the grouth) and that by the belly for a whole yere: besides that he gave us a certaine plot of grounde for our selves to sowe.[2] All which put us in marveilous comfort, if we could passe from Aprill, untill the beginning of July, (which was to have bene the beginning of their harvest,)* that then a newe supplie out of Englande or els our owne store would well inough maintayne us: All our feare was of the two moneths betwixt, in which meane space, if the Savages should not helpe us with Cassada, and Chyna, and that our weares should fayle us, (as often they did) wee might very well starve, notwithstanding the growing corne, like the starving horse in the stable, with the growing grasse as the proverbe is, which we very hardlye had escaped but onely by the hande of God, as it pleased him to try us. For within few dayes after, as before is sayde Ensensore our friende dyed, who was no sooner dead, but certaine of our great enemies about Pemisapan, as Osocan a Weroance, Tanaquiny and Wanchese most principally, were in hand again to put their old practises in ure[3] against us, which were readily imbraced, & al their former devises against us renewed, & new brought in question.

But that of starving us, by their forebearing to sowe, was broken by Ensenore in his life, by having made the king all at one instant to sowe his grounde not onely in the Islande but also at Addesmocopeia in the mayne, within two leagues over against us. Neverthelesse

* The beginning of their harvest in Julie.

there wanted no store of mischevous practises among them, and of all they resolved principally of this following.

First that Okisko, king of Weopomiok, with the Mandoages, should bee moved, and with great quantitie of copper intertayned to the number of seven, or 800 bowes to the enterprise the matter thus to be ordred.* They of Weopomiok should be invited to a certaine kind of moneths minde[1] which they do use to solemnise in their Savage maner for any great personage dead, and should have bene for Ensenore. At this instant also should the Mandoaks, who were a great people with the Chesepians, and their friends[2] to the number of 700. of them be armed at a day appoynted to the mayne of Addesmocopeio, and there lying close at the signe of fyers, which should interchangeably be made on both sides, when Pemisapan with his troup above named should have executed me, and some of our Weroances (as they called all our principall officers,) the mayne forces of the rest should have come over into the Iland where they ment to have dispatched the rest of the company, whome they did imagine to finde both dismayed and dispersed abroade in the Islande seeking of crabs, and fish to live withall. The manner of their enterprise was this.

Tarraquine and Andacon two principall men about Pemisapan, and very lustie fellowes with twentie more appointed to them had the charge of my person to see an order taken for the same, which they ment should in this sort have bene executed. In the dead time of the night they would have beset my house,[3] and put fire in the reedes, that the same was covered with: meaning (as it was likelye) that my selfe woulde have come running out of a sudden amazed in my shirt without armes, upon the instant whereof they woulde have knocked out my braynes.

The same order was given to certaine of his fellowes, for Master Herriots:[4] so for all the rest of our better sort, all our houses at one instant being set on fire as afore is sayde, and that as well for them of the forte, as for us at the towne. Now to the end that we might be the fewer in number together, and so be the more easilie dealt withall (for in deede ten of us with our armes prepared, were a terrour to a hundred of the best sort of them,)† they agreed and did immediatly

* The conspiracie of Pemisapan.
† The sufficiencye of our men to deale against the Savages, 10. to 100.

38

put it in practise, that they should not for any copper, sell us any victuals whatsoever: besides that in the night they should send to have our weares robbed, and also to cause them to be broken and once being broken never to be repayred againe by them. By this meanes the King stood assured, that I must bee enforced for lacke of sustenance, there to disband my company into sundry places to live upon shell fishe,* for so the Savages themselves doe, going to Ottorasko,[1] Crotoan, and other places fishing and hunting, while their grownds be in sowing, and their corne growing, which fayled not his expectation. For the famine grewe so extreeme among us, our weares fayling us of fish, that I was enforced to send captaine Stafford with 20. with him to Crotoan my lord Admirals Island[2] to serve two turnes in one, that is to say to feede himselfe, and his company, and also to keepe watch, if any shipping came upon the coast to warne us of the same. I sent master Pridiox with the Pynnesse to Otterasco, and ten with him, with the Provost Marshal to live there, and also to wayte for shipping: also I sent every weeke 16. or 20. of the rest of the companie to the mayne over against us,[3] to live of Casada, and oysters.

In the meane while Pemisapan went of purpose to Addesmocopeio for 3. causes, the one, to see his grounds there broken up, and sowed for a second croppe: the other to withdrawe himselfe from my dayly sending to him for supply of victuall for my company, for hee was afrayde to denye me any thing, neither durst he in my presence but by colour,[4] and with excuses, which I was content to accept for the time, meaning in the ende as I had reason, to give him the jumpe once for all: but in the meane whiles, as I had ever done before, I and mine bare all wrongs, and accepted of all excuses.

My purpose was to have relyed my selfe with Menatonon, and the Chaonists, who in truth as they are more valiant people and in greater number then the rest, so are they more faithfull in their promises, and since my late being there, had given many tokens of earnest desire they had to joyne in perfect league with us, and therefore were greatly offended with Pemisapan and Weopomiok for making him beleeve such tales of us.

The third cause of his going to Addesmacopeio was to dispatch his messengers to Weopomiok, and to the Mandoages, as aforesaid, al

* The savages live by fishing, and hunting, till harvest.

which he did with great impresse of copper in hand, making large promises to them of greater spoyle.

The answere within fewe dayes after, came from Weopomiok, which was devided into two parts. First for the King Okisko, who denyed to be of ye partie for himselfe, or any of his especial followers, and therefore did immediatly retyre[1] himselfe with his force into the mayne: the other was concerning the rest of the sayd province who accepted of it: and in like sort the Mandoags received the imprest.

The day of their assembly aforesayd at Roanoak, was appointed the 10. of July:[2] all which the premises were discovered by Skyco, the king Menatonon his sonne my prisoner, who having once attempted to run away, I laid him in the bylboes,[3] threatning to cut off his head, whome I remitted at Pemisapans request: whereupon he being perswaded that he was our enemie to the death, he did not only feede him with himselfe, but also made him acquainted with all his practises. On the other side, the yong man finding himself as well used at my hand, as I had meanes to shew, and that all my companie made much of him, he flatly discovered all unto me, which also afterwards was revealed unto me by one of Pemisapans owne men, ye night before he was slaine.

These mischiefes being al instantly upon mee, and my companie to be put in execution, stood mee in hand to study how to prevent[4] them, and also to save all others, which were at that time as aforesaid so farre from me: whereupon I sent to Pemisapan to put suspition out of his heade, that I ment presently to goe to Crotoan, for that I had heard of the arival of our fleete, (though I in trueth had neither heard nor hoped for so good adventure,) and that I meant to come by him, to borrow of his men to fish for my company, and to hunt for me at Crotoan, as also to buy some foure dayes provision to serve for my voyage.

He sent mee word that he would himselfe come over to Roanoak, but from day to day hee deferred, only to bring the Weopomioks with him, and the Mandoags, whose time appoynted was within 8. dayes after. It was the last of May, 1586. when all his owne savages began to make their assembly at Roanoak, at his commandement sent abroad unto them, and I resolved not to stay longer upon his comming over, since he ment to come with so good company, but thought good to go, and visite him with such as I had, which I resolved to do the

next day: but that night I ment by the way to give them in the Island
a Canuisado,[1] and at the instant to sease upon all the Canoas about the
Island to keepe him from advertisements.

But the towne tooke the allarum, before I ment it to them: the
occasion was this. I had sent the Master of the light horsemen[2] with
a few with him, to gather up all the Canoas in the setting of the sunne,
& to take as many as were going from us to Adesmocopeio, but to
suffer any that came from thence to land: he met with a Canoa, going
from the shoare, and overthrew the Canoa, and cut off 2. savages
heads:* this was not done so secretly but hee was discovered from the
shoare, whereupon the cry arose: for in trueth they, privie to their
owne villanous purposes against us, held as good espial upon us, both
day and night, as we did upon them.

The allarum given, they took themselves to their bowes, and we
to our armes: some three or foure of them at the first were slayne
with our shot, the rest fled into ye woods: The next morning with the
light horseman, & one Canoa, taking 25. with the Colonel of the
Chesepians, and the Serjeant major,[3] went to Adesmocopeio, and
being landed sent Pemisapan word by one of his owne savages that
met me at the shore, that I was going to Crotoan, and ment to take
him in the way to complaine unto him of Osocon, who the night past
was conveying away my prisoner, whom I had there present tied in an
handlocke: hereupon the king did abide my comming to him, and
finding my selfe amidst 7. or 8. of his principal Weroances, & followers, (not regarding any of the common sort) I gave the watchword
agreed upon, (which was Christ our victory,) and immediatly those
his chiefe men, and himselfe, had by the mercie of God for our
deliverance, that which they had purposed for us. The king himselfe
being shot thorow by the Colonell with a pistoll lying on the ground
for dead, & I looking as watchfully for the saving of Manteos friends,
as others were busie that none of the rest should escape, suddenly he
started up, and ran away as though he had not bene touched, insomuch
as he overrran all the companie, being by the way shot thwart the
buttocks by mine Irish boy with my Petronell.[4] In the end an Irish
man serving me, one Nugent and the deputie provost undertooke
him, and following him in the woods overtooke him, and I in some
doubt least we had lost both the king, and my man by our owne

* The slaughter, and surprise of the Savages.

negligence to have bene intercepted by the Savages, we met him returning out of the woods with Pemisapans head in his hand.*

This fell out the first of June, 1586. and the 8.[1] of the same came advertisement to me from captaine Stafford, lying at my lord Admirals Island, that he had discovered a great Fleete of 23. sailes: but whether they were friends or foes, he could not yet discerne, he advised me to stand upon as good gard as I could.

The 9. of the said moneth, he himself came unto me, having that night before, and that same day travelled by land 20. miles, and I must truly report of him from the first to the last, he was the gentleman that never spared labour or perill either by land or water, faire weather or fowle, to performe any service committed unto him.

He brought me a letter from the Generall sir Francis Drake,† with a most bountifull and honourable offer for the supplie of our necessities[2] to the performance of the action, we were entered into, and that not onely of victuals, munition and clothing, but also of barkes, pinnaces and boates, they also by him to be victualled, manned, and furnished to my contentation.

The 10. day hee arrived in the road of our bad harborough, and comming there to an anker, the 11. day I came to him, whom I found in deeds most honourably to performe that which in writing and message he had most curteously offered, he having aforehand propounded the matter to all the captains of his Fleete, and got their liking and consent thereto.

With such thanks unto him and his captaines for his care both of us and of our action, not as the matter deserved, but as I could both for my companie and my selfe, I (being aforehand) prepared what I would desire, craved at his hands that it would please him to take with him into England a number of weake, and unfit men for my good action, which I would deliver to him, and in place of them to supply me of his company, with oare men, artificers, and others.

That he would leave us so much shipping and victuall, as about August then next followyng, would cary me and all my companie into England, when we had discovered somwhat that for lacke of needfull provision in time left with us as yet remained undone.

That it would please him withall to leave some sufficient masters not onely to cary us into England, when time should be, but also to

* Pemisapan slaine.   † A letter from sir Francis Drake.

search the coast for some better harborow[1] if there were any, and especially to helpe us to some small boats and oare men.

Also for a supplie of calievers, handweapons, match and lead, tooles, apparell, and such like.

He having received these my requests according to his usuall commendable maner of governement (as it was told me) calling his captaines to counsell, the resolution was that I should send such of my officers of my companie,[2] as I used in such matters, with their notes to goe aboord with him, which were the master of the victuals, the keeper of the store, and the Vicetreasurer, to whom he appointed foorthwith for me the Francis, being a very proper barke of 70. tunnes, and tooke present order for bringing of victuall aboord her for 100 men. for foure moneths withall my other demaunds whatsoever, to the uttermost.

And further appointed for me two fine pinnaces, and 4. small boats, and that which was to performe all his former liberalitie towards us, was that he had gotten the full assents of two of as sufficient experimented masters as were any in his fleete, by judgement of them that knewe them, with very sufficient gings to tarie with mee, and to employ themselves most earnestly in the action, as I should appoynt them, untill the terme which I promised of our returne into England agayne. The names of one of those masters was Abraham Kendall, the other Griffith Herne.

While these things were in hand, the provision aforesayd being brought, and in bringing a boord, my sayd masters being also gone aboord, my sayd barkes having accepted of their charge, and mine owne officers with others in like sort of my company with them, all which was dispatched by the said Generall the 12. of the said moneth: the 13. of the same there arose such an unwonted storme, and continued foure dayes that had like to have driven all on shore, if the Lord had not held his holy hand over them, and the generall very providently foreseene the worst himselfe, then about my dispatch putting himselfe aboord: but in the ende having driven sundry of the Fleete to put to sea the Francis also with all my provisions, my two masters, and my company aboord, shee was seene to be free from the same, and to put cleare to sea.[3]

This storme having continued from the 13. to the 16. of the moneth, and thus my barke put away as aforesayd, the Generall comming a shore, made a new proffer to me, which was a shippe of 170. tunnes, called the Barke Bonner, with a sufficient master and guide to tarie with mee the time appointed, and victualled sufficiently to carie mee and my companie into England with all provisions as before: but hee tolde mee that hee would not for any thing undertake to have her brought into our harbour, and therefore hee was to leave her in the roade, and to leave the care of the rest unto my selfe, and advised mee to consider with my companie of our case, and to deliver presently unto him in writing, what I would require him to doe for us: which being within his power, hee did assure me as well for his Captaines, as for himselfe should be most willingly performed.

Hereupon calling such Captaines and Gentlemen of my companie as then were at hand, who were all as privie as my selfe to the Generals offer, their whole request was to mee, that considering the case that we stood in, the weaknesse of our companie, the small number of the same, the carying away of our first appointed barke, with those two especiall masters, with our principall provisions in the same, by the very hand of God as it seemed, stretched out to take us from thence: considering also, that his second offer, though most honourable of his part, yet of ours not to be taken, insomuch as there was no possibilitie for her with any safetie to be brought into the harbour: Seeing furthermore our hope for supplie with sir Richard Greenvill so undoubtedly promised us before Easter, not yet come,[1] neither then likely to come this yeere considering the doings in England[2] for Flaunders, and also for America, that therefore I would resolve my selfe, with my companie to goe into England in that Fleete, and accordingly to make request to the Generall in all our names, that he would bee pleased to give us present passage with him. Which request of ours by my selfe delivered unto him, hee most readily assented unto, and so hee sending immediately his pinnaces unto our Island for the fetching away of fewe[3] that there were left with our baggage, the weather was so boysterous, and the pinnaces so often on ground, that the most of all wee had, with all our Cardes, Bookes and writings, were by the Saylers cast over boord, the greater number of the Fleete being much agrieved with their long and daungerous abode in that miserable road.

From whence the Generall in the name of the Almightie, waying his ankers (having bestowed us among his Fleete) for the reliefe of whom hee had in that storme sustained more perill of wracke then in all his former most honourable actions against the Spaniards, with praises unto God for all, set saile the 19. of June, 1586. and arrived in Portesmouth, the 27. of Julie the same yeere.

VI

Thomas Harriot,

A briefe and true report of the new found land of Virginia (1588), as reprinted by Hakluyt in 1589

A BRIEFE and true report[1] of the new found land of Virginia: of the commodities there found and to be raised, as well merchantable as others:

Written by Thomas Harriot, servaunt to Sir Walter Raleigh, a member of the Colonie, and there imployed in discovering, a full twelvemoneth.

Rafe Lane one of her Majesties Equieres and Governour of the Colonie in Virginia above mentioned for the time there resident, To the gentle Reader, wisheth all hapinesse in the Lord.

Albeit (gentle Reader) the credite of the reports in this treatise contained, can litle be furthered by the testimonie of one as my selfe, through affection judged partiall, though without desert: Neverthelesse, forsomuch as I have bene requested by some my particular friends, who conceive more rightly of me, to deliver freely my knowledge of the same, not onely for the satisfying of them, but also for the true information of any other who soever, that comes not with a prejudicate minde to the reading thereof: Thus much upon my credite I am to affirme, that things universally are so truely set downe in this treatise by the authour thereof, an Actor in the Colonie and a man no lesse for his honestie then learning commendable, as that I dare boldly avouche, it may very well passe with the credite of trueth even amongst the most true relations of this age. Which as for mine owne part I am readie any way with my worde to acknowledge, so also (of the certaintie thereof assured by mine owne experience) with this my publique assertion, I doe affirme the same. Farewell in the Lord.[2]

To the Adventurers, Favourers, and Welwillers of the enterprise for the inhabiting and planting in Virginia.

Since the first undertaking by sir Walter Raleigh to deale in the action of discovering of that Countrey which is now called and knowen by the name of Virginia, many voiages having bene thither made at sundry times to his great charge, as first in the yeere 1584, and afterwards in the yeeres 1585, 1586, and now of late this last yeere of 1587. There have bene divers and variable reportes, with some slaunderous and shamefull speaches bruited abroad by many that returned from thence. Especially of that discoverie which was made by the Colonie transported by Sir Richard Greenvill in the yeere 1585, being of all the others the most principall and as yet of most effect, the time of their abode in the countrey being a whole yeere, when as in the other voiage before they staied but sixe weekes,[1] and the others after were onely for supplie and transportation, nothing more being discovered then had bene before. Which reports have not done a little wrong to many that otherwise would have also favoured and adventured in the action, to the honour and benefite of our nation, besides the particular profite and credite which would redound to themselves the dealers therein, as I hope by the sequell of events to the shame of those that have avouched the contrary shall be manifest, if you the adventurers, favourers and welwillers doe but either increase in number, or in opinion continue, or having bene doubtfull, renew your good liking and furtherance to deale therein according to the woorthinesse thereof alreadie found, and as you shall understand heereafter to be requisite. Touching which woorthinesse through cause of the diversitie of relations and reports, many of your opinions could not be firme, nor the mindes of some that are well disposed, be setled in any certaintie.

I have therefore thought it good beying one that have bene in the discoverie, and in dealing with the naturall inhabitaunts[2] specially imployed: and having therefore seene and knowen more then the ordinarie, to impart so much unto you of the fruits of our labours, as that you may know how injuriously the enterprise is slaundered, and that in publique manér at this present, chiefly for two respects.

First, that some of you which are yet ignoraunt or doubtfull of the state thereof, may see that there is sufficient cause why the chiefe enterpriser with the favour of her Majestie, notwithstanding such reportes, hath not onely since continued the action by sending into the countrey againe, and replanting this last yeere a new Colonie, but is also readie, according as the times and means will affoord, to folow and prosecute the same.

Secondly, that you seeing and knowing the continuance of the action, by the view hereof you may generally know and learne what the countrey is, and thereupon consider how your dealing therein if it proceed, may returne you profite and gaine, be it either by inhabiting and planting, or otherwise in furthering thereof.

And least that the substance of my relation should be doubtfull unto you, as of others by reason of their diversitie, I will first open the cause in a few words wherefore they are so different, referring my self to your favourable constructions, and to be adjudged of as by good consideration you shall find cause.

Of our companie that returned some for their misdemeanour and ill dealing in the countrey, have bene there woorthily punished, who by reason of their bad natures, have maliciously not onely spoken ill of their Governours, but for their sakes slaundered the countrey it selfe. The like also have those done which were of their consort.

Some being ignorant of the state thereof, notwithstanding since their returne amongst their friends and acquaintance, and also others, especially if they were in companie where they might not be gainesayd, would seeme to know so much as no men more, and make no men so great travellers as themselves. They stoode so much, as it may seeme, upon their credite and reputation, that having bene a twelve moneth in the countrey, it would have bene a great disgrace unto them as they thought, if they could not have sayd much whether it were true or false. Of which some have spoken of more than ever they sawe, or otherwise knew to be there: Other some have not bene ashamed to make absolute denial of that, which although not by them, yet by others is most certainly and there plentifully knowen, and other some make difficulties of those things they have no skill of.

The cause of their ignoraunce was, in that they were of that many, that were never out of the Island where wee were seated, or not farre, or at the least wise in few places els, during the time of our abode in the countrey, or of that many, that after golde and silver was not so soone found, as it was by them looked for, had litle or no care of any other thing but to pamper their bellies, or of that many which had litle understanding, lesse discretion, and more tongue then was needfull or requisite.

Some also were of a nice bringing up, only in cities or townes, or such as never (as I may say) had seene the world before. Because there were not to be found any English cities, nor such faire houses, nor at their owne wish any of their old accustomed daintie food, nor any soft beds of downe or feathers, the countrey was to them miserable, and their reports thereof according.

Because my purpose was but in briefe to open the cause of the varietie of such speeches, the particularities of them, and of many envious, malicious and slaunderous reports and devises els, by our owne countreymen besides, as trifles that are not woorthie of wise men to bee thought upon, I meane not to trouble you withal, but will passe to the commodities, the substance of that which I have to make relation of unto you.

The treatise whereof for your more readie view and easier understanding, I will divide into three speciall partes. In the first I will make declaration of such commodities there already found or to bee raised, which will not onely serve the ordinarie turnes of you which are and shall be the planters and inhabitaunts, but such an overplus sufficiently to be yeelded, or by men of skill to be provided, as by way of traffique and exchaunge with our owne nation of England, will enrich your selves the providers: those that shall deale with you, the enterprisers in generall, and greatly profite our owne countrymen, to supplie them with most things which heretofore they have bene faine to provide either of strangers or of our enemies, which commodities for distinction sake, I call Merchantable.

In the second, I will set downe all the commodities which we know the countrey by our experience doth yeeld of it selfe for victuall and sustenance of mans life, such as is usually fed upon by the inhabitants of the countreys, as also by us during the time we were there.

In the last part I will make mention generally of such other commodities besides, as I am able to remember, and as I shall thinke behoovefull for those that shall inhabite, and plant there to know of, which specially concerne building, as also some other necessarie uses: with a briefe description of the nature and maners of the people of the countrey.

The first part of Marchantable commodities.

Silke of grass, or grasse Silke.[1] There is a kinde of grasse in the countrey, upon the blades whereof there groweth very good Silke in forme of a thinne glittering skinne to bee stript off. It groweth two foote and an halfe high or better: the blades are about two foote in length, and halfe inch broad. The like groweth in Persia, which is in the selfe same climate as Virginia, of which very many of the Silke workes that come from thence into Europe are made. Hereof if it be planted and ordered as in Persia, it cannot in reason bee otherwise, but that there will rise in short time great profite to the dealers there-in, seeing there is so great use and vent thereof as well in our countrey as elsewhere. And by the meanes of sowing and planting it in good ground, it will be farre greater, better, and more plentifull then it is. Although notwithstanding there is great store thereof in many places of the countrey growing naturally and wild, which also by proofe here in England, in making a piece of silke Grogran,[1] we found to be excellent good.

Worme Silke. In many of our journeys wee found Silke wormes[2] faire and great, as big as our ordinarie Walnuts. Although it hath not bene our happe to have found such plentie as elsewhere to be in the countrey wee have heard of, yet seeing that the countrey doeth naturallie breed and nourish them, there is no doubt but if Arte be added in planting of Mulberie[3] trees and others fit for them in com-modious places, for their feeding and nourishing, and some of them carefully gathered and husbanded in that sort, as by men of skill is knowen to be necessarie; there will rise as great profit in time to the Virginians, as thereof doeth now to the Persians, Turkes, Italians and Spaniards.

Flaxe and Hempe.[4] The trueth is, that of Hempe and Flaxe there is no great store in any one place together, by reason it is not planted but as the soyle doeth yeeld of it selfe: and how so ever the leafe and stemme or stalke doe differ from ours, the stuffe by judgement of men of skill is altogether as good as ours. And if not, as further proofe should finde otherwise, we have that experience of the soyle, as that there cannot bee shewed any reason to the contrary, but that it will growe there excellent well, and by planting will bee yeelded plenti-fully, seeyng there is so much ground whereof some may well bee applied to such purposes. What benefite hereof may grow in cordage and linnens who cannot easily understand:

Allum.[5] There is a veine of earth along the sea coast for the space of fortie or fiftie miles, whereof by the judgement of some that have made triall here in England, is made good Allum, of that kind which is called Roche Allum. The richnesse of such a commoditie is so well knowen, that I neede not to say any thing thereof. The same earth doeth also yeeld White Copresse, Nitrum, and Alumen plumeum, but nothing so plentifully as the common Allum, which be also of price and profitable.

Wapeih. A kind of earth so called by the naturall inhabitants, very like to Terra sigillata,[1] and having bene refined, it hath bene found by some of our Phisitions and Chirurgions, to bee of the same kind of vertue, and more effectuall. The inhabitants use it very much for the cure of sores and wounds: there is in divers places great plentie, and in some places of a blew sort.

Pitch, Tarre, Rozen and Turpentine. There are those kindes of trees which yeeld them abundantly and great store. In the very same Island where we were seated, being fifteene miles of length, and five or six miles in breadth, there are few trees els[2] but of the same kind, the whole Island being full.

Sassafras.[3] Called by the inhabitants Winauk, a kinde of wood of most pleasaunt and sweete smell, and of most rare vertues in phisike for the cure of many diseases. It is found by experience to bee farre better and of more uses then the Wood which is called Guaiacum, or Lignum vitae. For the description, the maner of using, and the manifold vertues thereof, I referre you to the Booke of Monardus,[4] translated and entituled in English, The joyfull newes from the West Indies.

Cedar.[5] A very sweete wood and fine timber, whereof if nestes of chestes be there made, or timber thereof fitted for sweete and fine bedsteads, tables, deskes, lutes, virginals and many things els, (of which there hath bene proofe made alreadie) to make up fraight with other principal commodities, will yeeld profite.

Wine. There are two kindes of grapes[6] that the soile doeth yeeld naturally, the one is small and sowre of the ordinarie bignesse as ours in England, the other farre greater and of himselfe lushious sweete. When they are planted and husbanded as they ought, a principall commoditie of wines by them may be raised.

Oile. There are two sortes of Walnuts both holding oyle, but the one farre more plentifull then the other. When there are mils and other devises for the purpose, a commoditie of them may be raised because there are infinite store. There are also three severall kindes of Berries in the fourme of Oke akornes, which also by the experience and use of the inhabitaunts, wee finde to yeeld very good and sweete oyle. Furthermore, the Beares of the countrey are commonly very fat, and in some places there are many. Their fatnesse because it is so liquid, may well bee termed oyle, and hath many speciall uses.

Furres. All along the Sea coast there are great store of Otters, which being taken by weires and other engines made for the purpose, wil yeeld good profite. We hope also of Marterne furres,[1] and make no doubt by the relation of the people, but that in some places of the country there are store, although there were but two skins that came to our hands. Luzarnes[2] also wee have understanding of, although for the time we saw none.

Deere skinnes dressed after the maner of Chamoes or undressed, are to be had of the naturall inhabitants thousands yeerely by way of traffique for trifles, and no more waste or spoile of Deere then is and hath bene ordinarily in time before.

Civet cats.[3] In our travels there was found one to have bene killed by a salvage or inhabitant, and in another place the smell where one or more had lately bene before, whereby wee gather besides then by the relation of the people, that there are some in the countrey: good profite will rise by them.

Iron. In two places of the countrey specially, one about fourescore, and the other sixe score miles from the Forte or place where wee dwelt, wee founde neere the water side the ground to bee rockie, which by the triall of a Minerall man,[4] was found to holde iron[5] richly. It is found in many places of the countrey els, I know nothing to the contrarie, but that it may bee allowed for a good merchauntable commoditie, considering there the small charge for the labour and feeding of men: the infinite store of wood, the want of wood and deerenesse thereof in England, and the necessitie of ballasting of ships.

Copper.[6] An hundred and fiftie miles into the maine, in two townes we found with the inhabitaunts divers small plates of Copper, that had bene made as wee understoode by the inhabitaunts that dwell further into the Countrey, where as they say are mountaynes and Rivers that yeeld also white graines of mettall, which is to be deemed silver. For confirmation whereof, at the time of our first arrivall in the

Sir Francis Drake from a painting in the National Portrait Gallery: artist not known

Thomas Cavendish: the earliest published engraving. From
Franciscus Dracus redivivus, *Amsterdam, 1596*

country, I saw with some others with me, two small pieces of silver grosly beaten, about the weight of of[sic] a testrone, hanging in the eares of a Wiroans or Chiefe Lord that dwelt about fourescore miles from us: of whome through enquiry, by the number of dayes & the way, I learned that it had come to his hands from the same place or neere, where I after understood the copper was made, and the white graines of mettall found. The aforesaid copper we also found by triall to holde silver.[1]

Pearle: Sometimes in feeding on muscles we found some pearle: but it was our happe to meet with ragges, or of a pide colour: not having yet discovered those places where we heard of better and more plenty. One of our company, a man of skill in such matters, had gathered together from among the Savage people about five thousand: of which number he chose so many as made a fayre chaine, which for theyr likenesse and uniformity in roundnesse, orientnesse, and pide-nesse of many excellent colours, with equalitie in greatnesse, were very fayr and rare: and had therefore beene presented to her Majesty, had we not by casualty, and through extremity of a storme lost them,[2] with many things els in comming away from the countrey.

Sweet gummes of divers kindes, and many other Apothecary drugges, of which we will make speciall mention, when we shall receive it from such men of skill in that kinde, that in taking reason-able paines shall discover them more particularly then we have done, and then now I can make relation of, for want of the examples I had provided and gathered, and are now lost, with other things by casualty before mentioned.

Dies of divers kindes:[3] There is Shoemake well knowne, and used in England for blacke: the seed of an herbe called Wasebur, little small roots called Chappacor, and the barke of the tree called by the inhabitants Tangomockonomindge: which Dies are for divers sorts of red: theyr goodnesse for our English clothes remaine yet to be prooved. The inhabitants use them only for the dying of hayre, and colouring of theyr faces, and mantles made of Deere skinnes: and also for the dying of rushes to make artificiall works withall in theyr mats and baskets: having no other thing besides that they account of, apt to use them for. If they will not proove merchantable, there is no doubt but the planters there shall finde apt uses for them, as also for other colours which we know to be there.

Woad:[1] a thing of so great vent and uses amongst English Diers, which can not be yeelded sufficiently in our owne countrey for spare of ground, may be planted in Virginia, there being ground enough. The growth thereof neede not to be doubted, when as in the Islands of the Asores it groweth plentifully, which is in the same climate. So likewise of Madder.

We caryed thither Suger canes to plant, which being not so well preserved as was requisite, and besides the time of the yeere being past for theyr setting when we arrived, we could not make that proofe of them as we desired. Notwithstanding, seeing that they grow in the same climate,[2] in the South part of Spaine, and in Barbary, our hope in reason may yet continue. So likewise for Orenges and Limmons: there may be planted also Quinses. Whereby may grow in reasonable time if the action be diligently prosecuted, no small commodities in Sugers, Suckets, and Marmelades.

Many other commodities by planting may there also be raised, which I leave to your discreet and gentle considerations: and many also may be there, which yet we have not discovered. Two more commodities of great value, one of certainty, and the other in hope, not to be planted, but there to be raised, and in short time to be provided and prepared, I might have specified. So likewise of those commodities already set downe, I might have said more: as of the particular places where they are found, and best to be planted and prepared: by what meanes, and in what reasonable space of time they might be raised to profit, and in what proportion: but because others then welwillers might be therewithall acquainted, not to the good of the action, I have wittingly omitted them: knowing that to those that are well disposed, I have uttered according to my promise and purpose, for this part sufficient.

The second part of such commodities as Virginia is knowen to yeeld, for victuall and sustenance of mans life, usually fed upon by the naturall inhabitants: as also by us, during the time of our aboad. And first of such as are sowed and husbanded.

Pagatowr,[3] a kinde of graine so called by the inhabitants: the same in the West Indies is called Mayze: English men call it Guinney wheat, or Turkie wheat, according to the names of the countries from whence the like hath bene brought. The graine is about the bignesse of our ordinary English peaze, and not much different in forme and shape: but of divers colours: some white, some red, some yellow, and some blew. All of them yeeld a very white and sweete flowre: being used according to his kinde, it maketh a very good bread. We made of the same in the countrey some mault, whereof was brued as good ale as was to be desired. So likewise by the helpe of hops, thereof may be made as good beere. It is a graine of marvellous great increase: of a thousand, fifteene hundred, and some two thousand folde. There are three sorts, of which two are ripe in eleven and twelve weeks at the most, sometimes in tenne, after the time they are set, and are then of height in stalke about sixe or seven foot. The other sort is ripe in foureteene, and is about tenne foot high, of the stalks, some beare foure heads, some three, some one, and two: every head conteining five, sixe, or seven hundred graines, within a few more or lesse. Of these graines, besides bread, the inhabitants make victuall, either by parching them, or seething them whole untill they be broken: or boiling the flowre with water into a pappe.

Okingier, called by us Beanes, because in greatness and partly in shape they are like to the beanes in England, saving that they are flatter, of more divers colours, and some pide. The leafe also of the stemme is much different. In taste they are altogether as good as our English peaze.

Wickonzowr, called by us Peaze, in respect of the beanes for distinction sake, because they are much lesse, although in forme they little differ: but in goodnesse of taste much like, and are farre better then our English peaze. Both the beanes and peaze are ripe in tenne weeks after they are set. They make them victuall either by boiling them all to pieces into a broth, or boiling them whole untill they be soft, and begin to breake, as is used in England, either by themselves, or mixtly together: sometime they mingle of the wheat with them: sometime also, being whole sodden, they bruse or punne them in a morter, and thereof make loaves or lumps of dowish bread, which they use to eat for variety.

Macocquer, according to theyr several formes, called by us Pompions, Mellions,[1] and Gourds, because they are of the like formes as those kindes in England. In Virginia such of severall formes are of one taste, and very good, and do also spring from one seed.

There are of two sorts: one is ripe in the space of a moneth, and the other in two moneths.

There is an herbe which in Dutch is called Melden.[1] Some of those that I describe it unto, take it to be a kinde of Orage: it groweth about foure or five foot high; of the seed thereof they make a thicke broth, and pottage of a very good taste: of the stalke by burning into ashes they make a kinde of salt earth, wherewithall many use sometimes to season theyr broths: other salt they know not. We our selves used the leaves also for potherbs.

There is also another great herbe, in forme of a Marigolde, about sixe foot in height, the head with the floure is a spanne in bredth. Some take it to be Planta Solis:[2] of the seeds heereof they make both a kind of bread and broth.

All the aforesaid commodities for victuall are set or sowed, sometimes in grounds apart and severally by themselves, but for the most part together in one ground mixtly: the maner thereof, with the dressing and preparing of the ground, because I will note unto you the fertility of the soile, I thinke good briefly to describe.

The ground they never fatten with mucke, doong, or any other thing, neither plow nor digge it as we in England, but onely prepare it in sort as followeth. A few dayes before they sowe or set, the men with woodden instruments, made almost in forme of mattocks or hoes with long handles: the women with short peckers or parers, because they use them sitting, of a foot long and about five inches in bredth, doe onely breake the upper part of the ground to rayse up the weedes, grasse, and olde stubbes of corne stalkes with theyr roots. The which after a day or twoes drying in the Sunne, being scrapt up into many small heaps, to save them labour for carrying them away, they burne into ashes. (And whereas some may thinke that they use the ashes for to better the ground: I say that then they would either disperse the ashes abroad, which we observed they do not, except the heaps be too great: or els would take speciall care to set theyr corne where the ashes lie, which also we finde they are carelesse of.) And this is all the husbanding of theyr ground that they use.

Then theyr setting or sowing is after this maner. First for theyr corne, beginning in one corner of the plot, with a pecker they make a hole, wherein they put foure graines, with that care they touch not one another (about an inch asunder) and cover them with the moulde againe: and so throughout the whole plot, making such holes, and using them after such maner: but with this regard, that they be made in ranks, every ranke differing from other halfe a fathome or a yard, and the holes also in every ranke as much. By this meanes there is a yard spare ground betweene every hole: where according to discretion heere and there, they set as many beans and peaze: in divers places also among the seeds of Macocquer, Melden, and Planta solis.

The ground being thus set according to the rate, by us experimented, an English acre conteining fortie pearches in length, and foure in bredth, doth there yeeld in croppe or ofcome of corne, beanes and peaze, at the least two hundreth London bushels:[1] besides the Macocquer, Melden, and Planta solis: when as in England fortie bushels of our wheat yeelded out of such an acre, is thought to be much.

I thought also good to note this unto you, that you which shall inhabite, and plant there, may know how specially that countrey corne is there to be preferred before ours: Besides, the manifolde wayes in applying it to victuall, the increase is so much, that small labor and paines is needfull in respect that must be used for ours. For this I can assure you, that according to the rate we have made proofe of, one man may prepare and husband so much ground (having once borne corne before) with lesse then foure and twentie houres labour, as shall yeeld him victuall in a large proportion for a twelve moneth, if he have nothing else but that which the same ground will yeeld, and of that kinde onely which I have before spoken of: the sayd ground being also but of five and twentie yards square. And if need require, but that there is ground enough, there might be raised out of one and the selfesame ground two harvests or ofcomes: for they sow or set, and may at any time when they thinke good, from the midst of March untill the end of June: so that they also set when they have eaten of theyr first croppe. In some places of the countrey notwithstanding they have two harvests, as we have heard, out of one and the same ground.

For English corne neverthelesse, whether to use or not to use it, you that inhabite may do as you shall have farther cause to think best. Of the growth you need not to doubt: for barly, oats, and peaze, we have seene proofe of, not being purposely sowen but fallen casually in the woorst sort of ground, and yet to be as fayre as any we have ever seene heere in England. But of wheat, because it was musty, and had taken salt water, we could make no triall: and of rie we had none. Thus much have I digressed, and I hope not unnecessarily: now will I returne againe to my course, and intreat of that which yet remaineth apperteining to this chapter.

There is an herbe which is sowed apart by it selfe, and is called by the inhabitants Uppowoc: In the West Indies it hath divers names, according to the severall places and countryes where it groweth, and is used: the Spanyards generally call it Tobacco.[1] The leaves thereof being dried and brought into powder: they use to take the fume or smoke thereof, by sucking it through pipes made of clay, in to theyr stomacke and head: from whence it purgeth superfluous fleame and other gross humors, and openeth all the pores and passages of the body: by which meanes the use thereof not onely preserveth the body from obstructions, but also (if any be, so that they have not beene of too long continuance) in short time breaketh them: whereby theyr bodyes are notably preserved in health,[2] and know not many grievous diseases, wherewithall we in England are oftentimes afflicted.

This Uppowoc is of so precious estimation amongst them, that they thinke theyr gods are marvellously delighted therewith: where-upon sometime they make hallowed fires, and cast some of the powder therein for a sacrifice: being in a storme upon the waters, to pacifie theyr gods, they cast some up into the ayre and into the water: so a weare for fish being newly set up, they cast some therein and into the ayre: also after an escape of danger, they cast some into the ayre likewise: but all done with strange gestures, stamping, sometime dancing, clapping of hands, holding up of hands and staring up into the heavens, uttering therewithall, and chattering strange words and noises.

We our selves during the time we were there, used to sucke it after theyr maner, as also since our returne,[3] and have found many rare and woonderfull experiments of the vertues thereof: of which the relation would require a volume by it selfe: the use of it by so many of late, men and women of great calling as else, and some learned Physicians also, is sufficient witnesse.

And these are all the commodities for sustenance of life that I know and can remember they use to husband: all else that follow are found growing naturally or wilde.

Of Roots.

Openauk[1] are a kinde of roots of round forme, some of the bignesse of walnuts, some farre greater, which are found in moist and marish grounds growing many together one by another in ropes, or as though they were fastened with a string. Being boiled or sodden they are very good meat.

Okeepenauk[2] are also of round shape, found in drie grounds: some are of the bignesse of a mans head. They are to be eaten as they are taken out of the ground, for by reason of theyr drinesse they will neither roste nor seethe. Theyr taste is not so good as of the former roots, notwithstanding for want of bread, and sometimes for variety the inhabitants use to eat them with fish or flesh, and in my judgement they do as well as the housholde bread made of rie heere in England.

Kaishucpenauk[3] a white kinde of roots about the bignesse of henne egges, and neere of that forme: theyr taste was not so good to our seeming as of the other, and therefore theyr place and maner of growing, not so much cared for by us: the inhabitants notwithstanding used to boyle and eat many.

Tsinaw[4] a kinde of root much like unto that which in England is called the China root brought from the East Indies. And we know not any thing to the contrary but that it may be of the same kinde. These roots grow many together in great clusters, and do bring foorth a brier stalke, but the leafe in shape farre unlike: which being supported by the trees it groweth neerest unto, will reach or climbe to the top of the highest. From these roots while they be new or fresh, being chopt into small pieces, and stampt, is strained with water a juice that maketh bread, and also being boyled, a very good spoonemeat[5] in maner of a gelly, and is much better in taste if it be tempered with oile. This Tsinaw is not of that sort, which by some was caused to be brought into England for the China root, for it was discovered since, and is in use as is aforesaid: but that which was brought hither is not yet knowen, neither by us nor by the inhabitants to serve for any use or purpose, although the roots in shape are very like.

Coscushaw,[6] some of our company tooke to be that kinde of root which the Spanyards in the West Indies call Cassavy, whereupon also many called it by that name: it groweth in very muddie pooles, and moist grounds. Being dressed according to the countrey maner, it maketh a good bread, and also a good spoonemeat, and is used very much by the inhabitants: the juice of this root is poison, and therefore heed must be taken before any thing be made therewithall; either the roots must be first sliced and dried in the Sunne, or by the fire, and then being punned into floure, will make good bread: or els while they are greene they are to be pared, cut into pieces, and stampt: loaves of the same to be laid neere or over the fire untill it be sowre, and then being well punned againe, bread, or spoonemeat very good in taste and wholesome may be made thereof.

Habascon[1] is a root of hote taste, almost of the forme and bignesse of a parsnip, of it selfe it is no victuall, but onely a helpe being boiled together with other meats.

There are also Leeks, differing little from ours in England, that grow in many places of the countrey, of which, when we came in places where they were, we gathered and eat many, but the naturall inhabitants never.

Of Fruites.

Chestnuts,[2] there are in divers places great store: some they use to eat raw, some they stampe and boile to make spoonemeat, and with some being sodden, they make such a manner of dow bread as they use of theyr beanes before mentioned.

Walnuts:[3] there are two kindes of walnuts, and of them infinite store: in many places where are very great woods for many miles together, the third part of trees are walnut trees. The one kinde is of the same taste and forme, or little differing from ours of England, but that they are harder and thicker shelled: the other is greater, and hath a very ragged and hard shell: but the kernell great, very oily and sweet. Besides theyr eating of them after our ordinarie maner, they breake them with stones, and punne them in morters[4] with water, to make a milke which they use to put into some sorts of theyr spoonemeat: also among theyr sod wheat, peaze, beanes and pompions which maketh them have a farre more pleasant taste.

Medlars a kinde of very good fruit, so called by us chiefly for these respects: first in that they are not good untill they be rotten: then in that they open at the head as our medlars, and are about the same bignesse: otherwise in taste and colour they are farre different: for they are as red as cherries, and very sweet: but whereas the cherie is sharpe sweet, they are lushious sweet.

Mutaquesunnauk,[1] a kinde of pleasant fruit almost of the shape and bignesse of English peares, but that they are of a perfect red colour as well within as without. They grow on a plant whose leaves are very thicke, and full of prickles as sharpe as needles. Some that have bin in the Indies, where they have seene that kinde of red die of great price, which is called Cochinele, to grow, do describe [t]his plant right like unto this of Metaquesunnauk, but whether it be the true Cochenile or a bastard or wilde kinde, it can not yet be certified: seeing that also as I heard, Cochenile is not of the fruit, but found on the leaves of the plant:[2] which leaves for such matter we have not so specially observed.

Grapes there are of two sorts, which I mentioned in the merchantable commodities.

Straberies there are as good and as great as those which we have in our English gardens.

Mulberies, Applecrabs, Hurts or Hurtleberies, such as we have in England.

Sacquenummener[3] a kinde of berries almost like unto capers, but somewhat greater, which grow together in clusters upon a plant or herbe that is found in shallow waters: being boiled eight or nine houres according to theyr kinde are very good meat and wholesome, otherwise if they be eaten they will make a man for the time frantike or extremely sicke.

There is a kinde of Reed[4] which beareth a seed almost like unto our rie or wheat, and being boiled is good meat.

In our travels in some places we found Wilde peaze like unto ours in England, but that they were lesse, which are also good meat.

Of a kinde of fruit or berry in forme of Acornes.[5]

There is a kinde of berrie or acorne, of which there are five sorts that grow on severall kindes of trees: the one is called Sagatemener, the second Osamener, the third Pummuckoner. These kinde of acornes they use to drie upon hurdles made of reeds, with fire underneath, almost after the maner as we dry malt in England. When they are to be used, they first water them untill they be soft, and then being sod, they make a good victuall, either to eat so simply, or els being also pounded to make loaves or lumps of bread. These be also the three kindes, of which, I said before the inhabitants used to make sweet oile.

Another sort is called Sapummener, which being boiled or parched, doth eat and taste like unto chestnuts. They sometime also make bread of this sort.

The fift sort is called Mangummenauk, and is the acorne of theyr kinde of Oake, the which being dried after the maner of the first sorts, and afterward watered, they boile them and theyr servants, or sometime the chiefe themselves, either for variety or for want of bread, do eat them with theyr fish or flesh.

Of Beasts.

Deere, in some places there are great store: neere unto the sea coast they are of the ordinarie bignesse as ours in England, and some lesse: but further up into the countrey, where there is better food, they are greater: they differ from ours onely in this, their tailes are longer, and the snags of theyr hornes looke backward.

Conies, Those that we have seene, and all that we can heare of are of a grey colour like unto hares: in some places there are such plenty that all the people of some townes make them mantles of the furre or flue of the skinnes of those they usually take.

Saquenuckot and Maquowoc,[1] two kinds of small beasts, greater then conies, which are very good meat. We never tooke any of them our selves, but sometime eat of such as the inhabitants had taken and brought unto us.

Squirels which are of a grey colour, we have taken and eaten.

Beares which are all of blacke colour. The beares of this country are good meat: the inhabitants in time of winter do use to take and eat many, so also sometime did we. They are taken commonly in this sort. In some Islands or places where they are, being hunted for, as soone as they have spiall of a man, they presently runne away, and then being chased, they clime and get up the next tree they can, from whence with arrowes they are shot downe starke dead, or with those wounds that they may after easily be killed: we sometime shot them downe with our calivers.

I have the names of eight and twenty severall sorts of beasts,[2] which I have heard of to be here and there dispersed in the countrey,

62

especially in the maine: of which there are onely twelve kindes that we have yet discovered, and of those that be good meat we know only them before mentioned. The inhabitants sometime kill the Lyon, & eat him: and we sometime as they came to our hands of theyr Woolves or Woolvish dogges,[1] which I have not set downe for good meat, least that some would understand my judgement therein to be more simple then needeth, although I could allege the difference in taste of those kindes from ours, which by some of our company have beene experimented in both.[2]

Of Foule.

Turkie cocks and Turkie hennes: Stockdoves: Partridges: Cranes:[3] Hernes: and in winter great store of Swannes and Geese.[4] Of all sorts of foule I have the names in the country language, of fourescore and sixe, of which number, besides those that be named, we have taken, eaten, and have the pictures as they were there drawen, with the names of the inhabitants of severall strange sorts of water foule eight, and seventeene kindes more of land foule, although we have seene and eaten of many more, which for want of leasure there for the purpose, could not be pictured: and after we are better furnished and stored upon further discovery, with theyr strange beasts, fish, trees, plants, and herbs, they shall be also published.[5]

There are also Parrots, Faulcons, and Marlin hauks, which although with us they be not used for meat, yet for other causes I thought good to mention.

Of Fish.

For foure moneths of the yeere, February, March, Aprill and May, there are plenty of Sturgeons: And also in the same moneths of Herrings,[6] some of the ordinary bignesse as ours in England, but the most part farre greater, of eighteene, twentie inches, and some two foot in length and better: both these kindes of fish in those moneths are most plentifull, and in best season, which we found to be most delicate and pleasant meat.

There are also Trouts: Porpoises: Rayes:[7] Oldwives: Mullets: Plaice:[8] & very many other sorts of excellent good fish, which we have taken and eaten, whose names I know not but in the countrey language: we have of twelve sorts more the pictures, as they were drawen in the countrey, with theyr names.

The inhabitants use to take them two manner of wayes, the one is by a kinde of weare made of reeds, which in that countrey are very strong. The other way, which is more strange, is with poles made sharpe at one end, by shooting them into the fish after the maner as Irish men cast darts,[1] either as they are rowing in theyr boats, or els as they are wading in the shallowes for the purpose.

There are also in many places plenty of these kindes which follow: Sea crabbes.[2] such as we have in England.

Oisters,[3] some very great, and some small, some round, and some of a long shape: they are found both in salt water and brackish, and those that we had out of salt water are far better then the other as in our countrey.

Also Muscles: Scalops:[4] Periwinkles: and Crevises.[5]

Seekanauk,[6] a kinde of crusty shell fish, which is good meat, about a foot in bredth, having a crustie taile, many legges like a crab, and her eyes in her backe. They are found in shallowes of waters, and sometime on the shoare.

There are many Tortoyses[7] both of land and sea kinde, theyr backs and bellies are shelled very thicke, theyr head, feet, and taile, which are in appearance, seeme ougly, as though they were members of a serpent or venemous beasts: but notwithstanding they are very good meat, as also theyr egges. Some have beene found of a yard in bredth and better.

And thus have I made relation of all sorts of victuall that we fed upon for the time we were in Virginia, as also the inhabitants themselves, as farre foorth as I know and can remember, or that are specially worthy to be remembred.

The third and last part of such other things as are behovefull for those which shall plant and inhabite to know of, with a description of the nature and maners of the people of the Countrey.

Of commodities for building and other necessary uses.

Those other things which I am more to make rehearsall of, are such as concerne building, and other mechanicall necessarie uses, as divers sorts of trees for house and shippe timber, and other uses els: Also lime, stone, and bricke, least that being not mentioned some might have bene doubted of, or by some that are malitious reported the contrary.

Okes, there are as faire, straight, tall, and as good timber as any can be, and also great store, and in some places very great.

Walnut trees, as I have said before very many, some have bene seene excellent faire timber of foure and five fathome, and above fourescore foote streight without bough.

Firre trees[1] fit for masts of ships, some very tall and great.

Rakiock,[2] a kinde of trees so called that are sweete wood, of which the inhabitants that were neere unto us doe commonly make their boates or Canoes of the forme of trowes, onely with the helpe of fire, hatchets of stones, and shels: we have knowen some so great being made in that sort of one tree that they have carried well 20. men at once, besides much baggage: the timber being great, tall, streight, soft, light, and yet tough ynough I thinke (besides other uses) to be fit also for masts of ships.

Cedar, a sweete wood good for seelings, chests, boxes, bedsteads, lutes, virginals, and many things els, as I have also said before. Some of our companie which have wandered in some places where I have not bene, have made certaine affirmation of Cyprus[3] which for such and other excellent uses, is also a wood of price and no small estimation.

Maple, and also Wich-hazle,[4] whereof the inhabitants use to make their bowes.

Holly a necessary thing for the making of birdlime.

Willowes good for the making of weares and wheles[5] to take fishe after the English maner, although the inhabitants use onely reedes, which because they are so strong as also flexible, do serve for that turne very well and sufficiently.

Beech and Ashe, good for caske hoopes: and if neede require, plowe worke, as also for many things els.

Elme.

Sassafras trees.

Ascopo[6] a kinde of tree very like unto Lawrel, the barke is hot in taste and spicie, it is very like to that tree which Monardus describeth to be Cassia Lignea[7] of the West Indies.

There are many other strange trees whose names I know not but in the Virginian language, of which I am not now able, neither is it so convenient for the present to trouble you with particular relation: seeing that for timber and other necessary uses I have named sufficient. And of many of the rest, but that they may be applied to good use, I know no cause to doubt.

Now for stone, bricke and lime, thus it is. Neere unto the Sea coast where wee dwelt, there are no kinde of stones to be found (except a fewe small pebbles[1] about foure miles off) but such as have bene brought from further out of the maine. In some of our voyages wee have seene divers hard raggie stones, great pebbles, and a kinde of grey stone like unto marble, of which the inhabitants make their hatchets to cleeve wood. Upon inquirie wee heard that a little further up into the Countrey were of all sortes very many, although of quarries they are ignorant, neither have they use of any store whereupon they should have occasion to seeke any. For if every houshold have one or two to cracke nuts, grinde shels, whet copper, and sometimes other stones[2] for hatchets, they have ynough: neither use they any digging, but onely for graves[3] about three foote deepe: and therefore no marveile that they knowe neither quarries, nor lime stones, which both may be in places neerer than they wot of.

In the meane time until there be discoverie of sufficient store in some place or other convenient, the want of you which are & shalbe the planters therin may be as well supplied by bricke: for the making whereof in divers places of the Countrey there is clay both excellent good, and plentie, and also by lime made of oyster shels,[4] and of others burnt, after the maner as they use in the Isles of Tenet and Shepy,[5] and also in divers other places of England: Which kinde of lime is well knowen to be as good as any other. And of oyster shels there is plentie ynough: for besides divers other particuler places where are abundance, there is one shallowe sounde along the coast, where for the space of many miles together in length, & two or three miles in breadth, the ground is nothing els,[6] being but halfe a foote or a foote under water for the most part.

Thus much can I say further more of stones, that about 120. miles from our fort neere the water in the side of a hil, was found by a Gentleman of our company, a great veine of hard ragge stones, which I thought good to remember unto you.

Of the nature and maners of the people.

It resteth I speake a worde or two of the naturall inhabitants, their natures and maners, leaving large discourse thereof untill time more convenient hereafter: nowe onely so farre foorth, as that you may knowe, howe that they in respect of troubling our inhabiting & planting, are not to be feared, but that they shall have cause both to feare and love us, that shall inhabite with them.

They are a people clothed with loose mantles made of deere skinnes, and aprons of the same round about their middles, all els naked, of such a difference of statures onely as we in England, having no edge tooles or weapons of yron or steele to offend us withal, neither knowe they howe to make any: those weapons that they have, are onely bowes made of Witchhazle, and arrowes of reedes, flat edged truncheons also of wood about a yard long, neither have they any thing to defend themselves but targets made of barks, and some armours made of sticks wickered together with thread.

Their townes are but small, and neere the sea coast but fewe, some contayning but tenne or twelve houses: some 20. the greatest that wee have seene, hath bene but of 30. houses:[1] if they bee walled, it is onely done with barkes of trees made fast to stakes, or els with poles onely fixed upright, and close one by another.

Their houses are made of small poles, made fast at the tops in rounde forme after the maner as is used in many arbories in our gardens of England, in most townes covered with barkes, and in some with artificial matts[2] made of long rushes, from the tops of the houses downe to the ground. The length of them is commonly double to the breadth, in some places they are but 12. and 16. yards long, and in other some we have seene of foure and twentie.

In some places of the Countrey, one onely towne belongeth to the government of a Wiroans or chiefe Lorde, in other some two or three, in some sixe, eight, and more, the greatest Wiroans[3] that yet we had dealing with, had but eighteene townes in his government, & able to make not above seven or eight hundreth fighting men at the most. The language of every government is different from any other, and the further they are distant, the greater is the difference.

Their maner of warres amongst themselves, is either by sudden surprising one an other most commonly about the dawning of the day, or moone light, or els by ambushes, or some subtile devises. Set battels are very rare, except it fall out where there are many trees, where either part may have some hope of defence, after the deliverie of every arrowe, in leaping behinde some or other.

If there fall out any warres betweene us and them, what their fight is likely to bee, wee having advantages against them so many maner of wayes, as by our discipline, our strange weapons and devises els, especially ordinance great and smal, it may easily be imagined, by the experience we have had in some places, the turning up of their heeles against us in running away was their best defence.

In respect of ùs they are a people poore, and for want of skill and judgement in the knowledge and use of our things, doe esteeme our trifles before thinges of greater value: Notwithstanding, in their proper maner (considering the want of such meanes as wee have,) they seeme very ingenious. For although they have no such tooles, nor any such craftes, Sciences, and artes as wee, yet in those thinges they doe, they shewe excellencie of wit.[1] And by howe much they upon due consideration shall finde our maner of knowledges and craftes, to exceede theirs in perfection, and speede for doing or execution, by so much the more is it probable that they shoulde desire our friendships and love, and have the greater respect for pleasing and obeying us. Whereby may be hoped, if meanes of good governement be used, that they may in short time be brought to civilitie, and the imbracing of true religion.

Some religion they have alreadie, which although it be farre from the trueth, yet being as it is, there is hope it may be the easier and sooner reformed.

They beleeve that there are many Gods, which they call Mantoac,[2] but of different sorts and degrees, one onely chiefe and great God, which hath bene from all eternitie. Who, as they affirme, when hee purposed to make the worlde, made first other gods of a principall order, to bee as meanes and instruments to be used in the creation and governmente to followe, and after the Sunne, Moone, and starres, as pettie gods, and the instruments of the other order more principall. First (they say) were made waters, out of which by the gods was made all diversitie of creatures that are visible or invisible.

For mankinde they say a woman was made first, which by the

Sir Martin Frobisher, from the portrait by Cornelis Ketel,
now in the Bodleian Library, Oxford

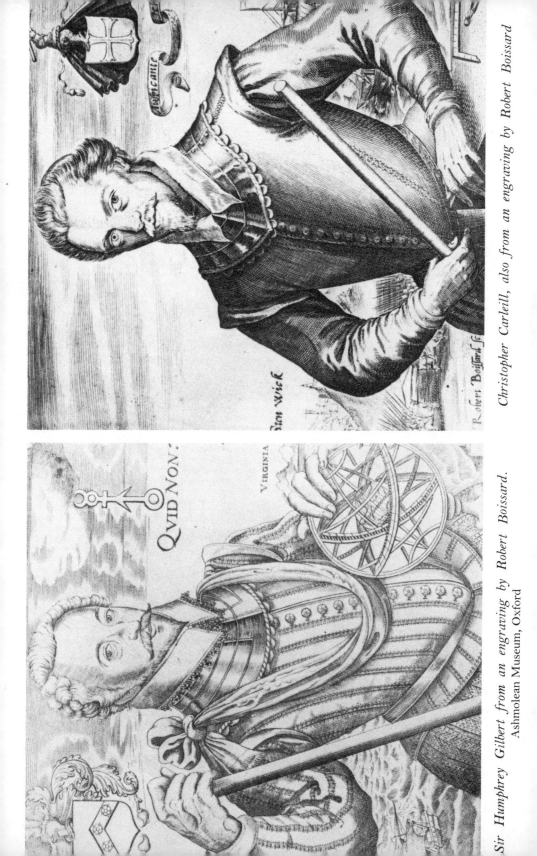

Sir Humphrey Gilbert from an engraving by Robert Boissard. Christopher Carleill, also from an engraving by Robert Boissard
Ashmolean Museum, Oxford

woorking of one of the goddes, conceived and brought foorth children: And in such sort they say they had their beginning.

But how many yeeres or ages have passed since, they say they can make no relation, having no letters nor other such meanes as we to keepe recordes of the particularities of times past, but onely tradition from father to sonne.

They thinke that all the gods are of humane shape, and therefore they represent them by images in the formes of men, which they call Kewasowok, one alone is called Kewas: them they place in houses appropriate or temples, which they call Machicomucke, where they worship, pray, sing, and make many times offering unto them. In some Machicomuck wee have seene but one Kewas, in some two, and in other some three. The common sort thinke them to bee also gods.

They beleeve also the immortalitie of the soule,[1] that after this life as soone as the soule is departed from the body, according to the workes it hath done, it is either caried to heaven the habitacle of gods, there to enjoy perpetuall blisse and happinesse, or els to a great pitte or hole, which they thinke to be in the furtherest partes of their part of the world towarde the Sunne set, there to burne continually: the place they call Popogusso.

For the confirmation of this opinion, they tolde mee two stories of two men that had bene lately dead and revived againe, the one happened but fewe yeeres before our coming into the Countrey of a wicked man, which having bene dead and buried, the next the earth of the grave being seene to moove, was taken up againe, who made declaration where his soule had bene, that is to say, very neere entring into Popogusso, had not one of the gods saved him, and gave him leave to returne againe, and teache his friendes what they shoulde doe to avoyde that terrible place of torment.

The other happened in the same yeere we were there, but in a towne that was threescore miles from us, and it was tolde mee for strange newes, that one being dead, buried, and taken up againe as the first, shewed that although his body had lien dead in the grave, yet his soule was alive, and had travailed farre in a long broade way, on both sides whereof grewe most delicate and pleasant trees, bearing more rare and excellent fruites, then ever hee had seene before, or was able to expresse, and at length came to most brave and faire houses, neere which hee mette his father, that had bene dead before, who gave

69

him great charge to goe backe againe, and shewe his friends what good they were to doe to enjoy the pleasures of that place, which when hee had done he should after come againe.

What subtiltie soever be in the Wiroances and priestes, this opinion worketh so much in many of the common and simple sort of people, that it maketh them have great respect to their Governours, and also great care what they doe, to avoyde torment after death, and to enjoy blisse, although notwithstanding there is punishment ordeined for malefactours, as stealers, whoremongers, and other sorts of wicked doers, some punished with death, some with forfeitures, some with beating, according to the greatnesse of the factes.

And this is the summe of their Religion, which I learned by having special familiaritie with some of their priestes. Wherein they were not so sure grounded, nor gave such credite to their traditions and stories, but through conversing with us they were brought into great doubts of their owne, and no small admiration of ours, with earnest desire in many, to learne more then wee had meanes for want of perfect utterance in their language to expresse.[1]

Most things they sawe with us, as Mathematicall instruments, sea Compasses, the vertue of the loadstone in drawing yron, a perspective glasse[2] whereby was shewed many strange sights, burning glasses, wilde fireworkes,[3] gunnes, bookes, writing and reading, spring clockes[4] that seeme to goe of themselves, and many other things that wee had, were so strange unto them, and so farre exceeded their capacities to comprehend the reason and meanes how they should be made and done, that they thought they were rather the workes of gods then of men, or at the leastwise they had bene given and taught us of the gods. Which made many of them to have such opinion of us, as that if they knewe not the trueth of God and religion alreadie, it was rather to bee had from us, whome God so specially loved then from a people that were so simple, as they found themselves to be in comparison of us. Whereupon greater credite was given unto that we spake of, concerning such matters.

Many times and in every towne where I came, according as I was able, I made declaration of the contents of the Bible, that therein was set foorth the true and onely God, and his mightie workes, that therein was conteined the true doctrine of salvation through Christ, with many particularities of Miracles and chiefe pointes of Religion, as I was able then to utter, and thought fit for the time. And although I tolde them the booke materially and of it selfe was not of any such vertue, as I thought they did conceive, but onely the doctrine therein conteined: yet woulde many bee glad to touche it, to embrace it, to kisse it, to holde it to their breastes and heades, and stroke over all their body with it, to shewe their hungrie desire of that knowledge which was spoken of.

The Wiroans with whome we dwelt called Wingina, and many of his people would be glad many times to be with us at our prayers, and many times call upon us both in his owne towne, as also in others whither he sometimes accompanied us, to pray and sing Psalmes, hoping thereby to be partaker of the same effects which we by that meanes also expected.

Twise this Wiroans was so grievously sicke that hee was like to die, and as he lay languishing, doubting of any helpe by his owne priestes, and thinking he was in such danger for offending us, and thereby our God, sent for some of us to pray and bee a meanes to our God that it woulde please him either that hee might live,[1] or after death dwell with him in blisse, so likewise were the requests of many others in the like case.

On a time also when their corne began to wither by reason of a drought which happened extraordinarily, fearing that it had come to passe by reason that in some thing they had displeased us, many would come to us and desire us to pray to our God of England, that hee woulde preserve their corne, promising that when it was ripe we also should be partakers of the fruite.

There coulde at no time happen any strange sickenesse, losses, hurtes, or any other crosse unto them, but that they woulde impute to us the cause or meanes thereof, for offending or not pleasing us.

One other rare and strange accident, leaving others, will I mention before I ende, which mooved the whole Countrey that either knewe or heard of us, to have us in wonderfull admiration.

There was no towne where we had any subtile devise practised against us, we leaving it unpunished or not revenged (because we sought by all meanes possible to win them by gentlenesse) but that within a fewe dayes after our departure from every such towne, the people began to die very fast, and many in short space, in some townes about twentie, in some fourtie and in one six score, which in trueth was very many in respect of their nombers. This happened in no place that we could learne, but where we had bene, where they used some practise against us, and after such time. The disease[1] also so strange, that they neither knew what it was, nor how to cure it, the like by report of the oldest men in the Countrey never happened before, time out of minde. A thing specially observed by us, as also by the natural inhabitants themselves.

Insomuch that when some of the inhabitants which were our friends, and especially the Wiroans Wingina, had observed such effects in foure or five townes to followe their wicked practises, they were perswaded that it was the worke of our God through our meanes, & that we by him might kil and slay whom we would without weapons, and not come neere them.

And thereupon when it had happened that they had understanding that any of their enemies had abused us in our journeys, hearing that we had wrought no revenge with our weapons, and fearing upon some cause the matter should so rest: did come and intreate us that wee woulde be a meanes to our God that they as others that had dealt ill with us might in like sort die, alleadging how much it would be for our credite and profite, as also theirs, and hoping furthermore that we would doe so much at their requests in respect of the friendship we professed them.

Whose entreaties although we shewed that they were ungodly, affirming that our God would not subject himselfe to any such prayers and requests of men: that in deede all thinges have bene and were to be done according to his good pleasure as hee had ordained: and that we to shewe our selves his true servants ought rather to make petition for the contrary, that they with them might live together with us, be made partakers of his trueth and serve him in righteousnesse, but notwithstanding in such sort, that wee referre that as all other things, to bee done according to his divine will and pleasure, and as by his wisedome he had ordained to be best.

Yet because the effect fell out so suddeinly and shortly after according to their desires, they thought neverthelesse it came to passe by our meanes, and that wee in using such speaches unto them, did but dissemble the matter, and therefore came unto us to give us thankes in their maner, that although wee satisfied them not in promise, yet in deedes and effect wee had fulfilled their desires.

This marveilous accident in all the Countrey wrought so strange opinions of us, that some people could not tel whether to thinke us gods or men, and the rather because that all the space of their sickenes, there was no man of ours knowen to die, or that was specially sicke: they noted also that we had no women amongst us, neither that we did care for any of theirs.

Some therefore were of opinion that wee were not borne of women, and therefore not mortall, but that wee were men of an olde generation many yeeres past, then risen againe to immortalitie.[1]

Some woulde likewyse seeme to prophecie, that there were more of our generation yet to come, to kill theirs and take their places, as some thought the purpose was, by that which was alreadie done.

Those that were immediatly to come after us they imagined to be in the ayre, yet invisible and without bodies, and that they by our intreatie and for the love of us, did make the people to die in that sort as they did, by shooting invisible bullets into them.

To confirme this opinion, their Phisitions (to excuse their ignorance in curing the disease,) would not bee ashamed to say, but earnestly make the simple people beleeve, that the strings of blood that they sucked[2] out of the sicke bodies, were the strings wherewithall the invisible bullets were tied and cast.

Some also thought that we shotte them our selves out of our pieces, from the place where wee dwelt, and killed the people in any such towne that had offended us as we listed, how farre distant from us soever it were.

And other some saide, that it was the speciall worke of God for our sakes, as wee our selves have cause in some sort to thinke no lesse, whatsoever some doe, or may imagine to the contrary, specially some Astrologers, knowing of the Eclipse of the Sunne[3] which we sawe the same yeere before in our voyage thitherward, which unto them appeared very terrible. And also of a Comet[4] which beganne to appeare but a fewe dayes before the beginning of the saide sickenesse. But to exclude them from being the speciall causes of so special an accident, there are further reasons then I thinke fit at this present to be alleadged.

These their opinions I have set downe the more at large, that it may appeare unto you that there is good hope they may be brought through discreete dealing and governement to the imbracing of the trueth, and consequently to honour, obey, feare and love us.

And although some of our companie towards the ende of the yeere, shewed themselves to fierce, in slaying some of the people, in some townes, upon causes that on our part, might easily ynough have bene borne withall: yet notwithstanding, because it was on their part justly deserved, the alteration of their opinions generally and for the most part concerning us is the lesse to be doubted. And whatsoever els they may be, by carefulnesse of our selves neede nothing at all to be feared.

The best neverthelesse in this, as in all actions besides is to bee endevoured and hoped, and of the worst that may happen notice to bee taken with consideration, and as much as may bee eschewed.

The Conclusion.

Nowe I have (as I hope) made relation not of so fewe and small thinges, but that the Countrey (of men that are indifferent and well disposed) may bee sufficiently liked: If there were no more knowen then I have mentioned, which doubtlesse and in great reason is nothing to that which remaineth to bee discovered, neither the soyle nor commodities. As wee have reason so to gather by the difference wee founde in our travailes, for although all which I have before spoken of, have bene discovered and experimented not farre from the Sea coast, where was our abode and most of our travailing: yet sometimes as wee made our journeis further into the maine and Countrey; we found the soile to be fatter, the trees greater and to growe thinner, the grounde more firme and deeper mould, more and larger champions, finer grasse, and as good as ever we saw any in England; in some places rockie and farre more high and hillie ground, more plentie of their fruites, more abundance of beastes, the more inhabited with people, and of greater pollicie and larger dominions, with greater townes and houses.

Why may we not then looke for in good hope from the inner partes of more and greater plentie, as well of other thinges, as of those which wee have alreadie discovered: Unto the Spaniards happened the like in discovering the maine of the West Indies. The maine also of this Countrey of Virginia, extending some wayes so many hundreth of leagues, as otherwise then by the relation of the inhabitants wee have most certaine knowledge of, where yet no Christian prince hath any possession or dealing, cannot but yeelde many kindes of excellent commodities, which we in our discoverie have not yet seene.

What hope there is els to bee gathered of the nature of the climate,[1] being answerable to the Island of Japan, the land of China, Persia, Jury, the Islands of Cyprus & Candy, the South parts of Greece, Italy, and Spaine, and of many other notable and famous Countreis, because I meane not to be tedious, I leave to your owne consideration.

Whereby also the excellent temperature of the aire there at all seasons, much warmer then in England, and never so vehemently hot, as sometimes is under and betweene the Tropikes, or neere them, cannot be knowen unto you without further relation.

For the holsomnesse thereof I neede to say but thus much: that for all the want of provision, as first of English victual, excepting for twentie dayes, we lived onely by drinking water, and by the victual of the Countrey, of which some sorts were very strange unto us, and might have bene thought to have altered our temperatures in such sort, as to have brought us into some grievous and dangerous diseases: Secondly the want of English meanes, for the taking of beastes, fishe, and foule, which by the helpe onely of the inhabitants and their meanes, could not be so suddenly and easily provided for us, nor in so great nomber and quantities, nor of that choise as otherwise might have bene to our better satisfaction and contentment. Some want also wee had of clothes. Furthermore, in all our travailes which were most speciall and often in the time of winter, our lodging was in the open aire upon the ground. And yet I say for all this, there were but foure of our whole companie (being one hundreth and eight) that died all the yeere and that but at the latter ende thereof and upon none of the aforesaid causes. For all foure, especially three were feeble, weake, and sickly persons before ever they came thither, and those that knewe them, much marveiled that they lived so long being in that case, or had adventured to travaile.

Seeing therefore the ayre there is so temperate and holsome, the soile so fertile, and yeelding such commodities, as I have before mentioned, the voyage also thither to and fro being sufficiently experimented, to be perfourmed twise a yeere with ease, and at any season thereof: And the dealing of Sir Walter Ralegh so liberall in large giving and graunting lande there, as is alreadie knowen, with many helpes and furtherances else: (The least that he hath graunted hath bene five hundreth acres[1] to a man only for the adventure of his person) I hope there remaines no cause whereby the action should be misliked.

If that those which shall thither travaile to inhabite and plant, be but reasonably provided for the first yeere, as those are which were transported the last, and being there, doe use but that diligence and care, as is requisite, and as they may with ease: There is no doubt, but for the time following, they may have victuals that are excellent good and plentie ynough, some more English sortes of cattell also hereafter, as some have bene before, and are there yet remayning, may, and shall be (God willing) thither transported. So likewise, our kinde of fruites, rootes, and hearbes, may be there planted and sowed, as some have bene alreadie, and proove well: And in short time also they may rayse of those sortes of commodities which I have spoken of, as shall both enriche themselves, as also others that shall deale with them.

And this is all the fruite of our labours, that I have thought necessary to advertise you of at this present: What else concerneth the nature and maners of the inhabitants of Virginia, the nomber with the particularities of the voyages thither made, and of the actions of such as have bene by Sir Walter Ralegh therein, and there imployed, many worthy to be remembred, as of the first discoverers of the Countrey: of our Generall for the time Sir Richard Greinvile, and after his departure of our Governour there Master Rafe Lane, with divers other directed and imployed under their governement: Of the Captaines and Masters of the voyages made since for transportation, of the Governour and assistants of those already transported, as of many persons, accidents, and things els, I have ready in a discourse by it selfe, in manner of a Chronicle,[2] according to the course of times: and when time shall be thought convenient, shall be also published.

Thus referring my relation to your favourable constructions, expecting good successe of the action, from him which is to be acknowledged the author and governour, not onely of this, but of all things els, I take my leave of you, this moneth of Februarie, 1588.

VII

Walter Bigges (etc.),
A summarie and true discourse of Sir Francis Drakes
West Indian voyage (Extract)[1]

AFTER three dayes spent in watering our Ships, wee departed now the second time from this Cape of S. Anthony the thirteenth of May, and proceeding about the Cape of Florida, wee never touched any where; but coasting alongst Florida, and keeping the shore still in sight, the 28. of May early in the Morning wee descried on the shore a place built like a Beacon, which was in deede a scaffold upon foure long mastes raised on ende, for men to discover to the seaward, being in the latitude of thirtie degrees, or very neere thereunto. Our Pinnesses manned, and comming to the shore, wee marched up alongst the river side, to see what place the enemie held there: for none amongst us had any knowledge thereof at all.

Here the Generall[2] tooke occasion to march with the companies himselfe in person, the Lieutenant generall[3] having the Vantguard; and going a mile up or somewhat more by the river side, we might discerne on the other side of the river over against us, a Fort[4] which newly had bene built by the Spaniards: and some mile or thereabout above the Fort was a little Towne or Village without walles, built of woodden houses, as the Plot doeth plainely shew. Wee forthwith prepared to have ordinance for the batterie; and one peece was a litle before the Evening planted, and the first shot being made by the Lieutenant generall himselfe at their Ensigne, strake through the Ensigne, as wee afterwards understood by a French man, which came unto us from them. One shot more was then made, which strake the foote of the Fort wall, which was all massive timber of great trees like Mastes. The Lieutenant generall was determined to passe the river this night with 4. companies, and there to lodge himselfe intrenched as neere the Fort, as that he might play with his muskets and smallest shot upon any that should appeare, and so afterwards to bring and plant the batterie with him: but the helpe of Mariners for that sudden to make trenches could not be had, which was the cause that this determination was remitted untill the next night.

In the night the Lieutenant generall tooke a little rowing Skiffe, and halfe a dozen well armed, as Captaine Morgan, and Captaine Sampson, with some others besides the rowers, & went to view what guard the enemie kept, as also to take knowledge of the ground. And albeit he went as covertly as might be, yet the enemie taking ye Alarme, grew fearefull that the whole force was approching to the assault, and therefore with all speede abandoned the place after the shooting of some of their peeces. They thus gone, and hee being returned unto us againe, but nothing knowing of their flight from their Fort, forthwith came a French man being a Phipher* (who had bene prisoner with them) in a litle boate, playing on his Phiph the tune of the Prince of Orenge his song;[1] and being called unto by the guard, he tolde them before he put foote out of the boate, what he was himselfe, and how the Spaniards were gone from the Fort,[2] offering either to remaine in hands there, or els to returne to the place with them that would goe.

Upon this intelligence, the Generall, the Lieutenant generall, with some of the Captaines in one Skiffe, and the Vice-admirall[3] with some others in his Skiffe, and two or three Pinnesses furnished of souldiers with them, put presently over towards the Fort, giving order for the rest of the Pinnesses to follow. And in our approch, some of the enemie bolder then the rest, having stayed behinde their company, shot off two peeces of ordinance at us: but on shore wee went, and entred the place without finding any man there.

When the day appeared, we found it built all of timber, the walles being none other but whole Mastes or bodies of trees set up right and close together in maner of a pale, without any ditch as yet made, but wholy intended with some more time; for they had not as yet finished al their worke, having begunne the same some three or foure moneths before: so as, to say the trueth, they had no reason to keepe it, being subject both to fire, and easie assault.

The platforme whereon the ordinance lay, was whole bodies of long pine trees, whereof there is great plentie, layd a crosse one on another, and some litle earth amongst. There were in it thirteene or

* Nicholas Borgoignon.

fourteene great peeces of Brasse ordinance, and a chest unbroken up, having in it the value of some two thousand pounds sterling by estimation of the kings treasure, to pay the souldiers of that place, who were a hundred and fiftie men.

The Fort thus wonne, which they called S. Johns Fort, and the day opened, wee assayed to goe to the towne, but could not by reason of some rivers and broken ground which was betweene the two places: and therefore being enforced to imbarke againe into our Pinnesses, wee went thither upon the great maine river, which is called as also the Towne, by the name of S. Augustin.

At our approching to land, there were some that began to shew themselves, and to bestow some few shot upon us, but presently withdrew themselves. And in their running thus away, the Sergeant Major[1] finding one of their horses ready sadled and brideled, tooke the same to follow the chase; and so overgoing all his company, was (by one layd behind a bush) shotte through the head: and falling downe therewith, was by the same and two or three more, stabbed in three or foure places of his body with swords and daggers, before any could come neere to his rescue. His death was much lamented, being in very deede an honest wise Gentleman, and a souldier of good experience, and of as great courage as any man might be.

In this place called S. Augustin, we understood the king did keepe, as is before said, one hundred and fiftie souldiers, and at another place some dozen leagues beyond to the Northwards, called S. Helena,[2] he did there likewise keepe an hundred and fiftie more, serving there for no other purpose, then to keepe all other nations from inhabiting any part of all that coast; the governement whereof was committed to one Pedro Melendez Marquesse, nephew to that Melendez the Admiral, who had overthrowen Master John Hawkins in the bay of Mexico some seventeen or eighteene yeeres agoe. This Governour had charge of both places, but was at this time in this place, and one of the first that left the same.

Heere it was resolved in full assembly of Captaines, to undertake the enterprise of S. Helena, and from thence to seeke out the inhabitation of our English countreymen in Virginia, distant from thence some six degrees Northward.

When wee came thwart of S. Helena,* the sholds appearing

* Santa Helena.

dangerous, and we having no Pilot to undertake the entrie, it was thought meetest to goe hence alongst. For the Admirall had bene the same night in foure fadome and a halfe, three leagues from the shore: and yet wee understood by the helpe of a knowen Pilot, there may and doe goe in Ships of greater burthen and draught then any we had in our Fleete.

We passed thus alongst the coast hard aboord the shore, which is shallow for a league or two from the shore, and the same is lowe and broken land for the most part.

The ninth of June upon sight of one speciall great fire (which are very ordinarie all alongst this coast, even from the Cape of Florida hither) the Generall sent his Skiffe to the shore, where they found some of our English countreymen (that had bene sent thither the yeere before by Sir Walter Ralegh) and brought them aboord: by whose direction wee proceeded along to the place which they make their Port.[1] But some of our ships being of great draught unable to enter, anchored without the harbour in a wilde roade at sea, about two miles from shore.

From whence the General wrote letters to master Ralfe Lane, being governour of those English in Virginia, and then at his Fort about six leagues from the Rode in an Island which they call Roanoac, wherein especially he shewed how ready he was to supply his necessities and wants, which he understood of, by those he had first talked withall.

The morrow after, Master Lane himselfe and some of his company comming unto him, with the consent of his captaines he gave them the choice of two offers, that is to say: Either he would leave a ship, a pinnesse, and certaine boates with sufficient Masters and Mariners, together furnished with a moneths victuall, to stay and make farther discovery of the countrey and coastes, and so much victuall likewise as might be sufficient for the bringing of them all (being an hundred and three persons) into England, if they thought good after such time, with any other thing they would desire, and that he might be able to spare.

Or els if they thought they had made sufficient discoverie already, and did desire to returne into England, he would give them passage. But they, as it seemed, being desirous to stay, accepted very thankefully and with great gladnesse, that which was offred first. Whereupon the ship being appointed and received into charge by some of their owne company sent into her by Master Lane, before they had received from the rest of the Fleete the provision appoynted them, there arose a great storme (which they sayd was extraordinary and very strange) that lasted three dayes together, and put all our Fleete in great danger, to bee driven from their anchoring upon the coast. For we brake many Cables, and lost many Anchors: and some of our Fleete which had lost all (of which number was the ship appointed for Master Lane and his company) was driven to put to sea in great danger, in avoyding the coast, and could never see us againe untill we mette in England. Many also of our small Pinnesses and boates were lost in this storme.

Notwithstanding after all this, the Generall offred them (with consent of his Captaines) an other ship with some provision, although not such a one for their turnes, as might have bene spared them before, this being unable to be brought into their Harbour. Or els if they would, to give them passage into England, although he knew we should performe it with greater difficultie then he might have done before.

But Master Lane with those of the chiefest of his company which hee had then with him, considering what should be best for them to doe, made request unto the General under their hands, that they might have passage for England: the which being graunted, and the rest sent for out of the countrey and shipped, we departed from that coast the 18. of June.

And so, God bee thanked, both they and wee in good safetie arrived at Portesmouth the 28. of July 1586. to the great glory of God, and to no small honour to our Prince, our Countrey, and our selves.

VIII

Depositions by Pedro Morales and
Nicolas Burgoignon, 1586

THE relation of Pedro Morales a Spaniard, which sir Francis Drake brought from Saint Augustines in Florida, where he had remayned sixe yeeres, touching the state of those partes, taken from his mouth by Master Richard Hakluyt 1586.

Three score leagues up to the Northwest from Saint Helena are the mountaines of the golde and Chrystall Mines, named Apalatci.[2]

The river of Wateri*[3] is thirtie leagues from S. Helena Northward, which is able to receive any Fleete of ships of great burden.

Wateri and Caiowa are two kings, and two rivers to the North of Saint Helena.

Oristou,
Ahoia,
Ahoiave,   } Kings and Rivers[4] to the South of Saint Helena.
Isamacon,
Icosa or Dicosa

The Spaniards have killed three hundred of the subjects of Potanou.

The greatest number of Spaniards that have bene in Florida this sixe yeeres, was three hundred, and now they were but two hundred in both the Forts.

There is a great City sixteene or twentie dayes journey from Saint Helena Northwestward, which the Spaniards call La grand Copal† which they thinke to bee very rich and exceeding great, and have bene within the sight of it, some of them.

They have offered in generall to the King to take no wages at all of him, if he will give them leave to discover this citie, and the rich

* Wateri a goodly river.   † La grand Copal a rich citie.

mountaines, and the passage to a sea or mighty Lake which they heare to be within foure and twenty dayes travel from Saint Helena, which is in 32. degrees of latitude: and is that river which the French called Port-royal.

He saith also that he hath seene a rich Diamond which was brought from the mountaines that lye up in the countrey Westward from S. Helena. These hils seeme wholy to be the mountaines of Apalatci, whereof the Savages advertised Laudonniere, and it may bee they are the hils of Chaunis Temoatam,[1] which Master Lane had advertisement of.

THE RELATION OF NICOLAS BURGOIGNON[2]

The relation of Nicholas Burgoignon, aliâs Holy, whom sir Francis Drake brought from Saint Augustine also in Florida, where he had remayned six yeeres,[3] in mine and Master Heriots hearing.

This Nicholas Burgoignon sayth, that betweene S. Augustine and S. Helen there is a Casique whose name is Casicôla which is lord of ten thousand Indians, and another casique whose name is Dicasca, and another called Touppekyn toward the North, and a fourth named Potanou toward the South, and another called Moscita toward the South likewise. Besides these he acknowledgeth Oristou, Ahoia, Ahoiaue, Isamacon, alledged by the Spaniard.[4]

He further affirmeth, that there is a citie Northwestward from S. Helenes in the mountaines, which the Spaniards call La grand Copal,[5] and is very great and rich, and that in these mountaines there is great store of Christal, golde, and Rubies, and Diamonds: And that a Spaniard brought from thence a Diamond which was worth five thousand crownes, which Pedro Melendes the marques nephew to olde Pedro Melendes that slew Ribault, & is now governer of Florida, weareth. He saith also, that to make passage unto these mountaines, it is needefull to have store of Hatchets to give unto the Indians, and store of Pickaxes to breake the mountaines, which shine so bright in the day in some places, that they cannot behold them, and therefore they travell unto them by night. Also corslets of Cotton, which the Spanyards call Zecopitz, are necessary to bee had against the arrowes of the Savages.

He sayth farther, that a Tunne of the sassafras of Florida is solde in Spaine for sixtie ducates:[6] and that they have there great store of Turkie cocks, of Beanes, of Peason, and that there are great store of pearles.

The things, as he reporteth, that the Floridians make most account of, are red Cloth, or redde Cotton to make baudricks[1] or gyrdles: copper, and hatchets to cut withall.

The Spaniards have all demaunded leave at their owne costs, to discover these mountaines, which the King denyeth, for feare lest the English or French would enter into the same action, once knowen.

All the Spaniards would passe up by the river of Saint Helena unto the mountaines of golde and Chrystall.

The Spaniards entring 50. leagues up Saint Helena, found Indians wearing golde rings at their nostrels and eares. They found also Oxen,[2] but lesse then ours.

Sixe leagues from Saint Helena toward the North, there is a poynt[3] that runneth farre into the sea, which is the marke to the Seamen to finde Saint Helena and Waterin.

Waterin is a river fortie leagues distant[4] Northward from Saint Helena, where any fleete of great ships may ride safely. I take this river to be that which we call Waren in Virginia,[5] whither at Christmasse last 1585. the Spaniards sent a barke with fortie men to discover where we were seated:[6] in which barke was Nicholas Burgoignon the reporter of all these things.

The Spaniards of S. Augustine have slaine three hundred of the subjects of Potanou. One Potassi is neighbour to Potanou. Oratina is he which the French history calleth Olata Outina.[7]

Calauai is another casique which they knowe.

The Tiger, *shown during the bombardment of the Castillo del Oro,
Smerwick Harbour, in 1580 (from a map in the Public Record
Office)*

Sir Richard Grenville's Tiger (*or possibly* Thomas Cavendish's
Elizabeth) *taken from John White's drawing of the encampment
at Guayanilla Bay, Puerto Rico, May 1585*

The arrival of the Englishmen in *Virginia*: from a drawing by John White, redrawn by Theodor de Bry

IX

Richard Hakluyt's
Narrative of the 1586 Virginia Voyages[1]

THE third voyage made by a Ship, sent in the yeere 1586. to the reliefe of the Colonie planted in Virginia, at the sole charges of Sir Walter Raleigh.

In the yeere of our Lord, 1586. sir Walter Raleigh at his owne charge prepared a ship of 100. tunnes,[2] fraighted with all maner of things in most plentiful maner for the supplie and relief of his Colonie then remaining in Virginia: but before they set saile from England, it was after Easter, so that our Colonie halfe dispaired of the comming of any supplie, wherefore every man prepared for himselfe, determining resolutely to spend the residue of their life time in that countrey, and for the better performaunce of this their determination, they sowed, planted, and set such things as were necessarie for their reliefe in so plentifull a manner, as might have suffised them two yeeres without any further labor: thus trusting to their owne harvest they passed the summer till the tenth of June, at which time their corne which they had sowed was within one fortnight of reaping, but then it happened, that Sir Frauncis Drake in his prosperous returne from the sacking of Saint Domingo, Cartagena, and Saint Augustines determined in his way homewarde to visit his countrymen the English Colonie then remayning in Virginia: so passing along the coastes of Florida, he fell with the partes, where our English Colony inhabited, and having espyed some of that company, there he ankered, and went alande where he conferred with them of their state and welfare, and howe thinges had past with them: they aunswered him that they lived all, but hitherto in some scarsitie, and as yet coulde here of no supplye out of England: therefore they requested him that he would leave with them some two or three shippes, that if in some reasonable time they heard not out of England, they might then return themselves: which hee agreed to: whilest some were then writing their letters to send into England, and some others making reportes of the accidentes of their travels each to other, some on lande, some on boord, a great storme arose, and drove the most of their fleete from their ankers to Sea, in which shippes, at that instant were the chiefest of the English Colony: the rest on land perceiving this, hasted to those three sayles which were appointed to be left there,[1] and for feare they should be left behinde, left all thinges so confusedly, as if they had bene chased from thence by a mightie armie, and no doubt so they were, for the hande of God came upon them[2] for the crueltie, and outrages committed by some of them against the native inhabitantes of that Countrie.

Immediatly after the departing* of our English Colonie out of this paradise of the worlde, the shippe above mentioned sent and set forth at the charges of Sir Walter Ralegh,[3] and his direction, arrived at Hatorask, who after some time spent in seeing our Colony up in the Countrie, and not finding them, returned with all the aforesayed provision into England.

About fourteene or fifteene daies after the departure of the aforesayd shippe, Sir Richard Grindfield† Generall of Virginia, accompanied with three shippes[4] well appointed for the same voyage arrived there, who not finding the aforesayd ship according to his expectation, nor hearing any newes of our English Colony, there seated, and left by him, Anno 1585. him selfe travailing up into divers places of the Countrey, as well to see if he could he are any newes of the Colony left there by him the yere before, under the charge of Master Lane his deputie, as also to discover some places of the Countrie: but after some time spent therein not hearing any newes of them, and finding the place which they inhabited desolate, yet unwilling to loose the possession of the Countrie, which Englishmen had so long helde: after good deliberation he determined to leave some men behinde to retaine possession of the Country: whereupon he landed 15. men[5] in the Ile of Roanoake furnished plentifully with all maner of provision for two yeeres, and so departed for England.

Not long after he fell with the Isles of Açores, on some of which Ilandes he landed, and spoyled the Townes of all such thinges as were worth cariage, where also he tooke divers Spanyardes: with these, and many other exploytes done by him in this voyage, as well outwarde as homeward, he returned into England.[6]

* June.   † Sir Richard Grindfields third voyage.

X

Hakluyt's Dedication to Ralegh,[1] 1587

TO the right honourable Sir Walter Ralegh Knight, Captaine of her Majesties Gard, Lord Warden of the Stanneries, and her Highnesse Lieutenant generall of the County of Cornewall, R. H. wisheth true felicite.

Sir, after that this historie, which had bene concealed many yeeres, was lately committed to print and published in France under your Name by my learned friend M. Martine Basanier of Paris, I was easily enduced to turne it into English, understanding that the same was no lesse gratefull to you here, then I know it to be acceptable to many great and worthie persons there. And no marvaile though it were very welcome unto you, and that you liked of the translation thereof, since no history hitherto set forth hath more affinitie, resemblance or conformitie with yours of Virginia, then this of Florida. But calling to minde that you had spent more yeeres in France then I,[2] and understand the French better then my selfe, I forthwith perceived that you approoved mine endevour, not for any private ease or commoditie that thereby might redound unto you, but that it argued a singular and especiall care you had of those which are to be employed in your owne like enterprise, whom, by the reading of this my translation, you would have forewarned and admonished aswell to beware of the gross negligence in providing of sufficiency of victuals, the securitie, disorders, and mutinies that fell out among the French, with the great inconveniences that thereupon ensued, that by others mishaps they might learne to prevent and avoyde the like,* as also might be put in minde, by the reading of the manifolde commodities and great fertilitie of the places herein at large described and so neere neighbours unto our Colonies, that they might generally bee awaked and stirred up

* Other mens misfortune ought to be our warning.

unto the diligent observation of every thing that might turne to the advancement of the action, wherinto they are so cheerefully entred. Many speciall poynts concerning the commodities of these partes, the accidents of the French mens government therein, the causes of their good or bad successe, with the occasions of the abandoning one of their forts, and the surprise of the other by the enemie are herein truely and faithfully recorded: Which because they be quoted by me in the margents, and reduced into a large alphabeticall table, which I have annexed to the ende of the worke, it shall be needlesse to recken up againe. And that the rather, because the same with divers other things of chiefest importance* are lively drawne in colours at your no smal charges by the skillfull painter James Morgues, sometime living in the Black-fryers in London (whom Monsieur Chastillion then Admirall of France sent thither with Laudonniere for that purpose) which was an eye-witnesse of the goodnesse and fertility of those regions, and hath put downe in writing many singularities which are not mentioned in this treatise: which since he hath published together with the purtraitures.[1] These foure voyages I knew not to whom I might better offer then to your selfe, and that for divers just considerations. First, for that as I have sayd before, they were dedicated unto you in French: secondly because now foure times also you have attempted the like upon the selfe same coast neere adjoyning: thirdly in that you have persed as farre up into the maine and discovered no lesse secrets in the partes of your aboad, then the French did in the places of their inhabiting lastly considering you are now also ready (upon the late returne of Captaine Stafford[2] and good newes which he brought you of the safe arrival of your last Colony in their wished haven) to prosecute this action more throughly then ever. And here to speake somewhat of this your enterprise, I affirme, that if the same may speedily and effectually be pursued, it will proove farre more beneficiall in divers respects unto this our realme, then the world, yea many of the wiser sort, have hitherto imagined. The particular commodities† whereof are wel knowen unto your selfe and some few others, and are faithfully and with great judgement committed to writing, as you are not ignorant, by one of your followers, which

* The chiefe things worthie observation in Florida are drawn in colours by James Morgues painter sometime living in the Black fryers in London.

† A collection of the commodities of Virginia.

remained there about a twelvemonth with your worshipful Lieutenant M. Ralph Lane, in the diligent search of the secrets of those Countreys. Touching the speedy and effectual pursuing of your action, though I wote well it would demaund a princes purse to have it throughly followed without lingring, yet am I of opinion, that you shall drawe the same before it be long to be profitable and gainful aswel to those of our nation there remaining, as to the merchants of England that shall trade hereafter thither, partly by certaine secret commodities already discovered* by your servants, & partly by breeding of divers sorts of beasts in those large and ample regions, and planting of such things in that warme climat as wil best prosper there, and our realme standeth most in need of. And this I find to have bin the course that both the Spaniards and Portugals tooke in the beginnings of their discoveries & conquests. For the Spaniards at their first entrance into Hispaniola found neither suger-canes nor ginger growing there, nor any kind of our cattel: But finding the place fit for pasture they sent kine & buls and sundry sorts of other profitable beasts thither, & transported the plants of suger-canes, and set the rootes of ginger:† the hides of which oxen, with suger and ginger, are now the chiefe merchandise of that Island. The Portugals also at their first footing in Madera, as John Barros writes in his first Decade,[1] found nothing there but mighty woods for timber, whereupon they called the Island by that name. Howbeit the climate being favourable, they inriched it by their own industry with the best wines and sugers in the world. The like maner of proceeding they used in the Isles of the Açores by sowing therin great quantity of Woad.‡ So dealt they in S. Thomas under the Equinoctial, and in Brasil, and sundry other places. And if our men will follow their steps, by your wise direction I doubt not but in due time they shall reape no lesse commoditie and benefit. Moreover there is none other likelihood but that her Majesty, which hath Christned, and given the name to your Virginia, if need require, will deale after the maner of honorable godmothers, which, seeing their gossips not fully able to bring up their children themselves, are wont to contribute to their honest education, the rather if they find any

---

* Meanes to raise benefit in new discoveries used by the Spaniards & Portugals.

† Kine, suger-canes and ginger transported into Hispaniola and Madera, &c.

‡ Woad and vines planted in the Azores.

towardlines or reasonable hope of goodnesse in them. And if Elizabeth Queene of Castile and Aragon, after her husband Ferdinando and she had emptied their cofers and exhausted their treasures in subduing the kingdome of Granada and rooting the Mores, a wicked weed, out of Spayne, was neverthelesse so zealous* of Gods honour, that (as Fernandus Columbus the sonne of Christopher Columbus recordeth in the history of the deedes of his father)[1] she layd part of her owne jewels, which she had in great account, to gage, to furnish his father foorth upon his first voyage, before any foot of land of all the West Indies was discovered; what may we expect of our most magnificent and gracious prince ELIZABETH of England, into whose lappe the Lord hath most plentifully throwne his treasures, what may wee, I say, hope of her forwardnesse and bounty in advancing of this your most honourable enterprise, being farre more certaine then that of Columbus, at that time especially, and tending no lesse to the glorie of God then that action of the Spanyardes? For as you may read in the very last wordes of the relation of Newe Mexico extant nowe in English,[2] the maine land, where your last Colonie meane to seate themselves, is replenished with many thousands of Indians, Which are of better wittes then those of Mexico and Peru, as hath bene found by those that have had some triall of them: whereby it may bee gathered that they will easily embrace the Gospell,† forsaking their idolatrie, wherein at this present for the most part they are wrapped and intangled. A wise Philosopher‡ noting the sundry desires of divers men, writeth, that if an oxe bee put into a medowe hee will seeke to fill his bellie with grasse, if a Storke bee cast in shee will seeke for Snakes, if you turne in a Hound he will seeke to start an Hare: So sundry men entring into these discoveries propose unto themselves severall endes. Some seeke authoritie and places of commandement, others experience by seeing of the worlde, the most part worldly and transitorie gaine, and that often times by dishonest and unlawfull meanes, the fewest number the glorie of God and the saving of the soules of the poore and blinded infidels. Yet because divers honest and well disposed persons are entred already into this your

* The great zeale of Elizabeth Queene of Castile and Aragon in advancing of new discoveries tending to Gods glory.

† The aptnesse of the people in the maine of Virginia to embrace Christianitie.

‡ Seneca.

businesse, and that I know you meane hereafter to sende some such good Churchmen thither, as may truely say with the Apostle to the Savages,* Wee seeke not yours but you: I conceive great comfort of the successe of this your action, hoping that the Lorde, whose power is wont to bee perfected in weakenesse, will blesse the feeble foundations of your building. Onely bee you of a valiant courage and faint not, as the Lorde sayd unto Josue,† exhorting him to proceede on forward in the conquest of the land of promise, and remember that private men have happily wielded and waded through as great enterprises as this, with lesser meanes then those which God in his mercie hath bountifully bestowed upon you, to the singuler good, as I assure my selfe, of this our Common wealth wherein you live. Hereof we have examples domesticall and forreine. Remember I pray you, what you find in the beginning of the Chronicle[1] of the conquest of Ireland newly dedicated unto your selfe.‡ Read you not that Richard Strangbow the decayed earle of Chepstow in Monmuthshire, being in no great favour of his soveraigne, passed over into that Island in the yere 1171. and accompanied only with certain of his private friends had in short space such prosperous successe, that he opened the way for king Henry the second to the speedy subjection of all that warlike nation to this crowne of England? The like conquest of Brasilia, and annexing the same to the kingdome of Portugall was first begun by meane and private men, as Don Antonio de Castillio, Ambassadour here for that realme, and by office keeper of all the records and monuments of their discoveries, assured me in this city in the yere 1581.[2] Now if the greatnes of the maine of Virginia, and the large extension thereof, especially to the West, should make you thinke that the subduing of it, were a matter of more difficulty then the conquest of Ireland, first I answere, that as the late experience§ of that skilfull pilote and Captaine M. John Davis to the Northwest[3] (toward which his discovery your selfe have thrise contributed with the forwardest) hath shewed a great part to be maine sea, where before was thought to be maine land, so for my part I am fully perswaded by Ortelius late reformation of Culuacan[4] and the gulfe of California, that the land on the backe part of Virginia extendeth nothing so far

* 2. *Cor*. 12.14.   † *Josue* 1.6.
‡ The good successe in Ireland of Richard Strangbow earle of Chepstow.
§ The happy late discoverie to the Northwest of Captaine Davis.

westward as is put downe in the Maps of those parts. Moreover it is not to be denied, but that one hundred men will do more now among the naked and unarmed people in Virginia, then one thousand were able then to do in Ireland against that armed and warlike nation in those daies. I say further, that these two yeres last experience hath plainly shewed, that we may spare 10000. able men without any misse. And these are as many as the kingdome of Portugal had ever in all their garrisons of the Açores, Madera, Arguin, Cape verde, Guinea, Brasill, Mozambique, Melinde, Zocotora, Ormus, Diu, Goa, Malaca, the Malucos, and Macao upon the coast of China. Yea this I say by the confession of singuler expert men of their own nation (whose names I suppresse for certain causes) which have bene personally in the East Indies, & have assured me that their kings* had never above ten thousand natural borne Portugals (their slaves excepted) out of their kingdome remaining in all the aforesaid territories. Which also this present yeere I saw confirmed in a secrete extract of the particular estate of that kingdome and of every governement and office subject to the same, with the several pensions thereunto belonging. Seeing therefore we are so farre from want of people, that retyring daily home out of the Lowe Countreys they go idle up and downe in swarms for lack of honest intertainment, I see no fitter place to employ some part of the better sort of them trained up thus long in service, then in the inward partes of the firme of Virginia against such stubborne Savages as shal refuse obedience to her Majestie. And doubtlesse many of our men will bee glad and faine to accept this condition, when as by the reading of this present treatie they shal understand the fertilitie and riches of the regions confining so neere upon yours, the great commodities and goodnesse whereof you have bin contented to suffer to come to light. In the meane season I humbly commend my selfe and this my translation unto you, and your selfe, and all those which under you have taken this enterprise in hand to the grace and good blessing of the Almighty, which is able to build farther, and to finish the good worke which in these our dayes he hath begun by your most Christian and charitable endevour. From London the 1. of May 1587.[1]

Your L. humble at commandement. R. HAKLUYT.

* The kings of Portugal had never above ten thousand of their naturall subjects in all their new conquered dominions.

XI

John White's

Narrative of the 1587 Virginia Voyage[1]

THE fourth voyage made to Virginia, with three shippes, in the yeere, 1587. Wherein was transported the second Colonie.[2]

In the yeere of our Lorde, 1587. Sir Walter Ralegh intending to persevere in the planting of his Countrey of Virginia, prepared a newe Colonie of one hundred and fiftie men to be sent thither, under the charge of John White, whom he appointed Governour, and also appointed unto him twelve Assistants, unto whome he gave a Charter, and incorporated them by the name of Governour, and Assistants of the Citie of Ralegh[3] in Virginia.

Aprill.

Our Fleete being in number three saile, viz. the Admirall,[4] a shippe of one hundred and twentie tunnes: a Flie boate, and a Pinnesse,[5] departed the sixe and twentieth of Aprill from Portesmouth, and the same day came to an anker at the Cowes, in the Isle of Wight, where wee staied eight daies.

Maye.

The 5. of Maye, at nine of the clocke at night, we came to Plymmouth, where we remained the space of two daies.

The 8. we waied anker at Plymmouth, and departed thence for Virginia.

The 16. Simon Ferdinando Master of our Admirall, lewdly forsooke our Flie boate,[6] leaving her distressed in the Baye of Portingall.

June.

The 19. we fell with "Dominica,* and the same evening we sailed betweene it, and Guadalupe: the 21. the Flie boat also fell with Dominica.

The 22. we came to an anker at an Isle, called Santa Cruz, where all the planters were set on land, staying there till the 25. of the same moneth. At our first landing on this Island, some of our women, and men, by eating a small fruite, like greene apples,¹ were fearefully troubled with a sudden burning in their mouthes, and swelling of their tongues so bigge, that some of them could not speake. Also a child by sucking one of those womens breast[s], had at that instant his mouth set on such a burning, that it was strange to see how the infant was tormented for the time: but after 24. howres, it ware away of it selfe.

Also the first night of our being on this Island, we tooke five great Torteses, some of them of such bignes, that sixteene of our strongest men were tired with carrying of one of them but from the Sea side, to our cabbins. In this Island we found no watring place, but a standing ponde, the water whereof was so evill, that many of our companie fell sicke with drinking thereof: and as many as did but wash their faces with that water, in the morning before the Sunne had drawen away the corruption, their faces did so burne, and swell, that their eies were shut up, and could not see in five or sixe daies or longer.

The second day of our abode there, we sent foorth some of our men to search the Island for fresh water, three one way, and two another way. The Governour also, with sixe others, went up to the toppe of an high hill, to view the Island, but could perceave no signe of any men, or beastes, nor any goodnes, but Parots, and trees of Guiacum. Returning backe to our Cabbins another way, he found in the discent of a hill, certaine potsheards of savage making, made of the earth of that Island: whereupon it was judged, that this Island was inhabited with Savages, though Fernando had tolde us for certaine, the contrarie. The same day at night, the rest of our companie very late returned to the Governour. The one companie affirmed, that they had seene in a valley, eleven Savages, and divers houses halfe a mile distant from the steepe, or toppe of the hill where they staied. The

* "One of the Isles of the Indias, inhabited with Savages.

other companie had found running out of a high rocke, a very faire spring of water, whereof they brought three bottles to the companie: for before that time, wee dranke the stinking water of the pond.

.The same second day at night, Captaine Stafford, with the pinnesse, departed from our fleete, riding at Santa Cruz, to an Island, called Beake, lying neere S. Johns, being so directed by Ferdinando, who assured him he should there finde great plentie of sheepe. The next day at night, our planters left Santa Cruz, and came all aboord, and the next morning after, being the 25. of June, we waied anker, and departed from Santa Cruz.

The seven and twentieth we came to anker at Cottea,[1] where we found the pinnesse riding, at our comming.

The 28. we waied anker at Cottea, and presently came to anker at S. Johns in Musketas Bay, where we spent three daies unprofitably in taking in freshe water, spending in the meane time more beere, then the quantitie of the water came unto.

Julie.

The first we waied anker at "Muskitoes Baye,* where were left behind two Irish men of our companie, Darbie Glaven,[2] and Denice Carrell,[3] bearing along the coast of S. Johns, till evening, at which time we fell with Rosse Baye.[4] At this place Fernando had promised wee should take in salt, and had caused us before, to make and provide as many sackes for that purpose, as we could. The Governour also, for that he understoode there was a Towne in the bottome of the Baye, not farre from the salt hils, appointed thirtie shotte, ten pikes, and ten targets, to man the pinnesse, and to goe a land for salt. Fernando perceaving them in a readines, sent to the Governour, using great perswasions with him, not to take in salt there, saying that he knewe not well, whether the same were the place or not: also, that if the pinnesse went into the Bay, she could not without great danger come backe, till the next day at night, and that if in the meane time any storme should rise, the Admirall were in danger to be cast away. Whilest he was thus perswading, he caused the lead to be cast, and having craftily brought the shippe in three fathome, and a halfe water,

* "Musketas Baye, is a harbour upon the South side of S. Johns Island, where we take in fresh water.

he suddenly began to sweare, and teare God in peeces, dissembling great danger, crying to him at the helme, beare up hard, beare up hard: so we went off, and were disappointed of our salt, by his meanes.

The next day, sailing along the West ende of S. Johns, the Governour determined to goe a land in S. Germans "Baye,* to gather yong plants of Oringes, Pines, Mameas, and Platonos, to set at Virginia, which we knewe might easily be had, for that they growe neere the shoare, and the places where they grewe, well knowen to the Governour,[1] and some of the planters: but our Simon denied it, saying: he would come to an anker at Hispaniola, and there lande the Governour, and some other of the Assistants, with the pinnesse, to see if he could speake with his friend Alanson,[2] of whome he hoped to be furnished both of cattell, and all such thinges as wee woulde have taken in at S. Johns: but hee meant nothing lesse, as it plainely did appeare to us afterwards.

The next day after, being the third of Julie, wee sawe Hispaniola, and bare with the coast all that day, looking still when the pinnesse should be prepared to goe for the place where Fernando his friend Alanson was: but that day passed, and we sawe no preparation for landing in Hispaniola.

The 4. of Julie, sailing along the coast of Hispaniola, untill the next day at noone, and no preparation yet seene for the staying there, we having knowledge that we were past the place where Alanson dwelt, and were come with Isabella: hereupon Fernando was asked by the Governour, whether he meant to speake with Alanson, for the taking in of cattell, and other things, according to his promise, or not: but he answered, that he was now past the place, and that Sir Walter Ralegh tolde him, the French Ambassador certified him, that the king of Spaine had sent for Alanson into Spaine: wherefore he thought him dead, and that it was to no purpose to touch there in any place, at this voyage.

The next day, we left sight of Hispaniola, and haled off for Virginia, about 4. of the clocke in the afternoone.

The sixt of Julie, wee came to the Islande Caycos, wherein Fernando saide were two salt pondes, assuring us if they were drie,

* "A pleasant and fruitfull Countrey, lying on the west ende of S. Johns Island 1ere groweth plentie of Oringes, Lemmons, Plantyns, and Pynes.

wee might find salt to shift with, untill the next supplie, but it prooved as true as the finding of sheepe at Beake. In this Island, whilest Ferdinando solaced himself a shoare, with one of the company, in part of the Island, others spent the latter part of that day in other parts of the Island, some to seeke the salt ponds, some fowling, some hunting Swannes, whereof we caught many. The next daye, earely in the morning we waied anker, leaving Caycos, with good hope, the first lande that wee sawe next, should be Virginia.

About the 16. of July, we fell with the maine of Virginia, which Simon Fernando tooke to be the Island of Croatoan, where we came to an anker, and rode there two or three daies: but finding himselfe deceaved, he waied, and bare along the coast, where in the night, had not Captaine Stafforde bene more carefull in looking out, then our Simon Fernando, wee had beene all cast away upon the breache, called the Cape of Feare,[1] for wee were come within two cables length upon it: such was the carelesnes, and ignorance of our Master.

The two and twentieth of Julie, we arrived safe at Hatoraske,[2] where our shippe and pinnesse ankered: the Governour went aboord the pinnesse, accompanied with fortie of his best men, intending to passe up to Roanoake foorthwith, hoping there to finde those fifteene Englishmen, which Sir Richard Greenvill had left there the yeere before, with whome he meant to have conference, concerning the state of the Countrey, and Savages, meaning after he had so done, to returne againe to the fleete, and passe along the coast, to the Baye of Chesepiok,[3] where we intended to make our seate and forte, according to the charge given us among other directions in writing, under the hande of Sir Walter Ralegh.[4] but assoone as we were put with our pinnesse from the shippe, a Gentleman by the meanes of Fernando, who was appointed to returne for England, called to the sailers in the pinnesse, charging them not to bring any of the planters backe againe, but leave them in the Island, except the Governour, and two or three such as he approved, saying that the Summer was farre spent,[5] wherefore hee would land all the planters in no other place. Unto this were all the sailers, both in the pinnesse, and shippe, perswaded by the Master, wherefore it booted not the Governour to contend with them,[6] but passed to Roanoake, and the same night, at Sunne set, went aland on the Island, in the place where our fifteene men were left, but we found none of them, nor any signe, that they had bene there, saving onely we found the bones of one of those fifteene, which the Savages had slaine long before.

The 23. of July, the Governour, with divers of his companie, walked to the North ende of the Island, where Master Ralfe Lane had his forte, with sundry necessarie and decent dwelling houses, made by his men about it the yeere before, where wee hoped to finde some signes, or certaine knowledge of our fifteene men. When we came thither, wee found the forte rased downe,[1] but all the houses standing unhurt, saving the neather roomes of them, and also of the forte,[2] were overgrowen with Melons of divers sortes, and Deere within them, feeding on those Mellons: so we returned to our companie, without hope of ever seeing any of the fifteene men living.

The same day order was given, that every man should be imploied for the repairing of those houses, which we found standing, and also to make other newe Cottages,[3] for such as shoulde neede.

The 25. our Flie boate, and the rest of our planters, arrived all safe at Hatoraske, to the great joye, and comfort of the whole companie: but the Master of our Admirall, Fernando grieved greatly at their safe comming: for he purposely left them in the Baye of Portingall, and stole away from them in the night, hoping that the Master thereof, whose name was Edward Spicer, for that he never had beene in Virginia, would hardly finde the place, or els being left in so dangerous a place as that was, by meanes of so many men of warre, as at that time were aboord,[4] they should surely be taken, or slaine: but God disappointed his wicked pretenses.

The eight and twentieth, George Howe, one of our twelve Assistants was slaine by divers Savages, which were come over to Roanoake, either of purpose to espie our companie,[5] and what number we were, or els to hunt Deere, whereof were many in the Island. These Savages beeing secretly hidden among high reedes, where oftentimes they finde the Deere asleepe, and so kill them, espied our man wading in the water alone, almost naked, without any weapon, save onely a small forked sticke, catching Crabs therewithall, and also being strayed two miles from his companie, shotte at him in the water, where they gave him sixeteene wounds with their arrowes: and after they had slaine him with their woodden swordes, beat his head in peeces, and fled over the water to the maine.

On the thirtieth of Julie, Master Stafford, and twentie of our men, passed by water to the Island of Croatoan, with Manteo, who had his mother, and many of his kinred, dwelling in that Island,[1] of whome we hoped to understande some newes of our fifteene men, but especially to learne the disposition of the people of the Countrey towards us, and to renew our olde friendshippe with them. At our first landing, they seemed as though they would fight with us: but perceaving us begin to marche with our shot towards them, they turned their backes, and fled. Then Manteo their countreyman, called to them in their owne language, whom, assoone as they heard, they returned, and threwe away their bowes, and arrowes, and some of them came unto us, embracing and entertaining us friendly, desiring us not to gather or spill any of their corne, for that they had but little. We answered them, that neither their corne, nor any other thing of theirs, should be diminished by any of us, and that our comming was onely to renew the olde love, that was betweene us, and them, at the first, and to live with them as brethren, and friendes: which answere seemed to please them well, wherefore they requested us to walke up to their Towne, who there feasted us after their manner, and desired us earnestly, that there might be some token or badge given them of us, whereby we might know them to be our friendes, when we met them any where out of the Towne or Island. They tolde us further, that for want of some such badge, divers of them were hurt the yeere before, beeing founde out of the Island by Master Lane his companie,[2] whereof they shewed us one, which at that very instant laye lame, and had lien of that hurt ever since: but they said, they knew our men mistooke them, and hurt them in steade of Winginoes men, wherefore they held us excused.

August.

The next day, we had conference further with them, concerning the people of Secota, Aquascogoc, & Pomiock, willing them of Croatoan, to certifie the people of those townes, that if they would accept our friendship, we would willingly receave them againe, and that all unfriendly dealings past on both partes, should be utterly forgiven, and forgotten. To this the chiefe men of Croatoan answered, that they would gladly doe the best they could, and within seven daies, bring the Weroances, and chiefe Governours of those townes with them, to our Governour at Roanoak, or their answere. We also understoode of the men of Croatoan, that our man Master Howe, was slaine by the remnant of Winginoes men, dwelling then at Dasamongueponke, with whom Winchese kept companie: and also we understood by them of Croatoan, how that the 15. Englishmen left at Roanoak the yeere before, by Sir Richard Greenvill, were suddenly set upon, by 30. of the men of Secota, Aquascogoc, and Dasamongue-ponke, in manner following. They conveied themselves secretly behind the trees, neere the houses, where our men carelesly lived: and having perceaved that of those 15. they could see but 11. onely, two of those Savages appeared to the 11. Englishmen, calling to them by friendly signes, that but two of their chiefest men should come unarmed to speake with those two Savages, who seemed also to be unarmed. Wherefore two of the chiefest of our Englishmen, went gladly to them: but whilest one of those Savages traitorously embraced one of our men, the other with his sword of wood, which he had secretly hidden under his mantell, stroke him on the head, and slewe him, and presently the other eight and twentie Savages shewed themselves: the other Englishman perceaving this, fled to his companie, whome the Savages pursued with their bowes, and arrowes, so fast, that the Englishmen were forced to take the house, wherein all their victuall, and weapons were: but the Savages foorthwith set the same on fire, by meanes whereof, our men were forced to take up such weapons as came first to hand, and without order to runne foorth among the Savages, with whome they skirmished above an howre. In this skirmish, another of our men was shotte into the mouth with an arrowe, whereof he died: and also one of the Savages was shot into the side by one of our men, with a wild fire arrowe, whereof he died presently. The place where they fought, was of great advantage to the Savages, by meanes of the thicke trees, behinde which the Savages through their nimblenes, defended themselves, and so offended our men with their arrowes, that our men being some of them hurt, retired fighting to the water side, where their boate lay, with which they fled towards Hatorask. By that time they had rowed but a quarter of a mile, they espied their foure fellowes comming from a creeke thereby, where they had bene to fetch Oysters: these foure they receaved into their boate, leaving Roanoake, and landed on a little Island on the right hand of our entrance into the harbour of

Their rype corne

Their greene corne

Corne newly sprong

Their sitting at meate

The house wherin the Tombe of their Herounds standeth.

SECOTON

A Ceremony in their prayers wt strange testures andsoges danshing abowt posts carued on the topps lyke mens faces.

The village of Secotan by John White

The manner of their fishing.

A drawing by John White to show some of the ways in which Indians fish

Hatorask, where they remained a while, but afterward departed, whither, as yet we knowe not.[1]

Having nowe sufficiently dispatched our busines at Croatoan, the same day wee departed friendly, taking our leave, and came aboord the fleete at Hatoraske.

The eight of August, the Governour having long expected the comming of the Weroanses of Pomioake, Aquascoquoc, Secota, and Dasamongueponke, seeing that the seven daies were past, within which they promised to come in, or to send their answers by the men of Croatoan, and no tidings of them heard, being certainly also informed by those men of Croatoan, that the remnant of Wingino his men, which were left alive, who dwelt at Dasamongueponke, were they which had slaine George Howe, and were also at the driving of our eleven Englishmen[2] from Roanoake, he thought to differre the revenging thereof no longer. Wherefore the same night, about midnight, he passed over the water, accompanied with Captaine Stafford, and 24. men, whereof Manteo was one, whome wee tooke with us to be our guide to the place where those Savages dwelt, where he behaved himselfe toward us as a most faithfull English man.

The next day, being the ninth of August, in the morning so earely, that it was yet darke, wee landed neere the dwelling place of our enemies, and very secretly conveyed our selves through the woods, to that side, where we had their houses betweene us and the water: and having espied their fire, and some sitting about it, we presently sette on them: the miserable soules herewith amased, fledde into a place of thicke reedes, growing fast by, where our men perceaving them, shotte one of them through the bodie with a bullet, and therewith wee entred the reedes, among which wee hoped to acquite their evill doing towards us, but wee were deceaved, for those Savages were our friendes, and were come from Croatoan, to gather the corne, and fruite of that place, because they understoode our enemies were fledde immediatly after they had slaine George Howe, and for haste had left all their corne, Tabacco, and Pompions standing in such sorte, that all had beene devoured of the birdes, and Deere, if it had not beene gathered in time: but they had like to have paide deerely for it: for it was so darke, that they beeing naked, and their men and women apparelled all so like others, we knewe not but that they were all men: and if that one of them, which was a Weroans wife, had not had her childe at her backe, she had beene slaine in steede of a man, and as happe was, another Savage knewe Master Stafford, and ranne to him, calling him by his name, whereby he was saved. Finding our selves thus disappointed of our purpose, wee gathered all the corne, Pease, Pumpions, and Tabacco, that we found ripe, leaving the rest unspoiled, and tooke Menatoan his wife, with the yong childe, and the other Savages with us over the water to Roanoak. Although the mistaking of these Savages somewhat grieved Manteo, yet he imputed their harme to their owne follie, saying to them, that if their Weroans had kept their promise in comming to the Governour, at the day appointed, they had not knowen that mischance.

The 13. of August, our Savage Manteo, by the commandement of Sir Walter Ralegh, was christened[1] in Roanoak, and called Lord therof, and of Dasamongueponke, in reward of his faithfull service.[2]

The 18. Elenora, daughter to the Governour, and wife to Ananias Dare, one of the Assistants, was delivered of a daughter in Roanoak, and the same was christened there the Sunday following,[3] and because this childe was the first Christian borne in Virginia, she was named Virginia. By this time our shippes had unlanded[4] the goods and victuals of the planters, and began to take in wood, and fresh water, and to newe calke and trimme them for England: the planters also prepared their letters, and tokens, to send backe into England.

Our two shippes, the Lyon, and the Flieboate, almost ready to depart, the 21. of August, there arose such a tempest at northeast,[5] that our Admirall then riding out of the harbour, was forced to cut his cables, and put to Sea, where he laye beating off and on, sixe dayes before hee coulde come to us againe, so that wee feared hee had beene cast away, and the rather, for that at the tyme that the storme tooke them, the moste, and best of their Saylers, were left aland.

At this time some controversies rose betweene the Governour, and Assistants,[6] about choosing two out of the twelve Assistants, which should goe backe as factors[7] for the companie into England: for every one of them refused, save onely one, which all the other thought not sufficient: but at length, by much perswading of the Governour, Christopher Cooper onely agreed to goe for England: but the next day, through the perswasion of divers of his familiar friendes, he changed his minde, so that now the matter stoode as at the first.

The next day, the 22. of August, the whole companie, both of the

Assistants, and planters, came to the Governour, and with one voice requested him to returne himselfe into England, for the better and sooner obtaining of supplies, and other necessaries for them: but he refused it, and alleaged many sufficient causes, why he would not: the one was, that he could not so suddenly returne backe againe, without his great discredite, leaving the action, and so many, whome he partly had procured through his perswasions to leave their native Countrey, and undertake that voyage, and that some enemies to him, and the action at his returne into England, would not spare to slander falsely both him,[1] and the action, by saying he went to Virginia, but politikely, and to no other ende, but to leade so many into a Countrey, in which he never meant to stay himselfe, and there to leave them behind him. Also he alleaged, that seing they intended to remove 50. miles further up into the maine[2] presently he being then absent, his stuffe and goods, might be both spoiled, and most of it pilfered away in the carriage, so that at his returne, hee should be either forced to provide himselfe of all such things againe, or els at his comming againe to Virginia, finde himselfe utterly unfurnished, whereof already he had found some proofe, beeing but once from them but three daies.[3] Wherefore he concluded, that he would not goe himselfe.

The next day, not onely the Assistants, but divers others, as well women, as men, beganne to renewe their requests to the Governour againe, to take uppon him to returne into England for the supplie, and dispatch of all such thinges, as there were to be done, promising to make him their bonde under all their handes, and seales, for the safe preserving of all his goods for him at his returne to Virginia, so that if any part thereof were spoiled, or lost, they would see it restored to him, or his Assignes, whensoever the same should be missed, and demanded: which bonde, with a testimonie under their handes, and seales, they foorthwith made, and delivered into his hands. The copie of the testimonie, I thought good to set downe.

May it please you, her Majesties Subjects of England, wee your friendes and Countrey men, the planters in Virginia, doe by these presents let you, and every of you to understande, that for the present and speedie supplie of certaine our knowen, and apparent lackes, and needes, most requisite and necessarie for the good and happie planting of us, or any other in this lande of Virginia, wee all of one minde, and consent, have most earnestly intreated, and uncessantly requested

John White, Governour of the planters in Virginia, to passe into England, for the better and more assured helpe, and setting forward of the foresayde supplies: and knowing assuredly that he both can best, and will labour, and take paines in that behalfe for us all, and hee not once, but often refusing it, for our sakes, and for the honour, and maintenance of the action, hath at last, though much against his will, through our importunacie, yeelded to leave his government, and all his goods among us, and himselfe in all our behalfes to passe into Englande, of whose knowledge, and fidelitie in handling this matter, as all others, wee doe assure our selves by these presents, and will you to give all credite thereunto. the five and twentieth of August.[1]

The Governour beeing at the last, through their extreame intreating, constrayned to returne into England, having then but halfe a daies respit to prepare him selfe for the same, departed from Roanoake, the seven and twentieth of August in the morning: and the same daye about midnight, came aboord the Flie boate, who already had waied anker, and rode without the barre, the Admirall riding by them, who but the same morning was newly come thither againe. The same day,[2] both the shippes waied anker, and sette saile for England: at this waying their ankers, twelve of the men which were in the Flieboate, were throwen from the Capestone,[3] which by meanes of a barre that brake, came so fast about upon them, that the other two barres thereof stroke and hurt most of them so sore, that some of them never recovered it: neverthelesse they assaied presently againe to waigh their anker, but being so weakened with the first fling, they were not able to weigh it, but were throwen downe, and hurt the seconde time. Wherefore having in all but fifteene men aboord and most of them by this infortunate[4] beginning so bruised, and hurt, they were forced to cut their Cable, and leese[5] their anker. Neverthelesse, they kept companie with the Admirall, untill the seventeenth of September, at which time wee fell with Corvo, and sawe Flores.

September.

The eighteenth, perceaving of all our fifteene men in the Flie boate, there remained but five, which by meanes of the former mischance, were able to stande to their labour: wherefore understanding that the Admirall meant not to make any haste for England, but linger about the Islande of Tercera for purchase,[1] the Flie boate departed for Englande with letters, where we hoped by the helpe of God to arrive shortly: but by that time wee had continued our course homeward, about twentie dayes, having had sometimes scarse, and variable windes, our fresh water also by leaking almost consumed, there arose a storme at Northeast, which for 6. dayes ceased not to blowe so exceeding, that we were driven further in those 6. then wee could recover in thirteene daies: in which time others of our saylers began to fall very sicke, and two of them dyed, the weather also continued so close, that our Master sometimes in foure daies together could see neither Sunne nor starre, and all the beverage we could make, with stinking water, dregges of beere, and lees of wine which remained, was but 3. gallons, and therefore now we expected nothing but by famyne to perish at Sea.

October.

The 16. of October we made land, but we knew not what land it was, bearing in with the same land at that day: about Sunne set we put into a harbour, where we found a Hulke of Dublin, and a pynesse of Hampton ryding, but we knew not as yet what place this was, neither had we any boate to goe a shoare,[2] untill the pinnesse sent off their boate to us with 6. or 8. men, of whom we understood we were in Smewicke in the west parts of Ireland: they also releeved us presently with fresh water, wyne, and other fresh meate.

The 18. the Governour, and the Master ryd to Dingen Cushe,[3] 5. myles distant, to take order of the new victualling of our Flye boate for England, and for reliefe of our sicke and hurt men, but with 4. dayes after the boatswane, the steward, and the boatswanes mate dyed aboord the flyeboate, and the 28. the Masters mate and two of our chiefe Saylers were brought sicke to Dingen.

November.

The first the Governour shipped him selfe in a ship called the Monkie, which at that time was readie to put to Sea from Dingen for England, leaving the Flyeboat and all his company in Ireland, the same day we set sayle, and on the third day we fel with the Northside of the lands end, and were shut up the Severne, but the next day we doubled the same, for Monts Bay.

The 5. the Governour landed in England at Martasew, neere Saint Michaels mount in Cornewall.

The 8. we arrived at Hampton, where we understood that our consort the Admirall was come to Portsmouth, and had bene there three weekes before: and also that Fernando the Master with all his company were not onely come home without any purchase, but also in such weaknesse by sicknes, and death of their cheefest men, that they were scarse able to bring their ship into the harbour, but were forced to let fall anker without, which they could not way againe, but might all have perished there, if a small barke by great hap had not come to them to helpe them. The names of the chiefe men that dyed are these, Roger Large, John Mathew, Thomas Smith, and some other saylers, whose names I know not at the writing hereof. Anno Domini 1587.[1]

XII

The Names of the 1587 Virginia Colonists[1]

THE names of all the men, women and Children, which safely arrived in Virginia, and remained to inhabite there. 1587.

Anno Regni Reginae Elizabethae .29.

John White [Governor].[2]
Roger Bailie [Assistant].
Ananias Dare [Assistant].[3]
Christopher Cooper [Assistant].
Thomas Stevens [Assistant].
John Sampson [Assistant].
Dyonis Harvie [Assistant].
Roger Prat [Assistant].
George Howe [Assistant].
Simon Fernando [Assistant].[4]
Nicholas Johnson.
Thomas Warner.
Anthony Cage.
John Jones.
John Tydway.
Ambrose Viccars.
Edmond English.
Thomas Topan.
Henry Berrye.
Richard Berrye.
John Spendlove.
John Hemmington.
Thomas Butler.
Edward Powell.
John Burden.
James Hynde.

William Willes.
John Brooke.
Cutbert White.
John Bright.

Clement Tayler.
William Sole.
John Cotsmur.
Humfrey Newton.
Thomas Colman.
Thomas Gramme.
Marke Bennet.
John Gibbes.
John Stilman.
Robert Wilkinson.
Peter Little.
John Wyles.
Brian Wyles.
George Martyn.
Hugh Pattenson.
Martyn Sutton.
John Farre.
John Bridger.
Griffen Jones.
Richard Shaberdge.

Thomas Ellis.
William Browne.

Michael Myllet.
Thomas Smith.
Richard Kemme.
Thomas Harris.
Richard Taverner.
John Earnest.
Henry Johnson.
John Starte.
Richard Darige.
William Lucas.
Arnold Archard.
John Wright.
William Dutton.
Morris Allen.
William Waters.
Richard Arthur.
John Chapman.
William Clement.

Robert Little.
Hugh Tayler.
Richard Wildye.
Lewes Wotton.
Michael Bishop.
Henry Browne.
Henry Rufoote.
Richard Tomkins.
Henry Dorrell.
Charles Florrie.
Henry Mylton.

Henry Payne.
Thomas Harris.
William Nicholes.
Thomas Phevens.

John Borden.
Thomas Scot.

James Lasie.[1]
John Cheven.
Thomas Hewet.
William Berde.

Women
Elyoner Dare.
Margery Harvie.
Agnes Wood.
Wenefrid Powell.
Joyce Archard.
Jane Jones.
Elizabeth Glane.
Jane Pierce.
Audry Tappan.
Alis Chapman.
Emme Merrimoth.
Colman.
Margaret Lawrence.
Joan Warren.
Jane Mannering.
Rose Payne.
Elizabeth Viccars.

Boyes and Children.
John Sampson.
Robert Ellis.
Ambrose Viccars.
Thomas Archard.
Thomas Humfrey.
Tomas Smart.
George Howe.
John Prat.
William Wythers.

Children born in Virginia.
Virginia Dare.
Harvye.

Savages.

Manteo.[1] ⎱
Towaye.[2] ⎰ That were in Englande and returned home into Virginia with them.

XIII

John White's
Narrative of the Abortive Virginia Voyage 1588[1]

THE first[2] voyage intended for the supply of the Colonie planted in Virginia by John White which being undertaken in the yeere 1588 by casualtie tooke no effect.

After the Governors returne[3] out of Virginia the 20. of November 1587.[4] he delivered his letters and other advertisments concerning his last voyage and state of the planters to Sir Walter Ralegh: whereupon he foorthwith appointed a pinnesse[5] to be sent thither with all such necessaries as he understood they stood in neede of: and also wrote his letters unto them, wherein among other matters he comforted them with promise, that with all convenient speede he would prepare a good supply of shipping and men with sufficience of all thinges needefull, which he intended, God willing, should be with them the Sommer following. Which pinnesse and fleete were accordingly prepared in the West Countrey at Bidiforde under the chardge of Sir Richard Greenevil. This fleete being now in a reddinesse only staying but for a faire wind to put to Sea, at the same time there was spred throughout all England such report of the wonderfull preparation and invincible fleetes made by the king of Spaine joyned with the power of the Pope for the invading of England, that most of the ships of warre then in a readines in any haven in England were stayed for service at home: And sir Richard Greenevil[6] was personally commanded not to depart out of Cornewall. The voyage of Virginia by these meanes for this yere thus disappointed, the Governour notwithstanding labored for the reliefe of the planters so earnestly, that he obtained two small pinnesses the one of them being of 30. tonnes called the Brave,[7] the other of 25. called the Roe,[8] wherein 15. planters and all their provision, with certaine reliefe for those that wintered in the Countrie was to be transported.

Thus the 22. of Aprill 1588. we put over the barre at Biddiford in the edge of the Northside of Cornewal, and the same night we came to an anker under the Isle of Lundy, where some of our company went on land: After we had roade there about the space of three howers we wayed anker againe and all that night we bare along the coast of Cornewall.

The next day being S. Georges day and the 23. of Aprill stil bearing along the coast we gave chase to 4. ships, & borded them & forced them all to come to anker by us in a smal bay at the lands end, out of these ships we tooke nothing but 3. men, & the same night we weighed & put to Sea.

The 24. day we gave chase to 2. ships, the one of them being a Scot the other a Breton. These we borded[1] also & tooke from them whatsoever we could find worth the taking, & so let them goe.

The 26. of April we escried a ship on sterne of us, for whom we strooke our toppe sayle, and stayed for it. By that time he came with us we saw in his flagge a redd crosse: wereupon we helde him for an Englishman, & gave over our preparation to fight with him. But when he was come neere to us we perceived his flagge not to be a right S. George: whereupon we were somewhat amased having so farre mistaken, for it was a very tall ship, and excellently well appointed & now readie to clap us aboord. And it was not now neede to bid every man to bestirre himselfe, for each one prepared with all speed to fight. In the meane time we hayled them whence they were: They answered of Flushing, bound for Barbarie. And they perceiving us to be Englishmen of warre bare from us and gave us a piece, and we gave them two pieces and so departed.

The 27. day in the morning we were come with the heigth of cape Finister, the winde being still at Northeast.

The 28. day the wind shifted: about foure of the clocke in the afternoone the same day we escried a sayle to the weather of us, whom we kept so neere unto us as we could all that night.

The 29. in the morning we gave chase to the same ship being then to the wind of us almost as farre as we could ken. Assoone as our pinnes, came up to them, the pinnes fought with the ship, & it was an Hulke of 200. tonnes & more, but after a few great shot bestowed on both sides, the pinnesse perceiving her consort not able to come to ayd her left the Hulke & came roome with the Brave againe. At their comming they desired the Captaine & Master of the Brave to lend them some men and other things whereof they had neede. Which things put aboord them they returned againe to the chase of the Hulke[1] earnestly, and with ful purpose to boord her. But the Hulke bare all night in with the coast of Spaine, and by morning were so neere land, that we fearing eyther change of wind or to be calmed gave over the fight and put off to Sea againe.

May

The first day of May being Wedensday the wind came large at Northeast.

The 3. being friday we gave chase to another tal ship, but it was night before we spake with her: and the night grew darke sodenly in such sort, that we lost sight both of the great ship & of our consort also, having thus in the darke lost our pinnesse, & knowing our barke so bad of sayle that we could neither take nor leve, but were rather to be taken or left of every ship we met, we made our course for the Isle of Madera, hoping there to find our pinnesse abiding for us.

The same day following being the 5. of May we spake with a man of warre of Rochel of 60. tons, very wel manned & bravely appointed being bound, as he said for Peru: having hailed ech other, we parted frindly in outward shew, giving ech other a voley of shot & a great piece: but nevertheles we suspected y^t which followed: for this Rocheller having taken perfect view of our ship, men, & ordinance, towards evening fell on sterne of us: and assoone as it was darke left us, and returned to his consort which was a tal ship of 100. tonne lying then on hull to weather of us out of ken, having 84. men in her, whereof 50. were smal shot, and 12. muskets, and in the ship 10. peeces of ordinance. This ship being this night certified by her consort that viewed us, of what force we were and how bad of sayle, this greater ship tooke in 20. of the chiefest men that were in the smallest ship, and presently gave us chase.

The next morning being Monday and the 6. of May, we escried them in the weather of us, so that it was in vaine to seeke by flight, but rather by fight to helpe our selves. The same day about 2. of the clocke in the afternoone they were come with us. We hayled them, but they would not answere. Then we waved them to leewardes of us, and they waved us with a sword amayne, fitting their sailes to clappe us aboord, which we perceiving gave them one whole side: with one of our great shot their Master gonners shoolder was stroken away, and our Master gonner with a smal bullet was shot into the head. Being by this time grappled and aboord each of other the fight continued without ceasing one houre and a halfe. In which fight were hurt & slaine on both sides 23. of the chiefest men,[1] having most of them some 6. or 8. woundes, and some 10. or 12. woundes. Being thus hurt and spoiled they robbed us of all our victuals, powder, weapons and provision, saving a smal quantity of biskuit to serve us scarce for England. Our Master and his Mate were deadly wounded, so that they were not able to come forth of their beds. I my selfe was wounded twise in the head, once with a sword, and another time with a pike, and hurt also in the side of the buttoke with a shot. Three of our passengers were hurt also, whereof one had 10. or 12. woundes our Master hurt in the face with a pike and thrust quite through the head. Being thus put to our close fights, and also much pestred with cabbens[2] and unserviceable folkes we could not stirre to handle our weapons nor charge a piece: againe having spent all the powder in our flaskes and charges which we had present for our defence, they cut downe our netting and entred so many of their men as could stand upon our poope and forecastle, from whence they played extremely upon us with their shot. As thus we stood resolved to die in fight, the Captaine of the Frenchmen cried to us to yeld and no force should be offred. But after we had yelded, they knowing so many of their best men to be hurt and in danger of present death, began to grow into a new furie, in which they would have put us to the sword had not their Captaine charged them, and persuaded them to the contrary. Being at length pacified they fell on all handes to rifling and carying aboord all the next day until 4. of the clock: at which time by over greedy lading both their owne boate and ours, they sunke the one and split the other by the ships side: by meanes whereof they left us two cables and ankers, all our ordinance and most part of our sailes, which otherwise had ben taken away also. Furthermore they doubting the wind would arise, and night at hand, & a tal ship al that day by meanes of the calme in sight, they came aboord us with their ship, and tooke in their men that were in us, who left us not at their departing any thing worth the carying away. Being thus ransacked and used as is aforesaid in all sorts, we determined (as our best shift in so hard a case) to returne for England, and caused all our able and unhurt men, to fal to newe rigging & mending our sailes, tacklings, and such things as were spilled in our fight. By this occasion, God justly punishing our former theeverie of our evil desposed mariners, we were of force constrained to break of our voyage intended for the reliefe of our Colony left the yere before in Virginia, and the same night to set our course for England, being then about 50. leagues to the Northeast of Madera.

The 7. of May¹ being Wednesday in the forenoone the wind came large at East northeast and we haled off as farre west and by north as we could untill the 10. of May, fearing to meete with any more men of warre, for that we had no maner of weapons left us.

The 11. the wind larged more, and thence forth we continued our due course for England.

The 17. of May we thrust our selves west of Usshant, & sounded, but found no ground at 110 fathoms. The same day at night we sounded againe, and found ground at 80. fathoms.

The 20. being Sonday we fell with the coast of Ireland.

The 21. in the forenoone we saw the Northside of Cornewal at the lands end.

The 22. of May we came to an anker betweene Lunday and Harting point neere unto Chavell key,² where we road untill the next tyde, and thence we put over the barre, and the same day landed at Biddeford.

Our other pinnesse whose company we had lost before the last cruell fight, returned also home into Cornwall within fewe weekes after our arrival, without performing our entended voyage for the reliefe of the planters in Virginia, which thereby were not a litle distressed.

XIV

John White to Richard Hakluyt,[1] 4 February 1593

TO the Worshipful and my very friend Master Richard Hakluyt, much happinesse in the Lord.

Sir, as well for the satisfying of your earnest request, as the performance of my promise made unto you at my last being with you in England, I have sent you (although in a homely stile, especially for the contentation of a delicate eare) the true discourse of my last voyage into the West Indies, and partes of America called Virginia, taken in hand about the end of Februarie, in the yeere of our redemption 1590.[2] And what events happened unto us in this our journey, you shall plainely perceive by the sequele of my discourse. There were at the time aforesaid three ships[3] absolutely determined to goe for the West Indies, at the speciall charges of Master John Wattes of London Marchant. But when they were fully furnished, and in readinesse to make their departure, a generall stay was commanded of all ships thorowout England.[4] Which so soone as I heard, I presently (as I thought it most requisite) acquainted Sir Walter Ralegh therewith, desiring him that as I had sundry times afore bene chargeable and troublesome unto him, for the supplies and reliefes of the planters in Virginia: so likewise, that by his endevour it would please him at that instant to procure license for those three ships to proceede on with their determined voyage, that thereby the people in Virginia (if it were Gods pleasure) might speedily be comforted and relieved without further charges unto him. Whereupon he by his good meanes obtained license of the Queenes Majestie,[5] and order to be taken, that the owner of the 3 ships should be bound unto Sir Walter Ralegh or his assignes, in 3000 pounds,[6] that those 3 ships in consideration of their releasement should take in, & transport a convenient number of passengers, with their furnitures and necessaries to be landed in Virginia. Neverthelesse that order was not observed, neither was the bond taken according to the intention aforesaid. But rather in contempt of the aforesaid order, I was by the owner and Commanders of the ships denied to have any passengers, or any thing els transported in any of the said ships, saving only my selfe & my chest; no not so much as a boy to attend upon me, although I made great sute, & earnest intreatie aswell to the chiefe Commanders, as to the owner of the said ships. Which crosse and unkind dealing, although it very much discontented me, notwithstanding the scarsity of time was such, that I could have no opportunity to go unto Sir Walter Ralegh with complaint: for the ships being then all in readinesse to goe to the Sea, would have bene departed before I could have made my returne. Thus both Governors, Masters, and sailers, regarding very smally the good of their countreymen in Virginia; determined nothing lesse[1] then to touch at those places, but wholly disposed themselves to seeke after purchase & spoiles, spending so much time therein, that sommer was spent before we arrived at Virginia. And when we were come thither, the season was so unfit, & weather so foule, that we were constrained of force to forsake that coast, having not seene any of our planters, with losse of one of our ship-boates, and 7 of our chiefest men: and also with losse of 3 of our ankers and cables, and most of our caskes with fresh water left on shore, not possible to be had aboord. Which evils & unfortunate events (as wel to their owne losse as to the hinderance of the planters in Virginia) had not chanced, if the order set downe by Sir Walter Ralegh[2] had bene observed, or if my dayly & continuall petitions for the performance of the same might have taken any place. Thus may you plainely perceive the successe of my fift & last voiage to Virginia,[3] which was no lesse unfortunately ended then frowardly begun, and as lucklesse to many, as sinister to my selfe. But I would to God it had bene as prosperous to all, as noysome to the planters; & as joyfull to me, as discomfortable to them. Yet seeing it is not my first crossed voyage, I remaine contented. And wanting my wishes, I leave off from prosecuting that whereunto I would to God my wealth were answerable to my will.[4] Thus committing the reliefe of my discomfortable company the planters in Virginia, to the merciful help of the Almighty, whom I most humbly beseech to helpe & comfort them, according to his most holy will & their good desire, I take my leave from my house at Newtowne in Kylmore[5] the 4 February, 1593.

Your most welwishing friend,

John White.

John White's drawing of a terrapin

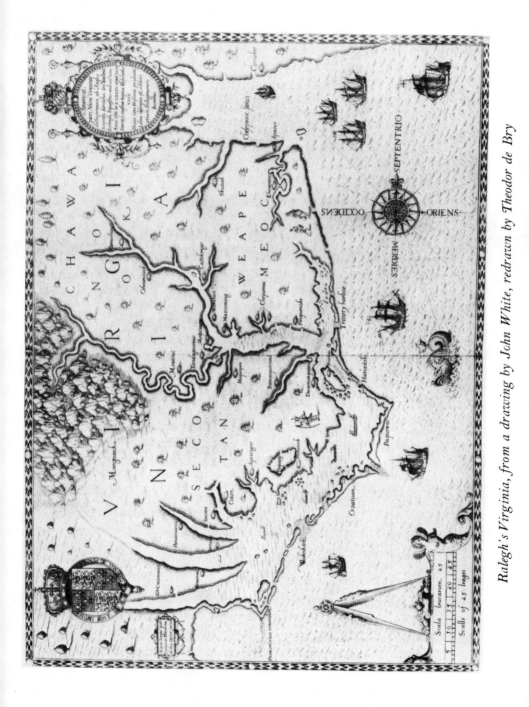

Ralegh's Virginia, from a drawing by John White, redrawn by Theodor de Bry

XV

John White's

Narrative of the 1590 Virginia Voyage[1]

THE fift voyage of Master John White into the West Indies and parts of America called Virginia, in the yeere 1590.

The 20 of March the three shippes the Hopewell,[2] the John Evangelist, and the Little John, put to Sea from Plymmouth with two small Shallops.

The 25 at midnight both our Shallops[3] were sunke being towed at the ships stearnes by the Boatswaines negligence.

On the 30 we saw a head us that part of the coast of Barbary, lying East of Cape Cantyn, and the Bay of Asaphi.[4]

The next day we came to the Ile of Mogador, where rode, at our passing by, a Pinnesse of London called the Mooneshine.

Aprill.

On the first of Aprill we ankored in Santa Cruz rode, where we found two great shippes of London lading in Sugar, of whom we had 2 shipboats to supply the losse of our Shallops.

On the 2 we set sayle from the rode of Santa Cruz, for the Canaries.

On Saturday the 4 we saw Alegranza, the East Ile of the Canaries.

On Sunday the 5 of Aprill we gave chase to a double flyboat,[5] the which, we also the same day fought with, and tooke her, with losse of three of their men slaine, and one hurt.

On Munday the 6 we saw Grand Canarie, and the next day we landed and tooke in fresh water on the Southside thereof.

On the 9 we departed from Grand Canary, and framed our course for Dominica.

The last of Aprill we saw Dominica, and the same night we came to an anker on the Southside thereof.

117

May.

The first of May in the morning many of the Salvages came aboord our ships in their Canowes, and did traffique with us; we also the same day landed and entered their Towne from whence we returned the same day aboord without any resistance of the Salvages;[1] or any offence done to them.

The 2 of May our Admirall and our Pinnesse[2] departed from Dominica leaving the John our Viceadmirall playing off and on about Dominica, hoping to take some Spaniard outwardes bound to the Indies; the same night we had sight of three smal Ilands called Los Santos, leaving Guadalupe and them on our starboord.

The 3 we had sight of S. Christophers Iland, bearing Northeast and by East off us.

On the 4 we sayled by the Virgines, which are many broken Ilands, lying at the East ende of S. Johns Iland; and the same day towards evening we landed upon one of them called Blanca, where we killed an incredible number of foules: here we stayed but three houres, & from thence stood into the shore Northwest, and having brought this Iland Southeast off us, we put towards night thorow an opening or swatch, called The passage, lying betwene the Virgines,[3] and the East end of S. John: here the Pinnesse left us and sayled on the South side of S. John.

The 5 and 6 the Admirall sayled along the Northside of S. John, so neere the shore that the Spaniards discerned us to be men of warre; and therefore made fires along the coast as we sailed by, for so their custome is, when they see any men of warre on their coasts.

The 7 we landed on the Northwest end of S. John, where we watered in a good river called Yaguana, and the same night following we tooke a Frigate of tenne Tunne comming from Gwathanelo laden with hides and ginger. In this place Pedro a Mollato, who knewe all our state, ranne from us to the Spaniards.

On the 9 we departed from Yaguana.

The 13 we landed on an Iland called Mona, whereon were 10 or 12 houses inhabited of the Spaniards; these we burned & tooke from them a Pinnesse, which they had drawen a ground and sunke, and carried all her sayles, mastes, and rudders into the woods, because we should not take him away; we also chased the Spaniards over all the

Iland; but they hid them in caves, hollow rockes, and bushes, so that we could not find them.

On the 14 we departed from Mona, and the next day after wee came to an Iland called Saona, about 5 leagues distant from Mona, lying on the Southside of Hispaniola neere the East end: betweene these two Ilands we lay off and on 4 or 5 dayes, hoping to take some of the Domingo fleete[1] doubling this Iland, as a neerer way to Spaine then by Cape Tyburon, or by Cape S. Anthony.

On Thursday being the 19 our Viceadmirall, from whom we departed at Dominica, came to us at Saona, with whom we left a Spanish Frigate, and appointed him to lie off and on other five daies betweene Saona and Mona to the ende aforesaid; then we departed from them at Saona for Cape Tyburon.[2] Here I was enformed that our men of the Viceadmirall, at their departure from Dominica brought away two young Salvages, which were the chiefe Casiques sonnes of that Countrey and part of Dominica, but they shortly after ran away from them at Santa Cruz Iland, where the Viceadmirall landed to take in ballast.

On the 21 the Admirall came to the Cape Tyburon, where we found the John Evangelist our Pinnesse staying for us: here we tooke in two Spaniards almost starved on the shore, who made a fire to our ships as we passed by. Those places for an 100 miles in length are nothing els but a desolate and meere wildernesse, without any habitation of people, and full of wilde Bulles and Bores, and great Serpents.

The 22 our Pinnesse came also to an anker in Aligato Bay at cape Tyburon. Here we understood of Master Lane,* Captaine of the Pinnesse; how he was set upon with one of the kings Gallies[3] belonging to Santo Domingo, which was manned with 400 men, who after he had fought with him 3 or 4 houres, gave over the fight & forsooke him, without any great hurt done in eyther part.

The 26 the John our Vizadmirall came to us to cape Tyburon, and the Frigat which we left with him at Saona. This was the appointed place where we should attend for the meeting with the Santo Domingo Fleete.

On Whitsunday[4] Even at Cape Tyburon one of our boyes ranne away from us, and at ten dayes end returned to our ships almost starved for want of food. In sundry places about this part of Cape Tyburon we found the bones and carkases of divers men, who had

* Master William Lane.

perished (as wee thought) by famine in those woods, being either stragled from their company, or landed there by some men of warre.

June.

On the 14 of June we tooke a smal Spanish frigat which fell amongst us so suddenly, as he doubled the point at the Bay of Cape Tyburon, where we road, so that he could not escape us. This Frigat came from Santo Domingo, and had but 3 men in her, the one was an expert Pilot, the other a Mountainer, and the third a Vintener,[1] who escaped all out of prison at Santo Domingo, purposing to fly to Yaguana which is a towne in the West parts of Hispaniola where many fugitive Spaniards* are gathered together.

The 17 being Wednesday Captaine Lane was sent to Yaguana with his Pinnesse and a Frigat to take a shippe, which was there taking in fraight, as we understood by the old Pylot, whom we had taken three dayes before.

The 24 the Frigat returned from Captaine Lane at Yaguana, and brought us word to cape Tyburon, that Captaine Lane had taken the shippe,[2] with many passengers and Negroes in the same; which proved not so rich a prize as we hoped for, for that Frenchman of warre had taken and spoyled her before we came. Neverthelesse her loading was thought worth 1000 or 1300 pounds, being hides, ginger, Cannafistula, Copperpannes, and Casavi.

July.

The second of July Edward Spicer whom we left in England came to us at Cape Tyburon,[3] accompanied with a small Pinnesse, whereof one Master Harps was Captaine.[4] And the same day we had sight of a fleete of 14 saile[5] all of Santo Domingo, to whom we presently gave chase, but they upon the first sight of us fled, and separating themselves scattered here and there: Wherefore we were forced to divide our selves and so made after them untill 12 of the clocke at night. But then by reason of the darknesse we lost sight of ech other, yet in the end the Admirall and the Moonelight happened to be together the same night at the fetching up of the Vizadmirall of the Spanish fleete,[6] against whom the next morning we fought and tooke

* Spanish fugitives.

him,* with losse of one of our men and two hurt, and of theirs 4 slaine and 6 hurt. But what was become of our Viceadmirall, our Pinnesse, and Prize, and two Frigates,[1] in all this time, we were ignorant.

The 3 of July we spent about rifling, romaging and fitting the Prize to be sailed with us.[2]

The 6 of July we saw Jamayca the which we left on our larboord, keeping Cuba in sight on our starboord.

Upon the 8 of July we saw the Iland of Pinos, which lieth on the Southside of Cuba nigh unto the West end or Cape called Cape S. Anthony.[3] And the same day we gave chase to a Frigat, but at night we lost sight of her, partly by the slow sayling of our Admirall, & lacke of the Moonelight our Pinnesse,[4] whom Captaine Cooke[5] had sent to the Cape the day before.

On the 11 we came to Cape S. Anthony, where we found our consort the Moonelight and her Pinnesse abiding for our comming, of whom we understood that the day before there passed by them 22 saile, some of them of the burden of 300 and some 400 tunnes loaden with the Kings treasure from the maine, bound for Havana;[6] from this 11 of July untill 22 we were much becalmed: and the winde being scarse, and the weather exceeding hoat, we were much pestered with the Spaniards we had taken: wherefore we were driven to land all the Spaniards saving three, but the place where we landed them was of their owne choise on the Southside of Cuba[7] neere unto the Organes and Rio de Puercos.

The 23 we had sight of the Cape of Florida, and the broken Ilands thereof called the Martires.

The 25 being S. James day in the morning, we fell with the Matanças[8] a head-land 8 leagues towards the East of Havana, where we purposed to take fresh water in, and make our abode two or three dayes.

On Sunday the 26 of July plying too and fro betweene the Matanças, and Havana, we were espied of three small Pinnasses of S. John de Ullua bound for Havana, which were exceeding richly loaden.[9] These 3 Pinnasses came very boldly up unto us, and so continued untill they came within musket shot of us. And we supposed them to be Captain Harps pinnesse, and two small Frigats taken by Captain

* This fight was in sight of the Iland of Navaza.[10]

Harpe: wherefore we shewed our flag. But they presently upon the sight of it turned about & made all the saile they could from us toward the shore, & kept themselves in so shallow water, that we were not able to follow them, and therefore gave them over with expence of shot & pouder to no purpose. But if we had not so rashly set out our flagge, we might have taken them all three, for they would not have knowen us before they had bene in our hands. This chase brought us so far to leeward as Havana: wherfore not finding any of our consorts at ye Matanças,[1] we put over again to the cape of Florida, & from thence thorow the chanel of Bahama.

On the 28 the Cape of Florida bare West of us.

The 30 we lost sight of the coast of Florida, and stood to Sea for to gaine the helpe of the current which runneth much swifter a farre off then in sight of the coast.* For from the Cape to Virginia all along the shore are none but eddie currents, setting to the South and Southwest.[2]

The 31 our three ships were clearely disbocked,[3] the great prize, the Admirall, and the Mooneshine,[4] but our prize being thus disbocked departed from us without taking leave of our Admirall or consort, and sayled directly for England.[5]

August.

On the first of August the winde scanted, and from thence forward we had very fowle weather[6] with much raine, thundering, and great spouts, which fell round about us nigh unto our ships.

The 3 we stoode againe in for the shore, and at midday we tooke the height of the same.[7] The height of that place we found to be 34 degrees of latitude. Towards night we were within three leagues of the Low sandie Ilands West of Wokokon.† But the weather continued so exceeding foule, that we could not come to an anker nye the coast: wherefore we stood off againe to Sea untill Monday the 9 of August.[8]

On munday the storme ceased, and we had very great likelihood of faire weather: therefore we stood in againe for the shore: & came to an anker at 11 fadome in 35 degrees‡ of latitude,[9] within a mile of the shore, where we went on land on the narrow sandy Iland,

* The state of the currents from the cape of Florida to Virginia.
† Sandie Ilands West of Wokokon.   ‡ They land in 35 degrees.

being one of the Ilandes West of Wokokon: in this Iland we tooke in some fresh water and caught great store of fish in the shallow water. Betweene the maine (as we supposed) and that Iland it was but a mile over and three or foure foote deepe in most places.

On the 12 in the morning we departed from thence and toward night we came to an anker at the Northeast end of the Iland of Croatoan, by reason of a breach* which we perceived to lie out two or three leagues into the Sea:[1] here we road all that night.

The 13 in the morning before we wayed our ankers, our boates were sent to sound over this breach: our ships riding on the side thereof at 5 fadome; and a ships length from us we found but 4 and a quarter, and then deeping and shallowing for the space of two miles, so that sometimes we found† 5 fadome, and by & by 7, and within two casts with the lead 9, & then 8, next cast 5, & then 6, & then 4, & then 9 againe, and deeper; but 3 fadome was the least, 2 leagues off from the shore. This breach is in 35 degr. & a halfe,[2] & lyeth at the very Northeast point of Croatoan, wheras goeth a fret[3] out of the maine Sea into the inner waters, which part the Ilandes and the maine land.

The 15 of August towards Evening we came to an anker at Hatorask, in 36 degr.‡ and one third,[4] in five fadom water, three leagues from the shore.[5] At our first comming to anker on this shore we saw a great smoke rise in the Ile Raonoake neere the place where I left our Colony in the yeere 1587, which smoake[6] put us in good hope that some of the Colony were there expecting my returne out of England.

The 16 and next morning our 2 boates went a shore, & Captaine Cooke & Captain Spicer & their company with me, with intent to passe to the place at Raonoak where our countreymen were left. At our putting from the ship we commanded our Master gunner to make readie 2 Minions and a Falkon well loden, and to shoot them off with reasonable space betweene every shot, to the ende that their reportes might bee heard to the place where wee hoped to finde some of our people. This was accordingly performed, & our twoe boats put off unto the shore, in the Admirals boat we sounded all the way and found from our shippe untill we came within a mile of the shore nine,

---

* A breach 2 or 3 leagues into Sea.   † Great diversity of soundings.
‡ Hatorask in 36 degr. & a terce.

123

eight, and seven fadome: but before we were halfe way betweene our ships and the shore we saw another great smoke to the South-west of Kindrikers mountes:[1] we therefore thought good to goe to that second smoke first: but it was much further from the harbour where we landed,[2] then we supposed it to be, so that we were very sore tired before wee came to the smoke. But that which grieved us more was that when we came to the smoke, we found no man nor signe that any had bene there lately, nor yet any fresh water in all this way to drinke. Being thus wearied with this journey we returned to the harbour where we left our boates, who in our absence, had brought their caske a shore for fresh water, so we deferred our going to Roanoak untill the next morning, and caused some of those saylers to digge in those sandie hilles for fresh water[3] whereof we found very sufficient.* That night wee returned aboord with our boates and our whole company in safety.

The next morning being the 17 of August, our boates and company were prepared againe to goe up to Roanoak, but Captaine Spicer had then sent his boat ashore for fresh water, by meanes whereof it was ten of the clocke aforenoone before we put from our ships which were then come to an anker within two miles of the shore. The Admirals boat was halfe way toward the shore, when Captaine Spicer put off from his ship. The Admirals boat first passed the breach, but not without some danger of sinking, for we had a sea brake into our boat which filled us halfe full of water, but by the will of God and carefull styrage of Captaine Cooke we came safe ashore, saving onely that our furniture, victuals match and powder were much wet and spoyled. For at this time the winde blue at Northeast and direct into the harbour so great a gale, that the Sea brake extremely on the barre,[4] and the tide went very forcibly at the entrance. By that time our Admirals boate was halled ashore, and most of our things taken out to dry, Captaine Spicer came to the entrance of the breach with his mast standing up, and was halfe passed over, but by the rash and undiscreet styrage of Ralph Skinner his Masters mate, a very dangerous Sea brake into their boate and overset them quite, the men kept the boat some in it, and some hanging on it, but the next sea set the boat on ground, where it beat so, that some of them were forced to let goe their hold, hoping to wade ashore, but the Sea still beat them

* Fresh water found in sandy hilles.

downe, so that they could neither stand nor swimme, and the boat twise or thrise was turned the keele upward; whereon Captaine Spicer* and Skinner hung untill they sunke, & seene no more. But foure that could swimme a litle kept themselves in deeper water and were saved by Captain Cookes meanes,[1] who so soone as he saw their oversetting, stripped himselfe, and foure other that could swimme very well, & with all haste possible rowed unto them, & saved foure. They were a 11 in all, & 7 of the chiefest were drowned, whose names were Edward Spicer, Ralph Skinner, Edward Kelley, Thomas Bevis, Hance the Surgion, Edward Kelborne, Robert Coleman. This mischance did so much discomfort the saylers, that they were all of one mind not to goe any further to seeke the planters. But in the end by the commandement & perswasion of me and Captaine Cooke, they prepared the boates: and seeing the Captaine and me so resolute, they seemed much more willing. Our boates and all things fitted againe, we put off from Hatorask, being the number of 19 persons in both boates: but before we could get to the place, where our planters were left, it was so exceeding darke, that we overshot the place[2] a quarter of a mile: there we espied towards the North end of the Iland ye light of a great fire thorow the woods, to the which we presently rowed: when wee came right over against it, we let fall our Grapnel neere the shore, & sounded with a trumpet a Call, & afterwardes many familiar English tunes of Songs, and called to them friendly; but we had no answere, we therefore landed at day-breake, and comming to the fire, we found the grasse & sundry rotten trees burning about the place. From hence we went thorow the woods to that part of the Iland directly over against Dasamongwepeuk, & from thence we returned by the water side, round about the North-point of the Iland,[3] untill we came to the place where I left our Colony in the yeere 1586.[4] In all this way we saw in the sand the print of the Salvages feet of 2 or 3 sorts troaden that night, and as we entred up the sandy banke upon a tree, in the very browe thereof were curiously carved these faire Romane letters CRO: which letters presently we knew to signifie the place, where I should find the planters seated, according to a secret token agreed upon betweene them & me at my last departure from them, which was, that in any wayes they should not faile to write or carve on the trees or posts of the

* Captaine Spicer drowned.

dores the name of the place where they should be seated; for at my
comming away they were prepared to remove from Roanoak 50
miles into the maine.[1] Therefore at my departure from them in Anno
1587 I willed them, that if they should happen to be distressed in any
of those places, that then they should carve over the letters or name, a
Crosse ✠ in this forme, but we found no such signe of distresse.
And having well considered of this, we passed toward the place
where they were left in sundry houses,[2] but we found the houses
taken downe, and the place very strongly enclosed with a high palisado[3] of great trees, with cortynes and flankers very Fort-like, and
one of the chiefe trees or postes at the right side of the entrance had
the barke taken off, and 5 foote from the ground in fayre Capitall
letters was graven CROATOAN without any crosse or signe of
distresse; this done, we entred into the palisado, where we found many
barres of Iron, two pigges of Lead, foure yron fowlers, Iron sacker-
shotte, and such like heavie things,[4] throwen here and there, almost
overgrowen with grasse and weedes. From thence wee went along
by the water side, towards the poynt of the Creeke[5] to see if we could
find any of their botes or Pinnisse, but we could perceive no signe of
them, nor any of the last Falkons and small Ordinance[6] which were
left with them, at my departure from them. At our returne from the
Creeke, some of our Saylers meeting us, tolde us that they had found
where divers chests had bene hidden, and long sithence digged up
againe and broken up, and much of the goods in them spoyled and
scattered about, but nothing left, of such things as the Savages knew
any use of, undefaced. Presently Captaine Cooke and I went to the
place, which was in the ende of an old trench, made two yeeres past[7]
by Captaine Amadas: where wee found five Chests, that had been
carefully hidden of the Planters, and of the same chests three were
my owne, and about the place many of my things spoyled and broken,
and my bookes torne from the covers, the frames of some of my pictures and Mappes[8] rotten and spoyled with rayne, and my armour
almost eaten through with rust; this could bee no other but the deede
of the Savages our enemies at Dasamongwepeuk, who had watched
the departure of our men to Croatoan; and assoone as they were departed, digged up every place where they suspected any thing to be
buried: but although it much grieved me to see such spoyle of my
goods, yet on the other side I greatly joyed that I had safely found a

certaine token of their safe being at Croatoan,[1] which is the place where Manteo was borne, and the Savages of the Iland our friends.

When we had seene in this place so much as we could, we returned to our Boates, and departed from the shoare towards our Shippes, with as much speede as we could: For the weather beganne to overcast, and very likely that a foule and stormie night would ensue. Therefore the same Evening with much danger and labour, we got our selves aboard, by which time the winde and seas were so greatly risen, that wee doubted our Cables and Anchors would scarcely holde untill Morning; wherefore the Captaine[2] caused the Boate to be manned with five lusty men, who could swimme all well, and sent them to the little Iland on the right hand of the Harbour, to bring aboard sixe of our men, who had filled our caske with fresh water: the Boate the same night returned aboard with our men, but all our Caske ready filled they left behinde, unpossible to bee had aboard without danger of casting away both men and Boates; for this night prooved very stormie and foule.

The next Morning it was agreed by the Captaine and my selfe, with the Master and others, to wey anchor, and goe for the place at Croatoan, where our planters were: for that then the winde was good for that place, and also to leave that Caske with fresh water on shoare in the Iland untill our returne. So then they brought the cable to the Capston, but when the anchor was almost apecke,[3] the Cable broke, by meanes whereof we lost another Anchor, wherewith we drove so fast into the shoare, that wee were forced to let fall a third Anchor; which came so fast home that the Shippe was almost aground by Kenricks mounts: so that wee were forced to let slippe the Cable ende for ende. And if it had not chanced that wee had fallen into a chanell of deeper water, closer by the shoare then wee accompted of, wee could never have gone cleare of the poynt that lyeth to the Southwardes of Kenricks mounts.[4] Being thus cleare of some dangers, and gotten into deeper waters, but not without some losse; for wee had but one Cable and Anchor left us of foure, and the weather grew to be fouler and fouler; our victuals scárse, and our caske and fresh water lost: it was therefore determined that we should goe for Saint John[5] or some other Iland to the Southward for fresh water. And it was further purposed, that if wee could any wayes supply our wants of victuals and other necessaries, either at Hispaniola, Sant John, or

Trynidad, that then wee should continue in the Indies all the Winter following, with hope to make 2. rich voyages of one, and at our returne to visit our countrymen at Virginia.[1] The captaine and the whole company in the Admirall (with my earnest petitions) thereunto agreed, so that it rested onely to knowe what the Master of the Moone-light[2] our consort would doe herein. But when we demanded them if they would accompany us in that new determination, they alledged that their weake and leake Shippe was not able to continue it; wherefore the same night we parted,* leaving the Moone-light to goe directly for England, and the Admirall set his course for Trynidad,[3] which course we kept two dayes.

On the 28. the winde changed, and it was sette on foule weather every way: but this storme brought the winde West and Northwest, and blewe so forcibly, that wee were able to beare no sayle, but our fore-course halfe mast high, wherewith wee ranne upon the winde perforce, the due course for England, for that wee were dryven to change our first determination for Trynidad, and stoode for the Ilands of Açores, where wee purposed to take in fresh water, and also there hoped to meete with some English men of warre[4] about those Ilands, at whose hands wee might obtaine some supply of our wants. And thus continuing our course for the Açores, sometimes with calmes, and sometimes with very scarce windes, on the fifteenth of September the winde came South Southeast, and blew so exceedingly, that wee were forced to lye atry[5] all that day. At this time by account we judged our selves to be about twentie leagues to the West of Cuervo and Flores, but about night the storme ceased, and fayre weather ensued.

On Thursday the seventeenth wee saw Cuervo and Flores, but we could not come to anker that night, by reason the winde shifted. The next Morning being the eighteenth, standing in againe with Cuervo, we escryed a sayle ahead us, to whom we gave chase: but when wee came neere him, we knew him to be a Spanyard, and hoped to make sure purchase of him; but we understood at our speaking with him, that he was a prize, and of the Domingo fleete already taken by the John our consort, in the Indies.[6] We learned also of this prize, that our Viceadmirall and Pinnisse had fought with the rest of the Domingo fleete, and had forced them with their Admirall to flee unto Jamaica under the Fort for succour, and some of them ran them-

* They leave the coast of Virginia.

selves aground, whereof one of them they brought away, and tooke out of some others so much as the time would permit. And further wee understood of them, that in their returne from Jamaica about the Organes neere Cape Saint Anthony, our Viceadmirall mette with two Shippes of the mayne land, come from Mexico, bound for Havana, with whom he fought: in which fight our Viceadmirals Lieutenant was slaine, and the Captaines right arme strooken off,[1] with foure other of his men slaine, and sixteene hurt, But in the ende he entred, and tooke one of the Spanish shippes, which was so sore shot by us under water, that before they could take out her treasure, she sunke; so that we lost thirteene Pipes of silver* which sunke with her, besides much other rich marchandize. And in the meane time the other Spanish shippe being pearced with nine shotte under water, got away;[2] whom our Viceadmirall intended to pursue: but some of their men in the toppe made certaine rockes, which they saw above water neere the shoare, to be Gallies of Havana and Cartagena, comming from Havana[3] to rescue the two Ships; Wherefore they gave over their chase, and went for England. After this intelligence was given us by this our prize, he departed from us, and went for England.

On Saturday the 19. of September we came to an Ancre neere a small village on the North side of Flores, where we found ryding 5. English men of warre, of whom wee understood that our Viceadmirall and Prize were gone thence for England. One of these five was the Moonelight our consort, who upon the first sight of our comming into Flores, set sayle and went for England, not taking any leave of us.

On Sunday the 20. the Mary Rose,[4] Admirall of the Queenes fleete, wherein was Generall Sir John Hawkins, stood in with Flores, and divers other of the Queenes ships, namely the Hope, the Non-pareilia, The Rainebow, the Swift-sure, the Foresight,[5] with many other good merchants ships of warre, as the Edward Bonaventure, the Marchant Royal, the Amitie, the Eagle, the Dainty[6] of sir John Hawkins, and many other good ships and pinnisses, all attending to meete with the king of Spaines fleete,[7] comming from Terra firma of the West Indies.

The 22. of September we went aboard the Raynebow, and towards night we spake with the Swift-sure, and gave him 3. pieces. The captaines desired our company; wherefore we willingly attended on

* 13. Pipes of silver.

them: who at this time with 10. other ships stood for Faial. But the Generall with the rest of the Fleete were separated from us, making two fleetes, for the surer meeting with the Spanish fleete.

On Wednesday the 23. we saw Gratiosa, where the Admiral and the rest of the Queens fleete were come together. The Admirall put forth a flag of counsel, in which was determined that the whole fleete should go for the mayne, and spred themselves on the coasts of Spaine and Portugal,[1] so farre as conveniently they might, for the surer meeting of the Spanish fleete in those parts.

The 26. we came to Faial, where the Admiral with some other of the fleete ankred, othersome plyed up and downe betweene that and the Pico untill midnight, at which time the Antony[2] shot off a piece and weyed, shewing his light: after whom the whole fleete stood to the East, the winde at Northeast by East.

On Sunday the 27. towards Evening wee tooke our leave of the Admirall and the whole fleete, who stood to the East. But our shippe accompanied with a Flyboate stoode in againe with S. George, where we purposed to take in more fresh water, and some other fresh victuals.

On Wednesday the 30. of September, seeing the winde hang so Northerly, that wee could not atteine the Iland of S. George, we gave over our purpose to water there, and the next day framed our due course for England.

October.

The 2. of October in the Morning we saw S. Michaels Iland on our Starre board quarter.

The 23. at 10. of the clocke afore noone, we saw Ushant in Britaigne.

On Sunday the 24. we came in safetie, God be thanked, to an anker at Plymmouth.[3]

Explanatory Notes

Abbreviations

Analysis: Regina Flannery, *Analysis of coastal Algonquian culture* (Catholic University of America, Anthropological Series, no. 7). Washington, D.C., 1939

APC: *Acts of the Privy Council*

Further English voyages: Irene A. Wright, *Further English voyages to Spanish America, 1583–1594*, 1951

Gilbert: D. B. Quinn, *The voyages and colonising enterprises of Sir Humphrey Gilbert*, 2 vols. (Hakluyt Society, 2nd ser., LXXXIII–LXXXIV), 1940

Hakluyts: E. G. R. Taylor, *The writings and correspondence of the two Richard Hakluyts*, 2 vols. (Hakluyt Soc., 2nd ser., LXXVI–LXXVII), 1935

Indians: J. R. Swanton, *The Indians of the southeastern United States* (Smithsonian Institution, Bureau of American Ethnology, Bulletin no. 137) Washington, D.C., 1946

Northern voyages: S. E. Morison, *The discovery of America: the northern voyages*, 1971

Pilgrimes: Samuel Purchas, *Hakluytus posthumus or Purchas his pilgrimes*, 4 vols. 1625. Another edition, 20 vols., Glasgow, 1905–7.

PN (1589): Richard Hakluyt, *The principall navigations, voiages and discoveries of the English nation*, 1589

PN, III (1600): Richard Hakluyt, *The principal navigations, voyages traffiques & discoveries of the English nation*, 3 vols., 1598–1600.

PN, VIII, IX (1904): Another edition, 12 vols., Glasgow, 1903–5

RV: D. B. Quinn, *The Roanoke voyages*, 2 vols. (Hakluyt Soc., 2nd ser., CIV–CV), 1955

I

Page 1. (1) *Barlowe's narrative: PN* (1589), pp. 728–33, collated with III (1600), 246–51 (VIII (1904) 297–310).

Page 1. (2) *two barkes:* the ship, the flagship or admiral, had Philip Amadas as captain and Simon Ferdinando (or Fernandes) as master and pilot. She may well have been the *Bark Raleigh* of 200 tons which had been sent by Ralegh on Sir Humphrey Gilbert's 1583 voyage but had turned back (*Gilbert*, pp. 37, 84, 378–9, 383, 396). The pinnace, commanded by Arthur Barlowe, could have been Ralegh's *Dorothy*.

(3) *Philip Amadas:* Amadas was a member of Ralegh's household before the voyage. He was over sixteen at the death of his father, John Amadys of Plymouth on 27 February 1581 (*Visitations of Devon*, ed. J. L. Vivian (1895), p. 12).

(4) *Arthur Barlowe:* Barlowe had seen service as a soldier with Ralegh in Ireland.

(5) *west of England:* most probably from Plymouth.

(6) *needefull:* In margin 'A Southerly course not greatly needful for Virginia' (*PN*, III (1600), 246). Barlowe's meaning is not too clear, but he is making an anticipatory reference to his course through the Caribbean, not speaking of the Atlantic passage, though 'southeasterly' does not appear to make sense. He could mean that from Puerto Rico, doubting the capacity of the current to carry him through the Straits of Florida, he steered too easterly a course and so got involved in the Bahama group.

(7) *disbogging:* from 'disbogue', an early and rare form of 'disembogue', to emerge from a river or strait into open sea.

Page 2. (1) *Islands:* apart from the Spanish reference to this expedition apparently touching at Puerto Rico, the arrangements of the rendezvous in 1585 would indicate that the call was made on the southwestern shore of the island, at Guayanilla Bay (cp. *Further English voyages*, p. 175).

(2) *entrance, or river:* by 'English miles' he may mean land, not nautical miles. 120 miles between 2 and 13 July, with southerly following winds, is exceptionally slow progress. If, as seems likely, the inlet was that called Port Ferdinando, the first contact with the coast was made about midway between the modern Cape Lookout and Cape Hatteras along the Core Bank (cp. map at end).

(3) *we entred:* the landing was therefore made at the northern end of the island in the Banks called Hatarask.

(4) *ceremonies used in such enterprises:* Sir Humphrey Gilbert in 1583 had entered into possession of Newfoundland by having delivered to him '(after the custom of England) a rod & a turffe and after having the English arms, engraved on lead affixed to a pillar erected on the place' (*PN*, III (1600), 151).

(5) *we first landed:* the place would be some two miles east of Cedar Point on Bodie Island, now nearly a mile out to sea (see map at end).

(6) *water side:* it has usually been argued that Amadas and Barlowe landed on the Carolina Banks in the vicinity of Nags Head or further north and approached Roanoke Island from the north by way of Trinitie Harbour. Harriot's note to T. De Bry (*America*, Pt. I (1590), pl. 2) is contemporary evidence for a northerly approach, but his account is hard to reconcile, in other respects, with Barlowe's. On the other hand, the reported discovery of a harbour by Fernandes and the naming of Port Ferdinando after him in 1585 would support the southern approach, which seems preferable (see map at end).

(7) *Cedars:* it would seem from his discussion below that Barlowe could distinguish the scarcer red cedar from the swamp cypress which could well have been taken for cedar.

(8) *Europe:* this would suggest that Barlowe had been to the Levant or possibly farther east.

(9) *Sea side:* in margin 'The Isle of Wokokon' (*PN*, III (1600), 246). This is one of the less happy examples of Hakluyt's editing practice. Barlowe makes it clear (p. 9) that the island is not Wococon (see map at end).

(10) *hils . . . meane heighth:* Kindrickers Mounts, so called by White (see map at end).

Page 3. (1) *leagues:* 'miles' (*PN*, III (1600), 246). Hakluyt, having put in his identification of the island as Wococon (p. 2, n. 9), then proceeded to alter Barlowe's indication of its length, when, in fact, 20 leagues, or 60 miles, is a good approximation to the length of the island of Hatarask as shown on the map. (See map at end.)

(2) *tree . . . rinde of blacke Sinamon:* brought by John Winter from the Straits of Magellan in 1579, Winter's Bark passed into the pharmacopeia as *Cortex winteranus* (*Drimys winteri*). Bark from the magnolias had a similar combination of bitter and aromatic properties without astringency. This suggests that Barlowe may mean the sweet bay, *Magnolia virginiana*.

(3) *landes side:* 'the Island side' (*PN*, III (1600), 247), to the north-easterly tip of the island of Hatarask.

(4) *Ferdinando:* Simão Fernandes, a Portuguese pilot from Terceira in the Azores, who had become a protestant and married in England.

Page 4. (1) *Wingina:* a chief of the Roanoke tribe, who ruled one village on Roanoke Island where he lived and at least one village on the mainland, Dasemunkepeuc.

(2) *Virginia:* the name was conferred some time between the drafting of Ralegh's parliamentary bill to confirm his discoveries in December 1584 and 24 March 1585, the latter being the latest date compatible with the governor's seal which bears the date '1584'.

Page 4. (3) *Wingina:* since the 'King' was himself, at this time, called Wingina, Barlowe's naming of his opponent 'Wingina' can scarcely be other than a mistake, possibly by the printer. If we place a full stop after 'Countrey', and read 'He is called Wingina, and was shotte', we shall probably be correct.

(4) *other:* 'others' is meant.

Page 5. (1) *Chammoys:* dressed deer-skin.

(2) *Buffe:* here probably the more roughly used deer-skin. Buffalo skins cannot be entirely ruled out, but the appearance of the bison east of the mountains in modern Virginia and North Carolina was occasional only, though such skins could have been obtained by trade.

(3) *swordes:* these proceedings indicate that the coastal Indians were experienced traders and suggest that they were already familiar with the appearance and uses of European weapons, as they could have been from their contacts with shipwrecked Spaniards (p. 9).

(4) *a peece of the same:* the skirt was usually a short fringed skin covering the front only: sometimes a second skin was added at the back. The breasts were normally left bare.

(5) *forehead . . . white Corrall:* the forehead decoration was often painted on, but in this case was probably composed of shell or bone beads.

(6) *downe to her middle:* ear ornaments of such elaboration are not shown in any of White's drawings, though pearl necklaces were of great length.

(7) *pendants of copper . . . every eare:* both men and women are shown wearing ear-rings made from copper beads, but none of great size or elaboration.

(8) *plate of golde . . . bowe very easily:* here the Indian may be using his breast plaque, or gorget of copper to imitate an English helmet.

(9) *men but on one:* the women's hair-style is as indicated, though the front is fringed and the back caught up, but the men's is, characteristically, shaved at the sides, leaving a cock's comb, long, and caught up at the back.

(10) *colour yellowish:* the yellowish-brown skin-colour is well indicated in the White drawings.

(11) *haire:* the hair-colour in the White drawings is invariably black, and few early descriptions mention hair of other colours.

(12) *corrall:* shell, almost certainly conch.

Page 6. (1) *copper on their heades:* the gorgets noted above, normally worn on the chest, suspended by a string round the neck.

(2) *men . . . brought home:* the men were Manteo and Wanchese, whose names were not included in Hakluyt's 1589 version of Barlowe (p. 12).

(3) *fortie or fiftie women:* this is an exaggeration and is much too great a

number to come from such small villages as that on Roanoke Island and Dasemonkepeuc on the mainland.

(4) *approched:* fire or smoke signalling was common among the coastal Algonkian peoples though not confined to them.

(5) *wracke:* if the recollections of Manteo and Wanchese were personal ones they must have been men of mature age. The year 1564–5 for the date of the wreck was one of Franco–Spanish conflict in the southeast, and is a likely one in which a vessel would be lost in this latitude.

(6) *spikes:* Harriot did not encounter any surviving metal tools (p. 67).

(7) *rosen:* compare Harriot p. 51.

(8) *Worshippe . . . understand:* Barlowe is stating that a location for a pearl fishery had been found and communicated to Ralegh, but there is no clear indication that the expedition of the following year had any such knowledge (see p. 53).

Page 7. (1) *corne:* this, the earliest description of maize cultivation from this area, should be compared with Harriot's (pp. 54–5).

(2) *mattocke, or pickeaxe:* Harriot described the implements used by the men as long-handled mattocks or hoes, and the shorter ones of the women as peckers or parers.

(3) *Pease into the ground:* Harriot was, in 1585–6, unable to make more systematic cultivation experiments owing to damaged seed and plants (see pp. 54, 57–8).

(4) *oates:* here Barlowe is mistaken.

(5) *soile:* while cleared patches of ground along the sounds were, and are, very fertile, the greater part of the mainland accessible from the sounds was swamp or swamp-forest.

(6) *trees:* cp. Harriot's accounts of trees, pp. 51, 65–6.

(7) *twentie mile into the River:* if the identification of the landing-place, made on p. 132, is sound, the party apparently sailed from Port Ferdinando south-westwards into Pamlico Sound, then northwards through Croatan Sound, and changed course eastwards to round the northern end of Roanoke Island, making a journey of some 20 to 25 miles according to the precise course followed (see map at end).

(8) *village:* this is the only description we have of Roanoke. It was, like Pomeiooc, an enclosed village, but with fewer houses, the latter with a pole frame, mat-covered.

(9) *artificially:* very artfully or skilfully.

(10) *waters side:* apparently that now submerged off North West Point.

(11) *billoe:* the strong current from Albemarle Sound was the probable reason for such precautions.

(12) *five roomes:* Barlowe may be exaggerating. The long-houses could

Page 7. (12)—*contd.*
have been divided into rooms by reed or bark mats or screens, but there is no
other indication that they were divided into many compartments. An upper
floor, extending about half the length of the building, is shown in White's
drawing of an ossuary, and may have also been found in dwelling houses.

(13) *great fire:* no internal fires, nor smoke-holes for them, appear in
White's drawings.

Page 8. (1) *boord:* these were the sleeping-benches of timber or cane which
extended round the interior walls of the houses shown by White.

(2) *furmentie:* frumenty, wheat boiled in milk and seasoned. Here maize,
probably boiled with herbs for seasoning.

(3) *sodden:* stewed with corn and beans.

(4) *wine:* a mistake, since the absence of deliberately fermented beverages
in eastern North America was universal.

(5) *water ... sodden ... hearbes:* the making of highly seasoned drinks of
this sort is not elsewhere recorded for this area but appears authentic.

(6) *vessels:* White illustrates a typical, light-brown cooking vessel, and
one very similar has been found in the Roanoke fort site.

(7) *platters:* illustrated by White.

(8) *Idoll:* this would mean that the idol was kept in the same building, in
some further inner shrine. Such a location would be unusual.

Page 9. (1) *Occam:* the word refers, not to the waters of the Sound, but to
the land beyond them.

(2) *Schycoake:* Skicoak was situated, according to subsequent information,
near Chesapeake Bay (see map at end).

(3) *daies journey:* an absurd statement which Hakluyt (*PN*, III (1600),
249) tried to improve by substituting 'houres'.

(4) *Nomopana:* apparently the upper portion of Albemarle Sound.

(5) *Chowanoake:* located well up the Chowan River.

(6) *Menatoan:* clearly distinguished (p. 26) as the chief of the Chowanoac
tribe.

(7) *shippe cast away:* the date on this reckoning would be 1558, and the
ship most probably Spanish. It is likely to be distinct from that mentioned
on p. 6.

(8) *Wococon:* this is the first mention of it by name and the only definite
statement that it was not inhabited.

(9) *Island adjoyning:* either Endesokee on the south, or Croatoan on the
north, most probably the latter as Manteo's mother lived there and he is
likely to have contributed the story.

Page 10. (1) *breastplates:* this seems unlikely to be correct.

(2) *they carry . . . their Idoll:* this appears to be the only example for this area of an idol being carried into battle; among the south-eastern tribes it was usually an 'ark', a bundle of sanctified objects, which was so carried.

(3) *Countrey left desolate:* this is the earliest comment on the long series of often senseless wars, which continually disrupted Indian society except in a few instances where they led to relatively stable confederations, such as that ruled by Powhatan in the early seventeenth century.

(4) *Ponouike:* a tribe, probably Algonkian, living apparently between the Pamlico and Neuse rivers.

(5) *Lorde of Sequotan:* probably, though not certainly, meant to be Wingina.

(6) *their Towne:* apparently the village of Secotan.

Page 11. (1) *leave the Countrey:* Harriot (p. 47) says they were six weeks in the country.

Page 12. (1) *We brought . . . Manteo:* Hakluyt, *PN,* III (1600), 251, adds the last sentence, perhaps from a re-reading of the text manuscript, perhaps on his own authority.

II

Page 13. (1) *Journal of the 1585 Voyage: PN,* (1589), pp. 733–6, collated with III (1600), 251–3 (VIII (1904), 310–17). This was evidently prepared from a journal kept on the *Tiger* by an anonymous member of her company.

(2) *19. day of Maye:* corrected to '9. day of April' (*PN,* III (1600), 251). The mistaken date was that on which Cavendish in the *Elizabeth* joined the *Tiger* off Puerto Rico.

(3) *Tyger:* the *Tiger* was a royal vessel, adventured or hired by the queen, as the expedition's flagship. A vessel of some 150 tons, she had an armament of 12 heavy guns, carrying some 160 men; she had Grenville as captain (and general of the expedition), Fernandes as master (and chief pilot), Ralph Lane (as colonel on the military side) and Amadas (as admiral of Virginia). See T. Glasgow, 'H.M.S. Tiger', *North Carolina Historical Review,* LIII (1966), 115–21.

(4) *Pinnesses:* these would probably be undecked pinnaces of 20–30 tons, which could be carried on deck if need be: the *Tiger*'s was lost; the second probably acted as tender for the vice-admiral—either the *Roebuck* or the *Lion.*

(5) *Assistants for counsell:* the chief officers, together with a number of assistants, often twelve, made up the council of war, which the general was expected to consult and by which he was in some measure bound.

Page 13. (6) *15. day:* corrected to '12' (*PN*, III (1600), 251). It will be noted that they considered the date of their arrival to be 11 May. *RV*, I, 183.

(7) *Baye of Muskito:* the site was known to the Spaniards as Mosquetal or Guadianilla or Guardianilla.

(8) *forte:* the completed encampment is shown in great detail in John White's drawing. It was located at the mouth of the Rio Guayanilla, on Guayanilla Bay (see *Northern voyages* (1971), pp. 633–6).

(9) *pinnesse:* this was to replace the *Tiger*'s pinnace lost on the way out: it was considered essential to have one to explore the Carolina Sounds in case no other small vessels of the squadron rejoined Grenville.

Page 14. (1) *fet:* fetched.

(2) *8. horsemen:* this was evidently a patrol from San German: its report got back to the governor, Diego Menéndez Váldes, at Puerto Rico, on 25 May/4 June, who thereupon sent reinforcements to San German (*Further English voyages*, p. 9).

(3) *Spaniards . . . departed:* the Spanish contingent was headed by the lieutenant in charge at San German.

Page 15. (1) *Fort . . . was fired:* the Spaniards soon after inspected the deserted site but say nothing of its firing: they found cut into the bole of a tree an inscription intended to guide other vessels which came to the rendez-vous, which reads (after double translation): 'On May 11th we reached this place with the *Tiger* and on the 19th the *Elizabeth* came up and we are about to leave on the 23rd in good health, glory be to God. 1585.' (ibid. p. 12).

(2) *29. day:* this is evidently a mistake. The writer meant '23': Hakluyt or his printer altered it, not realizing that what happened was that the two vessels moved west to San German Bay, made contact with the civilian inhabitants and attempted, apparently with some success, to buy livestock from them for the Virginia settlement (ibid. p. 11).

(3) *Spanish Frigat . . . sight of us:* this was on the night of the 23rd, when one of the ships was patrolling in the Mona Channel near the small island of Mona. The bark was on its way from Santo Domingo to Puerto Rico (ibid. p. 9).

(4) *another Frigat:* 24 May. She was coming from Santo Domingo with a substantial cargo of cloth (recently brought out by the fleet from Spain) for the town of San Juan de Puerto Rico (ibid. pp. 9–10, 16).

(5) *Roxo bay:* Cape Rojo is the more easterly of the capes at the south-western tip of Puerto Rico, and Rojo Bay is either Salinas Bay between it and Pt Aguila or Boqueron Bay to the north of it, the former being the more probable.

(6) *Spanish pilot:* the pilot was probably from the smaller prize and she

was almost certainly the vessel shown in White's drawing just offshore from the salt-hills.

(7) *salt hils within the trench:* his elaborate entrenchments in the sand are shown by White, who also includes two tall mounds of salt, evidently gathered from local salt-pans, within the entrenchment.

(8) *mauger:* despite.

(9) *Isabella:* Isabela, on Columbus's Rio de Isabela, the Bahia Isabela being the harbour to the westward of Puerto de Plata in lat. 19°49′N, long. 70° 41′W. There they had tried to get horses, dogs, cattle and sheep (ibid. p. 11).

Page 16. (1) *Governor:* the governor of Isabela and captain of Puerto de Plata was, apparently, Rengifo de Angulo, and the place of meeting is described as four leagues below (i.e. east) of Puerto de Plata (ibid. p. 16).

(2) *commodities of the Iland:* the livestock (ibid. pp. 10–12, 16) and sugar (so far as it consisted of rooted cane) were (with banana plants etc.) designed for the use of the Virginia colonists; the hides, ginger, pearls, and tobacco were acquired for sale in England.

Page 17. (1) *Admirall:* the *Tiger.*

(2) *Portingall:* he is likely to have been Fernandes, whom the writer blames also for the grounding of the *Tiger.*

(3) *Cape of Feare:* Cape Feare was identified in De Bry's version of White's map with what is now Cape Lookout, though White himself distinguishes two capes, each with its dependent shoals, but does not name them. In this case the modern Cape Fear is the more probable.

(4) *Wocokon:* see map at end.

(5) *the Admirall . . . sunke:* the blame assigned to Fernandes by the writer (and apparently by Grenville as well as his friends) was not shared by Lane (*RV*, I, 201–2).

(6) *Aubry:* Captains Aubrey and Bonython were probably in command of the two Spanish prizes. Croatoan, being the island immediately to the north of Wococon, could be approached by sea and it is likely that they took their vessels outside Cape Hatteras to the Chacandepeco inlet north of the cape where there was an Indian settlement.

(7) *two of our men . . . at Wocokon:* Captain George Raymond had thus arrived with the *Lion* near Cape Hatteras on about 16 June. He left some men on shore and sailed to Newfoundland. It seems likely that other men left on Croatoan were found later.

(8) *Tilt boate:* a Thames boat with an awning over the bows to shelter passengers.

Page 18. (1) *Captaine Clarke:* if John Clarke was captain of the *Roebuck,* then at some time since Grenville's arrival at Wococon on 26 June he had been

Page 18. (1)—*contd.*

joined by some or all of the vessels with which he had long parted company, the *Roebuck*, the *Dorothy* and the second small pinnace.

(2) *John White:* this is the only external reference to John White's presence in Virginia in 1585, but the fact that he is named along with the high treasurer, Francis Brooke, indicates that he was not a humble craftsman but an official of some standing in the hierarchy.

(3) *Pomeioke:* this was some 30 miles from their starting point and was enclosed by a palisade.

(4) *Secotan:* Secotan, the chief village of the Secotan tribe was not enclosed. White's drawings of the village and its inhabitants were probably made on this occasion.

(5) *we burnt . . . Towne:* Philip Amadas, as admiral, was sent back with his boat to undertake these punitive operations (the first we hear of) against the Indians. Grenville, with the remaining boats, continued the exploration by identifying at least the mouths of the Neuse River and Core Sound (see map at end).

(6) *our fleete:* they came back to find the *Tiger* caulked and refloated and, with her consorts, anchored well off the treacherous shoals.

(7) *Hatoraske:* by this he means the inlet at the northern end of the island of Hatarask, which Lane called Port Ferdinando from its discovery by Simon Fernandes.

(8) *Grangino:* Granganimeo had probably come to invite Grenville to establish his settlement near the Indian village at the north-west end of Roanoke Island, and it was probably on this occasion that final decisions were taken on where the settlement should be and how many men were to stay in it. Manteo was needed as interpreter.

(9) *Admirall:* the admiral is here Philip Amadas and not the flagship. He returned before 8 September.

(10) *John Arundell:* he was probably sent in command of the fastest seaworthy vessel, possibly one of the prizes. We do not know when he arrived, but, as 'John Arondell, of Tolverne (at Richmond)' he was knighted on Thursday, 14 October (W. A. Shaw, *Knights of England*, II, 84), having by then, no doubt, delivered his report of the voyage to the queen.

(11) *The 25 . . . set saile for England:* the laconic passing over of three important weeks is unfortunate. During this time the essential tasks of transferring the settlers to the Island and getting the houses and fort started were carried out. Lane was at Port Ferdinando writing letters on 12 August but he evidently moved to his new headquarters on 17 August. Grenville had probably to delay some days longer than he intended: he left the *Roebuck* at least behind him, and she could not have sailed before 10 September.

Explanatory Notes

(12) *lost sight of the Tyger:* Enrique Lopez (*Further English voyages*, p. 14) says that Grenville came on board with thirty-six men and transferred twenty Spaniards to the *Tiger*, along with most of the foodstuffs from the *Santa Maria*. The ships sailed in consort from near Bermuda to within some 1,200 miles of the Azores, but were separated in a storm.

Page 19. (1) *received by . . . friends:* Ralegh was at Plymouth, but we do not know which of Grenville's other associates were there. The *Tiger* went to be 'well-repaired'. She was not available for Grenville's 1586 expedition.

III

Page 20. (1) *Lane's colonists: PN* (1589), pp. 736–7, collated with III (1600), 254 (VIII (1904), 317–18): the order was changed by the printer in 1600. Preliminary work on the identification of the members of the expedition and of the colony appears in W. S. Powell, 'Roanoke colonists and explorers: an attempt at identification', *North Carolina Historical Review*, XXXIV (1957), 202–26. Firm identification of persons with common names is extremely difficult, but it would seem that at least some progress is possible with the rank-and-file of the colonists apart from the well-known names represented in the expedition.

(2) *Constable:* Marmaduke Constable (Powell, op. cit., p. 218), is quite possibly the gentleman who entered Caius College, Cambridge, in 1581. If so, he is likely to be the man who put his name at the end of the dedication of the copy of Robert Record, *The whetstone of witte* (1557), (S.T.C. 20820), sig. A4, now in the Folger Library, Washington, D.C.

Page 21. (1) *Doughan Gannes:* he can be identified as the Joachim Gaunse (Joachim Ganz) who was associated in 1581 with George Nedham in the smelting of copper by improved methods at the Keswick works of the Mines Royal Company, and who shortly afterwards put forward plans for 'makeing of Copper, vitriall, and coppris, and Smeltinge of Copper and Leade ures' (S.P. 12/142, 88–9; *Elizabethan Keswick*, ed. W. G. Collingwood (1912), p. 202). He was apparently Joachim Gaunz, the Jew, born in Prague, but living in Blackfriars, London, who was examined at Bristol in September 1589 on charges of blasphemy by denying the divinity of Christ (S.P. 12/226, 40), and may have been the son of David Ganz, astronomer and historian, b. in Westphalia 1541, d. at Prague 1613 (see I. Abrahams, 'Joachim Gaunse: a mining incident in the reign of Queen Elizabeth', in *Trans. Jewish Historical Society*, IV (1903), 83–103).

(2) *John Twyt:* 'Twit' (*PN*, III (1600), 254). As John White remained in Virginia, which is almost certain (p. 168), this may have been he,

Page 21. (2)—*cont.*

although Twit and Tuite are surnames in their own right. Other alternatives are that he is mistakenly put down as William White, that he compiled the list himself and omitted his own name, or that he was simply omitted by a printer's error.

(3) *Haunce Walters:* just possibly 'Hance the Surgion' of the *Moonlight* in 1590, who was drowned at Port Ferdinando (p. 125).

IV

Page 22. (1) *Lane to Hakluyt the Elder: PN* (1589), p. 793, collated with III (1600), 254–5 (VIII (1904), 319–20). The only other known connection of the elder Hakluyt with the enterprise was his 'Inducements' (in Taylor, *Hakluyts*, II, 327–41), which were not printed by his younger cousin.

(2) *discovered the maine:* apparently as the result of the return of the expedition led by Philip Amadas to Weapemeoc on 2 August.

(3) *Guinie wheate:* 'Maiz or or [*sic*] Guinie wheate' (*PN*, III (1600), 254); a good example of Hakluyt's care in editing, and also of his willingness, where he thought it helpful, to alter his text. Lane did not know the word 'maize' (cp. p. 54), but his identification of it with an African grain was not shared by contemporary naturalists, who usually ascribed its origin to Asia (especially the Near East, hence 'Turkey wheat') and America, or either.

(4) *commodities . . . & such like:* as for oil (e.g. walnut-oil), resin, pitch, and currants, Lane's estimate was superficially adequate, though only the timber products were worth commercial exploitation, but the flax was doubtful and sugar more so, while frankincense was apparently a confusion with the sweet gum.

Page 23. (1) *course cloth . . . they also like wel of:* though the English wished to sell woollen cloth, it would be of little use to Indians in this climate except for mantles and blankets. Some of the more astute Indians may have recognized that canvas could usefully replace the bark and fibre mats with which their houses were covered.

(2) *copper . . . so it be made red:* copper was primarily a medium of exchange and adornment: it was not in use for making tools.

(3) *Fort:* this is the earliest reference to the fort on Roanoke Island. On 12 August its construction was not even mentioned.

(4) *this 3 September:* 'this third of' (*PN*, III (1600), 255). Since another letter dated 8 September (*RV*, I, 214) refers to a report about 'Gynneye wheate' which reached Lane on 5 September, the letter may have '3' as a mistake or misprint for '8'.

Page 24. (1) *Lane's narrative . . . 1585-6: PN* (1589), pp. 737-47, collated with III (1600), 255-64 (VIII (1904), 320-45).

(2) *17. of August . . . 18. of June 1586:* these dates represent the limits of Lane's command at the fort on Roanoke Island. The first of them may very well mark the date of Grenville's departure from the site of the colony for Port Ferdinando, preparatory to his sailing on 25 August.

(3) *directed to Sir Walter Ralegh:* this report could have been made to Ralegh at any time after Lane's arrival at Portsmouth on 27 July 1586, but it is not likely to have been long delayed.

Page 25. (1) *foure score miles:* about 100 miles (see map at end).

(2) *would not stirre for an oare:* Grenville had sailed the pinnace, built on Puerto Rico, to Secotan and elsewhere, so that Lane is probably exaggerating.

(3) *the discovery of those partes:* it would thus appear that no exploration of this region, other than that undertaken by Grenville, was attempted, though Lane's statement does not rule out altogether some further preliminary reconnaissance in the period after Grenville's departure and before the winter of 1585-6.

(4) *Chesepians:* the Chesapeake expedition probably did pass the winter at or near Chesepiuc (see map at end).

(5) *Weroances:* usually used for the chief men of a tribe and not the chief alone.

(6) *Colonie . . . resident there:* the absence of specific information on the organization and activity of this expedition is the most serious gap in our knowledge of the first colony. Its leader was evidently the 'Colonel of the Chesepians' referred to on p. 41.

(7) *navigable for good shipping:* the pinnace was taken to the head of Albemarle Sound and the rest of the journey up the Chowan River was made by boat. This expedition was apparently Lane's first after the end of winter, in March 1586, and probably followed the return of the Chesapeake Bay expedition to Roanoke Island.

(8) *Townes:* all are villages of the Weapemeoc tribe on or near the northern shore of Albemarle Sound, except possibly Metackwem which may have stood on the peninsula between the Roanoke and Chowan Rivers and may have been a Chawanoac village.

(9) *excellency . . . of Chesepiok:* Hakluyt's interest in this area is shown in this comment and it probably contributed somewhat to the attempted diversion of the 1587 colony to the Bay. The interior of the southern shore of Chesapeake Bay, westwards from Lynnhaven Bay, is very well wooded, but it is much broken up by swamps and waterways.

Page 26. (1) *Towne . . . 700. fighting men:* this would mean that the village had a total population of some 2,000, which is far too high. His earlier use of the figure 700 for the whole population of the Weapemeoc tribe is reasonable.

(2) *foure dayes journey . . . to a certaine Kings countrey:* it is assumed that it is a route to Chesapeake Bay which is being outlined, though Lane was not clear that this was so. Such a route is indicated on the map at the end.

Page 27. (1) *blacke Pearle . . . white Pearle:* this is possibly an attempt to distinguish between mussel and oyster pearl-fishing, though much of the blackening was due to the Indian practice of cooking the shell-fish in the shell.

(2) *white men . . . black Pearles:* this may reflect some echo of Spanish contacts with the Chesapeake Bay Indians between 1559 and 1572.

(3) *that king . . . many of men . . . fight very well:* the Kecoughtan tribe early in the seventeenth century had declined, becoming one of the weakest in the Powhatan group (J. Smith, *Travels and works,* ed. E. Arber (Birmingham, 1884), p. 345).

(4) *with two hundreth men:* Lane expected a substantial reinforcement by Easter (3 April), since he was reckoning to have 100 additional men to spare (in spite of having to leave a garrison on Roanoke Island for the time being) and to send a further expedition by sea. The size of Grenville's expedition suggests that he could have left sufficient men to do all that Lane proposed.

Page 28. (1) *sconse:* for some discussion and criticism of sconces as light fortifications see Humphrey Barwick, *Breefe discourse* (c. 1591), fo. 27v. and Sir John Smythe, *Certain discourses* (1590), pp. 11, 13. A corn field implied a village, and the leaving of small outposts of this sort, liable to become involved with superior numbers of Indians, does not appear very sound strategy.

(2) *from Roanoak . . . unto this other:* the plan for the 1587 expedition was to do just this (p. 97). Hakluyt's influence in continually stressing the Chesapeake Bay venture was probably a factor in the settlement of the 1607 colony in the James River, even though nothing came of the 1586 and 1587 ventures.

(3) *Morotico:* Lane is getting both his bearings and his distances confused, since the Roanoke River entered the head of Albemarle Sound from the west some 40 miles south of the place of which he was speaking (cp. map at end). The Roanoke River, rising in the Blue Ridge Mountains, does carry down appreciably more water than the Chowan. The downstream current did, therefore, indicate that it would better repay exploration than the more mature Chowan.

(4) *vale water:* ebb-tide.

(5) *salt and brackish:* rough water on lakes on the Roanoke River and some

knowledge of its origin in the mountains may lie behind the tale, but the indications that there was a salt sea may be due to a misunderstanding.

Page 29. (1) *two double whirries:* note the inconsistency with Lane's statement (p. 25) that he had only one four-oared boat which could take only fifteen men and their equipment. One of those used was a double wherry, the other a 'light horseman' (p. 32). Lane may have left the pinnace at the head of Albemarle Sound.

(2) *Mangoaks:* the Mangoak tribe, apparently the Iroquoian Tuscarora, was located behind the Moratuc and Chawanoac peoples on the Roanoke River.

(3) *changed his name:* no precise analogy to this name-changing has been found—unless Wingina was merely taking a new 'war-name' in anticipation of his victory over the English—but it may be a variation of the practice of the Creeks and certain other south-eastern tribes who 'adopted the names of their children, sometimes in succession as the elder children died' (*Indians*, pp. 671–4).

(4) *allyes to the number of 3000:* that the alliance should include an Iroquoian tribe from the interior as well as the coastal Algonkians is surprising, while numbers are substantially exaggerated, whether by Lane's informants or by himself.

(5) *meaning towards us:* the paragraph is a typical example of Lane's lack of lucidity in composition. Having given us a version of his visit to Chawanoac in March 1586, he now reverts to the background of that expedition, namely to Wingina's stimulation of a great Indian assembly of a hostile nature to receive him. He still leaves untold the circumstances in which he braved this assembly, took Menatonon prisoner, ransomed him (pp. 26, 31) and, finally, convinced him of his peaceful intentions.

Page 30. (1) *160. miles from home:* as it was some 60 miles from Roanoke Island to the head of Albemarle Sound this would bring Lane some 100 miles up the Roanoke River in three days' rowing against a strong current. This is probably an exaggeration.

(2) *Mangoaks . . . prisoners:* Lane reckoned that by this time he had passed through the Moratuc country into that of the Mangoaks.

Page 31. (1) *Chaunis Temoatan:* there was some native copper in the Roanoke River basin (at Virgilina) which may well have been worked by the Tuscarora. All the indications are that the reports which reached Lane, though not false, were much exaggerated.

(2) *at the first melting . . . oare:* washing of alluvium for copper nodules is not confirmed for the Roanoke River basin, though it is not improbable, but the Indians in this area were unable to smelt copper.

Explanatory Notes

Page 32. (1) *by water it is 7. daies:* the Roanoke River changes direction several times and Indians who followed its course might only have very vague ideas of their distance from the coasts.

Page 33. (1) *an Islande:* Sans Souci Island, around which the Roanoke River divides before flowing into Albemarle Sound.

    (2) *winde blewe so strongly:* from the east or north-east.

    (3) *Easter eve:* Saturday, 2 April 1586.

    (4) *light horsemen:* light horseman.

    (5) *a good mine . . . passage to the Southsea . . . good Marchandise:* Lane records the relative keenness of his men to take risks for the discovery of treasure, contrasting this with their lack of enthusiasm for agriculture or commerce. There were expectations that there might be passages through North America to the Pacific in temperate latitudes and clearly the discovery of such a passage to the Pacific would be of the utmost economic and strategic importance. In his view that commerce could only be a subsidiary factor in the maintenance of a colony Lane was probably correct.

Page 34. (1) *Harriots:* This reference does not necessarily mean that Harriot accompanied Lane on the Roanoke River expedition.

    (2) *copper:* lumps of copper which had been smelted and also part of a goldsmith's crucible have been found on the site of the Fort and may link up with Joachim Ganz's experiments.

    (3) *into the heart of the mayne 200. myles:* Lane is here giving his plan in reverse. If the fort is on Chesapeake Bay, then the route already marked by 'sconses' back to the Chowan River could be taken, and an overland route to the Roanoke River worked out, so that the journey farther up-stream, though requiring to be marked by additional 'sconses', would be greatly shortened, thus bringing Chaunis Temoatan within manageable distance of the port and avoiding sailing through the treacherous Carolina Sounds.

    (4) *second part:* this, like the first part, is mainly an apologia by Lane for his failure to achieve more than he did. Harriot was not so shamefaced about a not inconsiderable achievement.

Page 35. (1) *a savage father:* a foster-father, stepfather or, even, father-in-law?

    (2) *a meane to save us from hurt:* the influence which Granganimeo and Ensenore are alleged to have exercised as 'weroances' in Wingina's councils would suggest that the latter's authority was far from absolute.

    (3) *preserved from starving:* it is difficult to see how Lane could have come to this conclusion at that time, since he still expected a relief to arrive by Easter (cp. p. 27).

    (4) *weares for fishe:* the art of setting fish-traps would require rather

specialized craftsmanship, but the complete lack of confidence which Lane had in his men's skill is surprising, seeing that there were presumably some craftsmen amongst them (cp. pp. 13–14, 27–8).

(5) *the onely God:* cp. Harriot's account of the willingness of the Indians to listen to Christian teaching, pp. 68–71.

(6) *Renapoaks:* understood to be a generic name for Indians of eastern N. America, meaning 'the true men'.

Page 36. (1) *sisters husband:* Wingina's brother-in-law, or step-brother, not Tetepano's. This provides the only specific reference to the presence of these Indians.

(2) *his sonne:* Skiko. He was not brought by Lane, but sent back from the head of Albemarle Sound in the pinnace.

(3) *those whose very names were terrible:* he would appear to mean the members of the Mangoak (Tuscarora) tribe, but this is scarcely consistent with the statements that this tribe was at times allied to the coastal Algonkian tribes.

(4) *Weroanza of England:* Queen Elizabeth. The holding of chiefly (or other) office by a woman was not unfamiliar among the coastal Algonkian peoples.

Page 37. (1) *her Majestie their onely Soveraigne:* the episode throws some light on the hierarchical character of Indian chieftaincy in this area. Okisco was in some manner subordinate to Menatonon, and was therefore obliged to enter into a form of submission to the English on his orders.

(2) *grounde for our selves to sowe:* the weirs and the allocated plots both inside and outside the Indian cornfields were presumably all on Roanoke Island. We do not hear from Harriot how the colonists took to the unaccustomed agricultural labour, or what, besides corn, they planted in the land handed over to them. This inference shows clearly that there had been no purchase or appropriation of land by the English on Roanoke Island and that they held their position, formally at least, by the tolerance of the Indians.

(3) *in ure:* into effect.

Page 38. (1) *moneths minde:* the celebration of a monthly mass for the repose of the souls of the dead in the Roman Catholic church. No such similar ceremony is suggested from other sources as typical of coastal Algonkian tribal practice. He is clearly referring to normal funerary rites.

(2) *Chesepians, and their friends:* this is the sole estimate of the war-strength of the Chesepian tribe with its associates (the Tripanicks and Opossians?), and it is also the only indication that there was any close association between the Virginia and Carolina Algonkian tribes. Lane may

Page 38. (2)—*contd.*

have been exaggerating his peril by reference to almost all the tribes of which he knew.

(3) *beset my house*: the passage adds something to what is otherwise known of the settlement. The individual houses of the leading members of the expedition were outside the fort ditch, probably between it and the village.

(4) *Master Harriots*: the possession of a separate cottage by Harriot indicates that he enjoyed some considerable status amongst the settlers.

Page 39. (1) *Ottorasko*: Hatarask, the island lying south of Port Ferdinando, with Croatoan southward again from it. All early authorities are agreed that such a reversion to a primitive gathering economy was forced on the Algonkian tribes during the late spring and early summer.

(2) *my lord Admirals Island*: the naming of Croatoan after Lord Howard of Effingham, is not elsewhere indicated. The Earl of Lincoln died in February 1585, but Howard did not take up his duties as Lord High Admiral until May. The name may have been given after Lane's return. Taken with Ralegh's letter of 1602 (E. Edwards, *The Life of Sir Walter Ralegh* (1868) II, 252), it indicates that he was a subscriber to the expedition.

(3) *mayne over against us*: along the shore to the south-west between Dasemunkepeuc and Pomeiooc.

(4) *by colour*: outward appearance, show of reason.

Page 40. (1) *Okisko . . . did retyre*: once again we are handicapped by insufficiently detailed knowledge of the Indian polity. Lane appears to mean that Okisko, in view of his engagements to Menatonon and to Lane, led away his own immediate entourage in order to allow the subordinate chieftains of the Weapemeoc villages to associate with Wingina in return for receiving his bribe of copper.

(2) *10. of July*: corrected to 'June' (*PN*, III (1600), 262).

(3) *bylboes*: a long iron bar fastened by a lock to the floor, along which ran sliding leg-irons. This probably formed part of the gaol which Lane must have had (since he had both a provost marshal and a deputy) inside the fort enclosure.

(4) *prevent*: forestall.

Page 41. (1) *Canuisado*: usually 'camisado', a night attack, so called because the attackers allowed their shirt-tails to hang out behind so that they would not be fired on by their own men.

(2) *light horsemen*: light horseman (*PN*, III (1600), 262).

(3) *Colonel of the Chesepians . . . Serjeant major*: neither has been identified though the first may have been Thomas Harriot: both were posts of some seniority in a large expedition. In such a small one as this, we must suspect

Lane of a liking for military titles, rather than a respect for function.

(4) *Petronell*: a heavy cavalry pistol carried in the belt.

Page 42. (1) *first of June . . . the 8*: Lane appears to be one day out in his calculations, though he may be reckoning from midnight to midnight and Drake from noon to noon. There appears less reason to doubt the Drake narrative (p. 80) that the signal fires, apparently in the vicinity of modern Cape Hatteras, were seen on the 9th. Drake's ships were probably sighted on the 8th by Stafford's men and the news conveyed to the fort, a distance of some 60 miles, by the double wherry which can scarcely have arrived until well into the 9th.

(2) *supplie of our necessities*: the evidence that Drake had for some weeks been collecting materials and boats likely to be useful to the colony is clearly set out in *Further English voyages*. It is unfortunate that we have not the precise terms of Drake's offer, since in it he would have referred to liberated Indians and Negroes who were intended as a reinforcement to the colony's labour force. Drake, too, is likely to have expected to find Grenville there with a substantial fleet, capable of carrying out some of the longer-term plans against the Spanish Indies.

Page 43. (1) *search . . . for some better harborow*: Lane possibly hoped to rush through his expedition from the Chowan River overland to Chesapeake Bay while the rest of the settlers were being brought round by sea.

(2) *officers of my companie*: we have not the names of any of these officials. Their existence suggests that inside the fort ditch there was, besides a gaol, a granary or other food repository, a storehouse for reserves of equipment and possibly also of goods acquired by barter from the Indians, and a treasury, since it is probable that to maintain morale military wages were paid regularly. The cape merchant, Thomas Harvey, may well have been the keeper of the store. The high treasurer, Francis Brooke, had returned in September 1585.

(3) *Francis . . . put cleare to sea*: while the *Francis* was genuinely driven to sea, her failure to put back once the storm was over may have been due to the unwillingness of her company to stay away from home any longer and also possibly risk loss in the distribution of prize money on the return of the main fleet.

Page 44. (1) *sir Richard Greenvill . . . not yet come*: Grenville was by this time well on his way, while Ralegh's supply ship was ahead of him.

(2) *the doings in England*: how recent was Drake's news from home? According to the Spaniards (*Further English voyages*, pp. 313–14) he had for some time been apprehensive of a Spanish attack on England before his return. What the American plan was, except possibly that Drake expected a

Page 44. (2)—*contd.*

force to follow his track so as to occupy parts of the West Indies, cannot be indicated.

(3) *fetching away of fewe:* amongst the residue left behind were three of Lane's party—the first lost, or deserted, colonists. It is not unlikely that they had been sent after 1 June to conduct Skiko home to Chowanoac.

VI

Page 46. (1) *A briefe and true report:* the title-page of the first edition reads:

A briefe and true report of the new found land of Virginia: of the commodities there found and to be raysed, as well marchantable, as others for victuall, building and other necessarie uses for those that are and shalbe the planters there; and of the nature and manners of the naturall inhabitants: Discovered by the English Colony there seated by Sir Richard Greinvile Knight in the yeere 1585. which remained under the government of Rafe Lane Esquier, one of her Maiesties Equieres, during the space of twelve monethes: at the speciall charge and direction of the Honourable Sir Walter Raleigh Knight, Lord Warden of the stanneries; who therein hath beene favoured and authorised by her Maiestie and her letters patents:

Directed to the Adventurers, Favourers, and Welwillers of the action, for the inhabiting and planting there:

By Thomas Hariot; servant to the abovenamed Sir Walter, a member of the Colony, and there imployed in discovering.

Imprinted at London 1588.

PN (1589), pp. 748–64; III (1600), 266–80 (VIII (1904), 348–86).

(2) *Farewell in the Lord:* Lane presumably wrote this letter (or allowed Harriot to put his name to it) in February 1588.

Page 47. (1) *sixe weekes:* Barlowe does not, himself, say how long he stayed, so this is a small piece of additional evidence on the 1584 expedition.

(2) *dealing with the naturall inhabitaunts:* Harriot's special responsibility for dealing with the Indians was due, *inter alia,* to his having acquired some knowledge of the language from Manteo and Wanchese (to whom he may well have taught English) in the months after their arrival in England.

Page 49. (1) *grasse Silke:* this is clearly a Yucca.

Page 50. (1) *Grogran:* grosgrain is a coarse fabric made from silk, or from a mixture of wool and mohair or from a mixture of these three fibres, and often thickened with gum.

(2) *Silke wormes:* the silkworm is not native to North America. The larvae of the tent caterpillar or of the fall web-worm may be what was observed.

(3) *Mulberie:* common or red mulberry is indigenous. White mulberry was introduced by the Spaniards.

(4) *Flaxe and Hempe:* it is not certain what indigenous plant or plants the English called flax or hemp. This could be a wild flax (*Carthartolinium*) but the yellow flowers would be unfamiliar.

(5) *Allum:* there is no alum in the coastal clays of N. Carolina, nor any of the other mineral substances mentioned here. Copperas was iron sulphate and may have been identified but white copperas or protosulphate of zinc would not be found. The German 'mineral men' usually employed as prospectors were notoriously unreliable and could 'find' almost any mineral for which they were asked.

Page 51. (1) *Terra sigillata:* this was the term normally used for Lemnian earth (cp. Samian earth, p. 22). Kaolin and other earths were extensively used in Europe for their medicinal properties. There were many clays in the area which Harriot could have noticed.

(2) *few trees els:* the greater number of trees in the coastal area are coniferous, mainly pine, and North Carolina's nickname, 'The Turpentine State', was derived from intensive exploitation of these trees.

(3) *Sassafras: Sassafras officinale,* a slender, aromatic tree whose roots and bark were used medicinally. It was discovered by the French in Florida 1562–5, and described by Nicholas Monardes in 1571 and 1574. Guaiacum from Santo Domingo is also described by Monardes.

(4) *Booke of Monardus:* Nicholas Monardes, *Ioyful newes out of the newe founde worlde* . . . *Englished by Ihon Frampton, marchaunt* (1577), from *La historia medicinal de las cosas que se traen de nuestras Indias Occidentalis que se siruen en medicina,* Seville, 1574.

(5) *Cedar:* The American red cedar is a juniper and not a true cedar.

(6) *grapes:* the small sour grape and the large, sweet muscadine are the species probably referred to here. Other species in the coastal lands are summer grape and fox grape.

Page 52. (1) *Marterne furres:* possibly south-eastern mink. Muskrat is also possible but Harriot could have seen these as they are still common in the marshes north of Pamlico Sound.

(2) *Luzarnes:* bobcat is probably meant but they could have heard reports of the mountain lion. See p. 63.

(3) *Civet cats:* southern skunk or polecat but civet was not obtained from it.

(4) *a Minerall man:* almost certainly Joachim Ganz.

(5) *iron:* there are frequent traces and some deposits of 'bog ore' in the swamp forests and marshes, and other traces of iron on the banks of the Roanoke and Chowan rivers.

Page 52. (6) *Copper:* the plates of copper were apparently obtained at Chawanoac and were said to have been made of copper from Chaunis Temoatan.

Page 53. (1) *silver:* natural silver is rare in eastern North America.

(2) *lost them:* Lane records also the loss of a rope of pearls he had from Menatonon.

(3) *Dies of divers kindes:* black dye was obtained from the leaves of dwarf sumach and smooth sumach, the berries yielding a red dye. A possible plant for 'Wasebur' is pokeweed the source of a purplish dye. The roots of dogwood, of New Jersey tea and of pocone all yield a red dye. Dogwood would be found growing on the Carolina Banks but New Jersey tea probably not while the pocone root was traded in from the uplands.

Page 54. (1) *Woad:* in 1585 the elder Hakluyt recommended the bringing out of seeds or plants of woad as a quick crop 'of great gaine to this clothing realme'.

(2) *the same climate:* the cultivation limits in eastern North America were not identical with those in Europe.

(3) *Pagatowr:* the Indian word for 'things put in a kettle to boil' could—but probably did not—cover other things than maize (Indian corn) on which so much of the Indian polity depended. Roasted, boiled and taken as gruel it made an essential basis for most Indian dishes, but it was commonly cooked with meat, fish, and vegetables.

Page 55. (1) *Mellions:* pumpkins and gourds but not melons which were a later introduction. Bottle gourd can be identified while the common white bush scallop squash is also probable.

Page 56. (1) *Melden:* clearly a member of the genus *Atriplex*, known as oraches or salt-bushes.

(2) *Planta Solis:* sunflower, many species in North Carolina. The Indians dried the seeds and ground them for flour. When crushed the seeds were also boiled usually for the oil.

Page 57. (1) *two hundreth London bushels:* probably a considerable exaggeration.

Page 58. (1) *Tobacco:* it is generally accepted that the tobacco cultivated in eastern North America was *Nicotiana rustica* in a number of varieties.

(2) *bodyes . . . preserved in health:* the medicinal uses of tobacco were being stressed at this time. The earliest English work on tobacco A[nthony] C[hute], *Tabaco* (London, Adam Islip, 1595) states: 'I think that there is nothing that harmes a man inwardly from his girdle vpward, but may be taken away with a moderate vse of Tabacco.'

(3) *sucke it . . . since our returne:* Ralegh and the colonists alike did much to

popularize smoking but it was already an established custom. Harriot himself was a heavy smoker while Ralegh learnt to cure tobacco expertly. What
the colonists apparently introduced was the smoking pipe used on Roanoke
Island, as a model for English pipe-makers.

Page 59. (1) *Openauk:* ground-nut, Indian potato or marsh potato. The
openauk was confused by later writers with the potato (*Solanum tuberosum*),
on account of John Gerard's description of this potato in his *Herball* (1597),
pp. 335, 781, as having been received 'from Virginia, otherwise called
Norembega'. The sequence of information and misinformation is fully
traced in J. G. Hawkes, 'The History of the Potato' in *Journal of the Royal
Horticultural Society* (1967), XCII, 249–62.

(2) *Okeepenauk:* man-of-the-earth or wild potato vine with its yam-like
tap root is most probably what is meant here.

(3) *Kaishucpenauk:* one of the members of the water-plantain family,
especially the common arrow-head or duck potato, found on pond and river
margins and in marshes.

(4) *Tsinaw:* this is merely an Indian attempt to reproduce 'china'. The
plant is one of the woody smilaxes. Smilax china was already described in
1582 as 'The diet roote Chinea' by William Mount (R. T. Gunther, *Early
British Botanists* (Oxford, 1922), p. 258.)

(5) *spoonemeat:* the use of the roots to make a reddish flour, a jelly, and a
drink like sarsaparilla was widespread in the south-east of N. America.

(6) *Coscushaw:* a member of the arum family, apparently arrow-arum and
golden-club. Cassava was made in the Caribbean from the pressed root of
Manihot utilissima. For Lane's name 'Cassava' for the arum-root flour see
p. 37.

Page 60. (1) *Habascon:* possibly the cow-parsnip which was used by the
Indians as a salt substitute but which would have to be brought from inland.
Angelico has also been suggested.

(2) *Chestnuts:* the characteristic tree of this family found on or near the
coast is the small coastal Chinquapin.

(3) *Walnuts:* the smooth nut is probably the pig-nut hickory. The dark,
ragged-shelled sort might have been the black walnut because, though unusual near the coast, it tended to seed round Indian settlements.

(4) *morters:* these invaluable artifacts had to be traded from the interior.

Page 61. (1) *Mutaquesunnauk:* prickly pear.

(2) *leaves of the plant:* this is the Nopal Cactus of Mexico and Central
America which is host of the parasitic scale-insect. The crushed body of this
insect is cochineal.

(3) *Sacquenummener:* not identified.

Explanatory Notes

Page 61. (4) *Reed:* possibly cord grass.

(5) *Acornes:* these nuts were not necessarily from the oak alone and may include the Chinquapin, and the hazel-nut. The oaks with sweetish acorns are the live oak, the post oaks, the white oak and the basket oak. *Sapummener* is possibly the acorn of the swamp chestnut oak. L'Écluse (*Exoticorum*, p. 43) notes a large acorn said to have been brought from Virginia, which he regards as Harriot's *Mangummenauk.*

Page 62. (1) *Saquenuckot and Maquowoc:* the more probable beasts would be musk rat and mink. The common raccoon, the beaver and the common opossum are also recorded as having been eaten in North Carolina.

(2) *eight and twenty . . . beasts:* an indication of the extent of Harriot's Indian vocabulary now lost.

Page 63. (1) *Woolvish dogges:* Harriot's meaning is not quite clear, but it is probable that his 'of' is superfluous, and that he is proceeding directly from his discussion of lion-eating by the Indians to that of dog-eating by the settlers. The use of dogs as domestic pets, for hunting and for eating is discussed in G. M. Allen, 'Domesticated dogs of the American aborigines', *Bulletin of the Museum of Comparative Zoology, Harvard University* (1920), LXIII, 431–517.

(2) *experimented in both:* the reference is to the eating of the two English bull-mastiffs by Lane's men when on their Roanoke River expedition (pp. 32–3).

(3) *Cranes:* the Florida sub-species of the Sandhill Crane now only an occasional visitor to the North Carolina coastlands.

(4) *Swannes and Geese:* formerly the trumpeter swan appears to have been common but now it is the whistling swan which migrates in winter to the sounds, along with the common Canada goose, American brant and greater snow goose.

(5) *shall be also published:* this promise of publication shows that Harriot contemplated not only a chronicle (see p. 76), but an illustrated account of his survey of American natural history.

(6) *Herrings:* seven species of the alewife or river herring contribute to the fisheries in the sounds and rivers, including branch herring, glut herring, shad, and hickory shad.

(7) *Rayes:* eleven species of rays and skates are found off North Carolina.

(8) *Plaice:* flounders and soles, the most common being summer flounder, southern flounder and winter flounder.

Page 64. (1) *Irish men cast darts:* the long throwing darts were the characteristic weapon of the Irish kern, who made up the light infantry of Ireland.

Harriot may have seen them in Ireland or obtained the comparison from Lane or some of his Irish followers.

(2) *Sea crabbes:* the best known crab in the Chesapeake Bay area is the blue or soft-shelled crab.

(3) *Oisters:* oysters made up a substantial part of the Indians' food. Harriot may here be including the smaller clams.

(4) *Scalops:* several species of scallops as well as quahogs or hard-shell clams, soft-shell clams and razor clams. (Harden Taylor [etc.], *Survey of marine fisheries of North Carolina* (1951), pp. 205–18.)

(5) *Crevises:* the fresh-water crayfish. As 'Crevices', however, Harriot would include, according to the contemporary meaning of the word, the American lobster.

(6) *Seekanauk:* king-crab or horseshoe crab. The long sword-shaped tail-spine was used by the Indians in this area to tip their fish-spears.

(7) *Tortoyses:* these are land and sea turtles and terrapins.

Page 65. (1) *Firre trees:* loblolly pine, longleaf pine, and Pocoson pine are the most prominent 'firs' amongst the coastal trees.

(2) *Rakiock:* this is either the tulip tree or the white cypress, a variety of the swamp cypress.

(3) *Cyprus:* the true cypresses (*Cupressus* spp.) are not found in eastern North America. The swamp cypress (above) and the pond cypress are not evergreens.

(4) *Maple . . . Wich-hazle:* Carolina red maple is common but witch-hazel occurs only as a small shrub near the coast.

(5) *weares and wheles:* English weels (traps) were made from osiers or willow. The Indians used the cane (*Arundinaria macrosperma* the large variety and *A. tecta* the small).

(6) *Ascopo:* sweet bay.

(7) *Cassia Lignea:* for Monardes see page 151. *Joyfull Newes,* ed. Gaselee, I, 28-33, deals mainly with the infusion made from *Lignum vitae* which was used as a specific against syphilis.

Page 66. (1) *small pebbles:* consolidated rock is rare throughout the coastal plain.

(2) *household . . . stones:* the mortar-stones, traded from the interior, were among the most important possessions of a household. Sharp-bladed shells were used as knives and, especially, as razors. The whetting of copper would suggest that it was used for tools and weapons and probably that it was annealed. Other references do not bear this out (cp. pp. 5, 31), and it may be that the English taught the Indians to develop their decorative use of copper in this way.

Explanatory Notes

Page 66. (3) *graves:* inhumation was the common method of burial, with the preservation of the bones of chiefs in special ossuaries.

(4) *clay . . . lime . . . oyster shels:* there were many types of suitable clay and a supply of lime for mortar and plaster, down to the middle of the nineteenth century at least, came from the deep middens, mainly of oyster shells, left by the Indians.

(5) *Tenet and Shepy:* Thanet and Sheppey, both in Kent.

(6) *the ground is nothing els:* there are natural deposits of shell beds in many parts of the sounds.

Page 67. (1) *30. houses:* it seems likely that Chawanoac was the largest town of the Carolina Algonkians, but Harriot may have seen larger on Chesapeake Bay, e.g. Skicoac.

(2) *barkes . . . matts:* the bark was most probably cypress, though cedar and pine were used. The mats were of cane or rushes.

(3) *greatest Wiroans:* Menatonon of Chawanoac is probably the chief referred to.

Page 68. (1) *excellencie of wit:* Manteo at least gave a remarkable illustration of the capacity of some of them to master English speech and concepts.

(2) *Mantoac:* the ordinary term for spirit or supernatural being in the Algonquian languages is *manito* (*Analysis*, p. 155).

Page 69. (1) *immortalitie of the soule:* differential treatment in after-life according to conduct on earth is emphasized by many coastal Algonkian peoples.

Page 70. (1) *in their language to expresse:* Harriot's only specific admission that he could speak (however imperfectly) the Algonquian tongues.

(2) *perspective glasse:* this was either a primitive form of telescope—as it involved a combination of lenses—or (most probably) a magnifying glass which could be used with a concave mirror.

(3) *wilde fireworkes:* wildfire in the Middle Ages was an inflammable compound, easy to ignite and hard to extinguish and used in warfare. But by 1585 fireworks as decorative illuminants and projectiles were popular at court, and Harriot is probably noting the use of some of these.

(4) *spring clockes:* there are several ship-clocks of this period in the British Museum.

Page 71. (1) *to pray . . . that hee might live:* praying accorded with the Indian methods of treating diseases by the repetition of magical formulae, although to them they often added physical treatment.

Page 72. (1) *The disease:* this was most likely to have been measles or possibly smallpox though it could have been the common cold. Malaria was possibly brought out by Lane's men. The lethal effects of measles or colds would be quite inexplicable to the English, but they are likely to have recognized smallpox or malaria.

Page 73. (1) *immortalitie:* it is difficult to say whether the Indians regarded the English as supernatural beings or as men returned from the dead. While transmigration was a frequent belief it did not exclude the possibility of return as grown men.

(2) *blood that they sucked:* sucking appears to have played a more significant part in Carolina Algonkian medicine than, for example, among the Virginia Algonkians where it was preliminary to herbal treatment.

(3) *Eclipse of the Sunne:* for the eclipse of the sun forecast for 19 April 1585 see *RV*, I, 380–1.

(4) *Comet:* there was only one comet recorded in 1585, and it appeared for about a month (mid-October to mid-November) in the northern hemisphere.

Page 75. (1) *nature of the climate:* the illusion that lands in the same latitudes had necessarily identical climates and produced identical crops has already been encountered, and it is implied throughout the writings of both the Hakluyts. See pp. 54, 75.

Page 76. (1) *five hundredth acres:* as we do not know many of the details of Ralegh's agreement with the City of Ralegh settlers on 7 January 1587 (p. 93 and *RV*, II, 571) this information is of great value.

(2) *Chronicle:* this is the first and only reference to Harriot's chronicle, which has entirely disappeared, along with almost every scrap of his other papers on North America.

VII

Page 77. (1) *Bigges's discourse: PN*, III (1600), 546–8. *A summarie and true discourse of Sir Frances Drakes West Indian voyage* first appeared in England under Richard Field's imprint (two issues) in 1589, and reappeared under Roger Ward's (completely reset): it is probably from this that Hakluyt printed it in 1600 (it was not in the 1589 edition). The extract deals only with the latter parts of Drake's voyage from Cuba to Florida to Virginia and then back to England. He had set out in September 1585.

(2) *the Generall:* Drake, commanding the *Elizabeth Bonaventure*.

(3) *the Lieutenant generall:* Christopher Carleill, commanding the *Tiger*.

(4) *a Fort:* the fort of San Juan, located a little to the north of the open settlement of San Augustín (established 1565).

Page 78. (1) *Prince of Orenge his song:* the song was 'Wilhelmus van Nassouwe', 1569, attributed to Philips van Marnix, Count of Sainte Aldegonde.

Page 78. (2) *Spaniards were gone from the Fort:* Pedro Menéndez Marqués, the governor, had sensibly evacuated both fort and town, and had taken refuge with the nearby Indians (*Further English voyages*, passim, especially pp. 163–4).

(3) *the Vice-admirall:* Martin Frobisher, commanding the *Primrose*.

Page 79. (1) *the Sergeant Major:* Anthony Powell.

(2) *S. Helena:* Fort San Marcos, at Santa Elena, on Port Royal Sound, where Gutierre de Miranda commanded, was more like 60 than 12 leagues to the north.

Page: 80. (1) *their Port:* Fort Ferdinando, or Hatarask, in the Carolina Outer Banks, opposite the southern end of Roanoke Island where Lane's fort was.

VIII

Page 82. (1) *Relation ... Morales: PN,* III (1600) 361 (IX (1904), 112–13). Drake arrived with his prisoners at Plymouth at the end of July 1586, by which time Hakluyt was in England, and the deposition was made between then and his return to France. Morales was probably one of the Spanish deserters mentioned in *Further English voyages*, pp. 182, 186. The purpose of the interrogation was to obtain information on territories south and southwest of Virginia.

(2) *Apalatci:* the 'Montes Apalatci', with appropriate legends, appear on Jacques Le Moyne's map of Florida (De Bry, *America*, Pt. II (1591), pl. I). The name derived from the Apalachee tribe of Florida, and may have been added by Hakluyt as it is not apparently used by Spaniards at this time.

(3) *river of Wateri:* this and the following paragraphs largely represent the results of the Pardo-Moyano expeditions of 1566–7, see C. O. Sauer, *Sixteenth Century North America* (1971), p. 217. The area is mainly in modern South Carolina.

(4) *Kings and Rivers:* Ahoya, Ahoyabe, Uscamacu, and Coosa formed parts of the Cusabo, a South Carolina tribe.

Page 83. (1) *the hils of Chaunis Temoatam:* Hakluyt was right in essentials in that Lane's Roanoke River rose, like all the other important rivers of the eastern slope, in the Appalachians, but he had no idea of the distances involved. This sentence was Hakluyt's gloss on the deposition and was probably written at the time it was made rather than in 1600, since one purpose in taking the deposition was to obtain information useful for subsequent Virginia expeditions.

(2) *Nicolas Burgoignon: PN,* III (1600), 361–2 (IX (1904), 113–15). Evidently taken, like the foregoing, by Hakluyt after July 1586.

(3) *sixe yeeres:* he was apparently one of the four survivors of the French expedition of Gilberto Gil in 1580 (*Colonial Records of Spanish Florida, 1577-80*, ed. J. T. Connor (Florida State Hist. Soc., 1930), I, 318-23).

(4) *the Spaniard:* Pedro Morales.

(5) *La grand Copal:* Hakluyt (*PN*, III (1600), 311) identified La Grand Copal with Chiquola, which is Chicola on the Le Moyne map and is situated on a river which is either the Waccamaw-Pee Dee River entering Winyah Bay, or the Santee a little to the south.

(6) *sixtie ducates:* at 6s. the ducat this would give a price of £18 a ton. Its commercial value explains the emphasis put on Virginia sassafras by Harriot (p. 51).

Page 84. (1) *baudricks:* baldric, the transverse strapping from which a sword was suspended.

(2) *Oxen:* a confused reference to bison.

(3) *poynt:* Cape Romain (lat. 32° 58′N.), though the distance is not adequate.

(4) *Waterin . . . fortie leagues distant:* cp. 'Guatary' (the same?), 80 leagues from Santa Elena (*Georgia H.Q.*, XXXVIII, 79-80). Winyah Bay, much nearer, may be intended.

(5) *Waren in Virginia:* this is Hakluyt interpolating a personal comment. His 'Waren' is 'Warreā' of the Virginia colony, very much farther north (cp. *RV*, I. 215-16, II. 872).

(6) *to discover where we were seated:* Menéndez Marqués, when he returned from Havana to Florida in June, heard a rumour from the Indians of ships passing along the Florida coast and his letter to this effect reached Havana by 24 October (*Further English voyages*, p. xxii, n. 3). He appears to have waited until the hurricane season was over, and then sent an expedition northwards. We know nothing of it apart from what is said here, but again the presumption is that the vessel was instructed to search the harbours and estuaries north of Santa Elena. It is unlikely, in this event, that the reconnaissance was pursued north of Cape Fear (cp. *RV*, II. 744-5, 781).

(7) *Outina:* Laudonnière (*PN*, III (1600), 326-7, 339-45) gives a number of references to Utina. He and his tribe (the Timucua or Utina) dominated the middle course of the St. Johns River in Florida.

IX

Page 85. (1) *1586 Virginia Voyages: PN* (1589). pp. 747-8; III (1600), 265 collated with VIII (1904), 346-8. This is the only narrative of the American voyages in Hakluyt which is not a first-hand account. The natural assumption

Page 85. (1)—*contd.*
is that Hakluyt found himself, when he came to compile the *Principall navigations*, without any account of the two voyages made in 1586. He wrote this himself, though it is surprising that he did not obtain a more detailed account for his second edition.

(2) *a ship of 100. tunnes:* not identified.

Page 86. (1) *three sayles . . . to be left there:* there is nothing in this account of the end of the first colony that could not have been based on Lane and Bigges (pp. 42–5, 80–1), apart from the statement that after the storm there were still three ships with the colonists at Port Ferdinando, which were to have been left with them. In fact only the *Francis* was to have been left behind.

(2) *the hande of God came upon them:* this view fits in with that expressed by Harriot in the *Briefe and true report* (pp. 72–3).

(3) *the shippe . . . of Sir Walter Ralegh:* Drake sailed with the colonists on 18 or 19 June, so that the arrival of Ralegh's ship can probably be put before the end of June. The very vague statement of what was done and found suggests that Hakluyt merely learnt that the ship, after visiting Roanoke, still retained her stores on her return.

(4) *Sir Richard Grindfield . . . with three shippes:* the account of Grenville's visit suggests that Hakluyt had some more specific information than on the voyage of the first supply ship, but had still no detailed narrative before him at the time of writing. There seems no reason to doubt that Grenville had seven or eight ships in his squadron when he reached Madeira and that all of those accompanied him to Virginia (*RV*, II, 482, 788–9).

(5) *he landed 15. men:* Pedro Diaz, a Spanish pilot who was with Grenville, says the number was eighteen, two of whom were called Cofar (Coffin) and Chapman, and as his is direct evidence it may be the more reliable. He says Grenville left with them four pieces of artillery and supplies for eighteen men for one year (ibid., II, 791).

(6) *returned into England:* about 16/26 December.

X

Page 87. (1) *Dedication to Ralegh:* having published René de Laudonnière's *Histoire notable de la Floride* (on the French expeditions to Florida, 1562–8), Hakluyt translated it and had it published in England as *A notable historie* (T. Dawson, 1587), with an introduction linking it with the Virginia voyages sponsored by Ralegh. This is from his reprint, III (1600), 301–3.

(2) *more yeeres in France then I:* Ralegh was in France 1568–72 (P. Lefranc, *Ralegh écrivain* (Paris, 1968), p. 26); Hakluyt had first gone there in September 1583.

Page 88. (1) *James Morgues . . . hath published . . . with the purtraitures:* this was, in 1587, the first news of Ralegh's patronage of Le Moyne (d. 1588), whose drawings were posthumously engraved in T. de Bry, *America*, Pt. II (Frankfurt, 1591). Hakluyt in 1600 altered the last phrase from 'which he meaneth to publish together with the purtraitures before it be long' [Sig. [ ] 2v.].

(2) *late return of Captaine Stafford:* the probability is that Captain Edward Stafford was in command of the *Lion* when she returned from Virginia on October 18 (p. 105), so that Hakluyt cannot have completed the dedication before this time.

Page 89. (1) *John Barros . . . his first Decade:* João de Barros, *Asia*, the first Decade (Lisbon, 1552).

Page 90. (1) *Fernandus Columbus . . . history . . . of his father:* Fernando Colón, *Historie . . . dell' Ammiraglio D. Cristoforo Colombo* (Venice, 1571).

(2) *relation of Newe Mexico . . . in English:* the narration of the expedition of Antonio de Espejo in Juan González de Mendoza, *The historie of the great and mightie kingdome of China*, translated by Robert Parke (1588). Hakluyt republished Espejo in Spanish in 1586 and had it translated into French. He included his own translation in *PN*, III (1600), 389–96. It was not, however, 'extant now in English' in the sense of having been published in that language when Hakluyt wrote in 1587.

Page 91. (1) *the Chronicle:* in R. Holinshed, *Chronicles*, III (2nd ed., 1587), by John Hooker. This had very recently been published.

(2) *Antonio de Castillio . . . assured me in this city in . . . 1581:* in 1587 Hakluyt wrote 'within these six yeeres' (*A notable historie*, sig. [ ]4). His earliest reference to this meeting was in *Divers voyages* (1582), sig. ¶13.

(3) *John Davis to the Northwest:* the voyages of 1585–7 in search of a north-west passage, the narratives of which Hakluyt was to publish for the first time in *PN* (1589).

(4) *Culuacan:* Culiacan, Abraham Ortelius, *Theatrum orbis terrarum* (ed. of 1582), f. 7.

Page 92. (1) *London the 1. of May 1587:* Hakluyt was not in London on May 1, and he did not complete the dedication until, it would appear, after October 18. 1 November, not 1 May, would therefore be a likely date. Hakluyt may, however, have worked from a draft dated 1 May.

XI

Page 93. (1) *1587 Virginia Voyage: PN* (1589), pp. 764–70, collated with III (1600), 180–6 (VIII (1904), 386–402). This is the earliest narrative of

Page 93. (1)—*contd.*
White's we have and it was evidently compiled by him before 25 March 1588, using his journal as a basis.

(2) *The fourth voyage . . . second Colonie:* 1584, 1585, 1586 (two separate voyages were Hakluyt's three earlier voyages. White ranked this as his third (p. 166). To call this the second colony is to ignore the party left on Roanoke Island by Grenville in 1586.

(3) *Charter . . . of the Citie of Ralegh:* what is known of the charter of 7 January 1587 is given in *RV*, II, 506–12, but the document itself has not survived. The precise extent of Ralegh's activity in recruiting settlers remains in doubt. According to Harriot (p. 76) each man had a promise of 500 acres of land in Virginia for his personal adventure only: he was probably given a bonus if he brought wife and/or children, while it is probable that the colonists put in their own investment for their stores and equipment, probably also for additional land. Of the round figure of 150 only 108 plus two Indians were left on Roanoke Island (pp. 107–9).

(4) *the Admirall:* the *Lion,* John White captain, Simon Fernandes master.

(5) *a Flie boate, and a Pinnesse:* nothing is known of the flyboat's name or size, or of her captain. Her master, Edward Spicer, commanded William Sanderson's *Moonlight* in 1590. The pinnace is also not named: Edward Stafford was captain.

(6) *Simon Ferdinando . . . forsooke our Flie boate:* this is the first of a long series of charges against Fernandes, over whom White appears to have been able to exercise little or no control. The underlying conflict was clearly over Fernandes's desire to continue the privateering tradition and White's wish to spare the settlers from delays and fights with Spanish vessels.

Page 94. (1) *a small fruite, like greene apples:* apparently a poisonous species of pome, which it is not possible to identify on the data given but the effects of which as described are quite appropriate to such a fruit. Hakluyt adds (*PN*, III (1600), 281) in the margin, 'Circumspection to be used in strange places'.

Page 95. (1) *Cottea:* S. E. Morison (*Northern voyages,* p. 655) makes a case for it being Vieques.

(2) *Darbie Glaven:* the Darby Glande of the 1585–6 colony. For his own story of this episode and his subsequent career see *RV*, II, 834–8.

(3) *Denice Carrell:* Denis Carroll is the only other certain Irishman among the intending settlers, though Thomas Butler and James Lasie may also have been of Irish origin. The presence of an Irish group might point, very slightly, towards White having connections in Ireland.

(4) *Rosse Baye:* Rojo Bay was either Sucia Bay to the east of Cape Rojo or Salinas Bay to the west, between Point Aguila and Cape Rojo (cp. *West Indies pilot,* II, 38, 41).

Page 96. (1) *plants . . . well knowen to the Governour:* since he had gathered them and made drawings of them before in 1585. This is another small but telling pointer in identifying John White the painter with the governor.

(2) *his friend Alanson:* Philip's reactions to the news that trading was taking place had been sharp and apparently led to clearing the French merchants from Hispaniola, at least for the time being.

Page 97. (1) *Cape of Feare:* White was aware of the existence of a cape in the position of the modern Cape Fear, but he called what we now know as Cape Lookout 'Cape Feare'. His story of this landing would fit in with a position between the two capes, and on the Carolina Outer Banks.

(2) *Hatoraske:* formerly Port Ferdinando.

(3) *to the Baye of Chesepiok:* Hakluyt (*PN*, III (1600), 282) adds in the margin: 'An intent to plant in the Bay of Chesepiok'—an objective which he had himself urged. White evidently expected Coffin and Chapman's party to remain on the island after his own departure for Chesapeake Bay, and so would have left stores to enable them to do so. This part of Virginia would not in any case have come within the scope of the grant to White's company.

(4) *directions . . . of Sir Walter Ralegh:* the fact that Ralegh issued the instructions personally indicates how directly responsible he remained for the conduct of the expedition and the supervision of the colony.

(5) *Summer was farre spent:* for privateering (with the Spanish fleet due to reach the Azores in August or September) rather than for sailing.

(6) *booted not the Governour to contend with them:* White's story may betray a great lack of confidence in his own powers of leadership (which other passages in his narrative might be used to endorse), or it may reflect either his personal preference for Roanoke Island and its surroundings as site for a colony or his confidence that he could get to Chesapeake Bay with the colonists in any event.

Page 98. (1) *the forte rased downe:* the fort that was 'rased' was the earthwork and not the building inside it, as is made clear. But the fort building was most probably damaged by fire.

(2) *houses . . . also of the forte:* the fort building inside the earthworks. Apart from being higher, larger, and somewhat stouter, there is no reason to believe it differed substantially from the houses.

(3) *newe Cottages:* under Lane only the principal men in the colony had houses of their own. Now, the family make-up of part of the new colony required domestic housing.

(4) *aboord:* corrected to 'abroad' (*PN*, III (1600), 283).

(5) *divers Savages . . . to espie our companie:* Grenville in 1586 had the greatest difficulty in locating any Indians at all. It may well have been their

Page 98. (5)—*contd.*

absence for some considerable time which lulled the 1586 settlers into a false sense of security. They probably came down the westerly shore of the island, the side from which they could, by means of a shallow, islet-studded sound —now Croatan Sound—most easily approach Roanoke Island.

Page 99. (1) *many of his kinred, dwelling in that Island:* this passage is the best evidence that the Croatoan people formed a distinct tribe and had a fairly substantial population on the island. White said later that Manteo was born on Croatoan Island.

(2) *divers . . . were hurt . . . by Master Lane his companie:* evidently a skirmish additional to those mentioned by Lane, which must have taken place on 31 May or 1 June in the previous year.

Page 101. (1) *they . . . departed, whither . . . we knowe not:* their disappearance was the second in the story so far, three of Lane's men having been left behind, and not heard of again after June 1586.

(2) *eleven Englishmen:* White is confused about numbers. If two had been killed and four were on the Outer Banks the number which were driven from the island would appear to have been nine, unless the higher initial total of eighteen given by Diaz is correct.

Page 102. (1) *Manteo . . . was christened:* this is the first recorded admission of a North American Indian to the Church of England. It implied the presence possibly of a ship's chaplain, which the *Lion* might well have carried. There is no indication that there was a clergyman among the settlers.

(2) *in reward of his faithfull service:* this meant, in theory, that Ralegh, assuming proprietorial and feudal rights over Virginia on the basis of his 1584 patent, was installing Manteo as his feudal sub-tenant in the place which had formerly been occupied by Wingina.

(3) *Sunday following:* 18 August was a Monday and the Sunday following the 24th.

(4) *our shippes had unlanded:* the pinnace, with the ships' boats which were being left behind, evidently acted as a tender to convey goods from Port Ferdinando to the creek near the fort site.

(5) *a tempest at northeast:* this was a danger-point for vessels lying off the Banks since they were very likely to drive ashore or on to one of the capes or their attendant shoals.

(6) *controversies rose betweene the Governour, and Assistants:* lacking the full document of 7 January 1587 it is impossible to say whether the respective authority to be exercised by the governor and his assistants was set out in detail. Normally, the head of a company (or expedition) was expected to take the advice of his assistants (or council of war), but did not invariably do so.

(7) *factors:* there was an obvious need for the company to have factors in England, but three of the twelve assistants had already been left behind for this purpose.

Page 103. (1) *slander . . . him:* without knowing something of White's position in England we can say nothing about his personal enemies, but from Harriot's picture of the situation it is quite probable that he, as one of the supporters of continued colonization, had won the dislike of a number of Lane's men who had turned against the scheme.

(2) *to remove 50. miles . . . into the maine:* see p. 126.

(3) *beeing . . . from them but three daies:* presumably during the Dasemunkepeuc expedition and not on the earlier visit to Croatoan.

Page 104. (1) *five and twentieth of August:* 'the 25 of August 1587' (*PN*, III (1600), 285). This testimonial is the first formal document to survive which originated in an English settlement on the mainland of North America.

(2) *the same day:* White's calendar is somewhat confused, unless he is using a sea day, running from noon to noon.

(3) *Capestone:* capstan.

(4) *infortunate:* 'unfortunate' (*PN*, III (1600), 286).

(5) *leese:* lose.

Page 105. (1) *for purchase:* prize-taking.

(2) *any boate to goe a shoare:* all the ships' boats apparently having been left with the settlers.

(3) *Dingen Cushe:* 'Dingen a Cushe' (*PN*, III (1600), 286), Dingle, on the south side of the peninsula across which White rode.

Page 106. (1) *Anno Domini 1587:* the year is presumably that within which White completed his narrative, possibly before 31 December and certainly before 25 March 1588.

XII

Page 107. (1) *1587 Virginia Colonists: PN* (1589), pp. 770–1, collated with III (1600), 287 (VIII (1904), 420–3), where the order of the names has been altered. Internal evidence would suggest that only John White could have compiled the list in its present form. It may be suggested that he used as a basis a list drawn up before the settlers left England (forgetting to remove his own name, and those of George Howe and Simon Fernandes), to which he added the names of those born in Virginia before giving it to Hakluyt. No detailed evidence of the origin and social class of the settlers has yet been found, but William S. Powell, 'Roanoke colonists and explorers:

Page 107. (1)—*contd.*

an attempt at identification', *North Carolina Historical Review*, XXXIV (1957), 202–26, is suggestive on possible lines of research.

An elementary analysis suggests that there were fourteen families, comprising perhaps thirty-six people, among the settlers. It is curious that no girls, except Virginia Dare, are distinguished as such and that there is not more than one boy of the same surname. The implication (strengthened by the high proportion of unattached men) may well be that part of the family was, in a number of cases, left in England to be brought out later. The unattached boys and women are likely, in some cases at least, to have been servants. Final figures are eighty-five men, less one dead (George Howe) and two returned (John White and Simon Fernandes), seventeen women and eleven children, making 113 brought from England and 110 left by White, plus two children born on Roanoke Island and two Indians, the total left behind being 114.

(2) *John White:* all that is known or can be usefully suggested is in P. H. Hulton and D. B. Quinn, *The American drawings of John White*, I (1964), 12–24.

(3) *Ananias Dare:* W. S. Powell has established (loc. cit. pp. 225–6) that, son-in-law of John White, husband of Elenor and father of Virginia, he was a resident of St. Bride's, Fleet Street, before his departure, having fathered an illegitimate son John who applied for letters of administration in 1594, and was granted them in 1597 (when presumption of his father's death seemed sufficient).

(4) *Simon Fernando:* he did not, and was not intended to, remain. John Nichols, William Fullwood, and James Plat, the three remaining assistants, were apparently left to manage the company's supplies in England. Nichols was still active in 1589 (cp. *RV*, I, 571).

Page 108. (1) *James Lasie:* possibly Anglo-Irish, where the name Lacy was fairly common, though it could well be English. It is highly probable that he is the James Lasie of the 1585 settlement (p. 21), and the only member of Lane's colonists, apart from Wright, to remain with the 1587 settlers.

Page 109. (1) *Manteo:* he could have returned to England either with Lane in Drake's fleet or with Grenville.

(2) *Towaye:* he too may well have accompanied Lane or Grenville in 1586.

XIII

Page 110. (1) *Voyage 1588: PN* (1589), pp. 771–3 (not reprinted in 1600).

(2) *first:* a printer's error for 'fifth', i.e. since 1584.

(3) *the Governors returne:* White wrote this narrative, like that of the 1587 expedition, partly in the third, partly in the first, person.

(4) *20. of November 1587:* this is evidently the date of White's meeting with Ralegh, as he had reached Southampton on 8 November. Ralegh may have been in London at this date, but the evidence is not precise.

(5) *appointed a pinnesse:* from this it would appear that Ralegh expected the pinnace to leave within a very few weeks at most. It remains somewhat obscure why it did not sail. Probably it was feared that a small, unescorted vessel was unlikely to survive Spanish attacks.

(6) *sir Richard Greenevil:* Grenville's fleet of seven or eight vessels was ready to sail at the end of March: the privy council order of 31 March forbade him to do so, that of 9 April which instructed him to join Drake at Plymouth would permit the detachment of such vessels as Drake would release. (*APC, 1588*, pp. 7, 27.)

(7) *Brave:* described by White as a bark, she was probably a French ship, taken in 1586 by Melchior Yeo, the *Brave* of Fecamp, Adam Mannier master, with silks, olives, hides, wool, and cochineal (possibly one of two taken and sent home by Grenville).

(8) *Roe:* not identified. The additional information from Pedro Diaz is in *RV*, II, 793-4.

Page 111. (1) *2. ships . . . we borded:* indiscriminate attacks on vessels of any or every nationality would seem to support White's implication that the crews were particularly irresponsible, Grenville having kept the best sailors for action in home waters.

Page 112. (1) *returned . . . to the chase of the Hulke:* they were at this time, according to Diaz about 30 leagues from Madeira.

Page 113. (1) *slaine on both sides 23. of the chiefest men:* Diaz says that the French boarding party numbered thirty, and that the greater number on both sides had been killed and wounded.

(2) *cabbens:* cabins, provided for the planters, which in some way obstructed the field of fire against boarding parties.

Page 114. (1) *7. of May:* a slip, for the 8th, which was Wednesday and is required by the narrative.

(2) *Chavell key:* between Lundy Island and Hartland Point, near to Clovelly Quay.

XIV

Page 115. (1) *White to Hakluyt: PN,* III (1600), 287-8, enclosing the narrative of the 1590 voyage.

Page 115. (2) *yeere . . . 1590:* White's use of calendar dating here (rather than English style which would make this date 1589) would indicate that he is doing the same with the date of the letter (i.e. it is 4 February 1593, not 4 February 1593–4, English style).

(3) *three ships:* the *Hopewell, Little John,* and *John Evangelist.*

(4) *all ships thorowout England:* the 'restraint and staye' of all shipping was the result of instructions from the privy council on 1 February 1590 (*APC, 1589–90,* pp. 341–2; E. P. Cheyney, *History of England, 1588–1603,* I, 529–30).

(5) *license of the Queenes Majestie:* no such licence has been traced. William Sanderson's claim that he was responsible for obtaining the pass is not irreconcilable with White's story of his approach to Ralegh, since Sanderson was Ralegh's man of business and probably undertook the negotiation on his behalf. But Sanderson implies clearly that the licence was granted to him and to John Watts. (See *RV,* II, 705–6.)

(6) *3000 pounds:* Sanderson gives the sum as £5,000 and implies that the captains and masters of the ships were parties to the bond and that it was executed. White says nothing of the additional obligation to accept the consortship of the *Moonlight,* Sanderson's own ship, though he admits that they left her behind in England.

Page 116. (1) *nothing lesse:* for 'nothing more'? The prominence which the sailors gave to White in their dealings with the Spaniards and their frequent references to the intended relief of the colony (*Further English voyages,* pp. 253–4, 256) do not suggest, whatever the element of bluff involved, that they considered the Virginia visit of no importance.

(2) *the order set downe by Sir Walter Ralegh:* the *Moonlight,* being Sanderson's ship, and probably having some supplies for the colonists when she left in May, made no move to get to Virginia ahead of Watts's ships, and it is unlikely that the instructions, whether written by Ralegh or Sanderson, specified too particularly when the vessels must leave the Caribbean.

(3) *fift & last voiage to Virginia:* on the basis of our present knowledge (unless Hakluyt altered his text) White is a sound authority for his having been on the 1584 voyage as well as those of 1585–6, 1587, 1588, and 1590.

(4) *my wealth were answerable to my will:* the implications are that White had got all the money that the London syndicate of 1589, or Ralegh, would supply for the Virginia venture and had eaten substantially into his own resources.

(5) *Newtowne in Kylmore:* Newton in Kilmore, or the Great Wood, where he was a tenant of the Munster plantation undertaker, Hugh Cuffe, about 9 miles north-west of Edmund Spenser's castle of Kilcolman. A few traces of a castle, possibly that occupied by White, remain at Newton, barony of

Explanatory Notes

Orrery and Kilmore, Co. Cork. All further knowledge of White's life remains conjectural. (See P. H. Hulton and D. B. Quinn, *The American drawings of John White*, I (1964), 21–3.)

XV

Page 117. (1) *White's Narrative of the 1590 Voyage: PN*, III (1600), 288–95, being sent to Hakluyt by John White with the letter dated 4 February 1593.

(2) *Hopewell: alias* the *Harry and John* of London, Abraham Cocke captain, Robert Hutton master, the flagship of the squadron; the *John Evangelist* of London, William Lane captain, a pinnace; the *Little John, alias* the *John* of London, Christopher Newport captain. All three belonged to 'John Wattes and Company of London merchants' and held letters of reprisal against the Spaniards from the Lord High Admiral.

(3) *Shallops:* the shallop was a large boat or small pinnace used for coastal exploration. (See William A. Baker, *Sloops and shallops* (Barre, Mass., 1966), pp. 1–19.)

(4) *Cape Cantyn and the Bay of Asaphi:* Cape Cantin (32° 40′N. lat.) and the Bay of Safi (or Asfi) (32° 20′N. lat.).

(5) *a double flyboat:* this ship, taken by Captain Newport, was evidently sent home with a prize-crew.

Page 118. (1) *the Salvages:* for some account of the survival of the Island Caribs in Dominica see Sir Harry Luke, *Caribbean circuit* (1950), pp. 123–33.

(2) *Admirall and our Pinnesse: Hopewell* and *John Evangelist.*

(3) *passage, lying betwene the Virgines:* the Virgin Passage 'is situated between the islets and reefs of the eastern end of Culebra Island and Savana islet, about 8 miles eastward' (*West Indies Pilot*, II (1942), 98).

Page 119. (1) *hoping to take some of the Domingo fleete:* the Santo Domingo squadron normally joined the homeward bound fleets at Havana, proceeding by way of Cape San Antonio at the western end of Cuba. White here suggests that it was, however, anticipated that it might double eastwards through the Mona Channel, or might pass between Hispaniola and eastern Cuba to the north coast. Saona, off the western end of Hispaniola, was a suitable base for keeping watch for shipping leaving or entering Santo Domingo.

(2) *we departed . . . for Cape Tyburon:* the *Little John* and the Spanish frigate were assigned to watch the eastern end of Hispaniola while the *Hopewell* and the *John Evangelist* went on to the western end, presumably in case the Santo Domingo squadron evaded the patrol based on Saona.

(3) *the Pinnesse . . . set upon with one of the kings Gallies:* the governor of Hispaniola, Lope de Vega Portocarrero, reported, 'I compelled one galley

Explanatory Notes

Page 119. (3)—*contd.*
to go out, furnishing it some men from the townspeople. It met an English ship off the Island of Puerto Rico and fought her for a while using artillery. The ship was in good condition and the galley was poorly armed and so did not dare to come to close quarters. The result was to drive the Englishman from here, where he was on the course which must be followed by all vessels from Spain.' 24 June/4 July. (*Further English voyages*, p. 245.)

(4) *Whitsunday:* 6 June.

Page 120. (1) *an expert Pilot . . . a Mountainer . . . a Vintener:* the pilot was Anton Martin, a native of Tenerife in the Canaries. He had been jailed in Santo Domingo on a charge of casting away a ship, but was released on parole for Easter. He induced a resident of Santo Domingo to buy the frigate with the object of going on a salvage expedition to La Beata. He then slipped away with the Indian herdsman and the vintner. The latter were later released but Martin appears to have joined the *Hopewell*'s crew (ibid., pp. 250–1).

(2) *Captaine Lane had taken the shippe:* she was the *Trinidad*, of 60 tons by the Spanish reckoning, Blas Lopez master, Marcos de Escobar owner.

(3) *came to us at Cape Tyburon:* William Sanderson's *Moonlight*, Edward Spicer captain, sent out to aid the Roanoke Island colony. Spicer had been master of the flyboat in the 1587 voyage.

(4) *Pinnesse . . . Master Harps . . . Captaine:* the *Conclude*, Joseph Harris (not Harps) captain, owned by Thomas Middleton and his partners.

(5) *a fleete of 14 saile:* commanded by Captain Vicente González.

(6) *Vizadmirall of the Spanish fleete: Buen Jesus* for the capture of which see *RV*, II, 642–6, 695–703. The Spanish evidence is in *Further English voyages*, pp. lxxvii, 245–6, 249–54.

Page 121. (1) *what was become of our Viceadmirall . . . and two Frigates:* the *Conclude* was with them; the *Little John*, the *John Evangelist* and the two small frigates had chased González's ships to the harbour of San Juan de la Vega, Jamaica, but the *Trinidad* disappeared.

(2) *fitting the Prize to be sailed with us:* Robert Hallett was given command of the *Buen Jesus* with a prize crew drawn from the *Hopewell*, the *Moonlight*, and the *Conclude*.

(3) *Cape S. Anthony:* Cape San Antonio was evidently the next agreed rendezvous. It was well placed for watching for the fleets making for Havana. The galleys patrolling from Havana were not permitted to go beyond the Cape (ibid., p. 261).

(4) *Moonelight our Pinnesse:* White evidently wrote 'the Moonlight her Pinnesse', i.e. the *Conclude*.

170

(5) *Captaine Cooke:* Captain Abraham Cocke.

(6) *22 saile . . . bound for Havana:* this was the *galeones* fleet under Oribe de Appallua which reached Havana on 19/29 July (ibid., p. 253).

(7) *the Southside of Cuba:* correctly, on the north-west side of Cuba (ibid., p. 250).

(8) *Matanças:* Matanzas was evidently the next rendezvous. The headland is likely to have been the high hill, Pan de Matanzas (*West Indies Pilot,* III, 351–3).

(9) *three small Pinnasses . . . richly loaden:* if White is correct the pinnaces are likely to have been stragglers from de Rada's *flota* which had entered Havana on 3/13 July (*Further English voyages,* p. lxxviii).

(10) *Navaza:* this fixes the place (Navassa is about 30 miles west of Cape Tiburon) where the *Buen Jesus* was taken.

Page 122. (1) *not finding any of our consorts at yᵉ Matanças:* it appears that a brief call was made at Cape Hicados, east of Matanzas, probably in a last effort to try to link up with their missing consorts (who were now only a few days behind). There five Spaniards were put ashore (ibid., p. 253).

(2) *helpe of the current . . . eddie currents . . . to the South and Southwest:* the Gulf Stream in the Florida Channel is 95 nautical miles wide with a velocity of 3½ knots (R. E. Coker, *The great and wide sea* (1947), pp. 126–30). White's is the earliest recorded observation of the coastal counter current (cp. Henry Chapin and F. G. Walton Smith, *The ocean river* (1953), pp. 108, 140–1).

(3) *disbocked:* disembogued, emerging from a channel to open sea.

(4) *Mooneshine:* a slip for the *Moonlight.*

(5) *our prize . . . sayled directly for England:* White does not necessarily imply that the *Buen Jesus* was intended to go to Virginia, but merely that Hallett did not observe the usual courtesies at parting. Several witnesses later implied that it was intended she should sail directly home.

(6) *fowle weather:* typical of the hurricane season.

(7) *we tooke the height of the same:* taking the meridian height of the sun with the quadrant or cross-staff from which latitude was calculated.

(8) *Monday the 9 of August:* Monday was 10 August, so that White's reckoning was a day out.

(9) *35 degrees of latitude:* 35° N. is probably too high. The description would fit the Carolina Outer Banks either north or south of Cape Lookout at 34° 40′N.), although either Core Sound or Bogue Sound is now well over a mile wide (see map at end).

Page 123. (1) *a breach . . . into the Sea:* this is an inlet distinguished by water breaking on a bar or shoals nearby. In this instance the shoals are those of the

Page 123. (1)—*contd.*

modern Cape Hatteras and known as the Diamond and Outer Shoals. They have shifted south and west (see map at end).

(2) *This breach is in 35 degr. & a halfe:* the inlet, just north of the modern village of Buxton, which was probably known to the Indians as Chacandepeco. The true latitude was 35° 16′ N.

(3) *fret:* a strait or inlet.

(4) *Hatorask, in 36 degr. and one third:* Hatarask or Port Ferdinando was at 35° 50′ N.

(5) *three leagues from the shore:* probably a slip of White's for 'miles'.

(6) *smoake:* the fires may have been caused by Indians smoking out deer, but at this time of the year they are more likely to have been caused by the sun burning dried vegetation.

Page 124. (1) *Kindrikers mountes:* Kenricks Mounts were high sand dunes just north of Cape Kenrick, the 'false Hatteras' of White's maps, now represented by Wimble Shoals and a water-swept patch of bank north of the settlement of Rodanthe (see map at end). A Captain Kenrick was later in Ralegh's service, though the name could have come from an Indian source.

(2) *where we landed:* they had landed on the southern side of the Port Ferdinando Inlet and had walked southwards along Hatarask Island in the direction of Cape Kenrick.

(3) *digge in those sandie hilles for fresh water:* though there are no deep wells on the Banks some of the higher dunes contain more or less impermeable strata, creating, for example, the fresh-water pond, formerly much larger, behind the Kill Devil Dunes at Nags Head.

(4) *the Sea brake extremely on the barre:* Lane said in 1585 there was 12 ft. of water on the bar at high water, but with a north-easterly wind raising the water against the outgoing current high seas would be caused.

Page 125. (1) *were saved by Captain Cookes meanes:* Abraham Cocke's bravery and resourcefulness are a measure of his experience as well as of his character (cp. Sir William Foster, *The voyages of Sir James Lancaster to Brazil and the East Indies, 1591–1603* (1940)).

(2) *we overshot the place:* it is evident that they made their way up Roanoke Sound to the east of the island and not by Croatan Sound to the west. They intended to land on Shallowbag Bay, near Baum Point, from which the fort site would lie north-west.

(3) *Northpoint of the Iland:* North West Point.

(4) *1586:* sic for '1587'.

Page 126. (1) *to remove from Roanoak 50 miles into the maine:* either north to Chesapeake Bay or west and then north-west up the Chowan river.

(2) *in sundry houses:* the site of the houses has not been established by excavation, but it may probably be implied that they lay between the 1585 fort and the Indian village, the sequence from North West Point south-eastwards being—village, houses, fort, only the ditch of which has been excavated and the banks reconstituted.

(3) *enclosed with a high palisado:* the new enclosure (a stockade without a ditch) was some little distance from the old fort site, to the north-west of the fort ditch as excavated.

(4) *such like heavie things:* to have left cannon and shot was not surprising, as it could not easily be carried by boat, but to leave iron bars and pigs of lead, which were necessary for the forge, which the settlers are likely to have had, and for bullet-making, may argue some haste in departure.

(5) *the poynt of the Creeke:* to the east of the stockade, probably where a sandspit now projects into Roanoke Sound. The shoreline has, however, been substantially eroded.

(6) *Pinnisse . . . and small Ordinance:* this is the only indication that the pinnace had been left with the colonists. If she was at their disposal the colonists were clearly much more mobile than they would otherwise have been. The removal of the smaller pieces of artillery would have been easy with a pinnace.

(7) *made two yeeres past:* taken literally, 1588, which makes no sort of sense. Even if we take it to mean 1587 it appears very unlikely that Philip Amadas had been with the expedition of that year. What White is most likely to have meant is 'two years before I was here last', i.e. 1585.

(8) *Chests . . . carefully hidden . . . frames of some of my pictures and Mappes:* White's emphasis on the care of his belongings during his absence in England is recorded (p. 103), and it is clear that he did not blame the planters for leaving his possessions behind, as they had done their best to safeguard them. The equipment he specifies is that of a man of some education and position and is a slight sidelight on his biography. The fact that he mentions his framed maps and pictures ties the painter of the 1585–6 colony firmly with the governor of the 1587 settlement.

Page 127. (1) *their safe being at Croatoan:* White's assumption that the settlers had gone to Croatoan was a reasonable one and explains, amongst other things, why he described in detail the soundings recently made at the mouth of the channels dividing Hatarask and Croatoan Islands (p. 123). The main Indian settlement on Croatoan was near the southern side of the inlet, near the present village of Buxton. The Croatoan Indians formed a tribe separate from those of Roanoke Island. Manteo would have returned there in August 1587. But White's belief, and the likelihood that some of the

Page 127. (1)—*contd.*
settlers visited Manteo, do not point to the whole colony having moved south instead of north.

(2) *the Captaine:* Abraham Cocke.

(3) *apecke:* apeake.

(4) *Kenricks mounts:* Cape Kenrick (see map at end).

(5) *Saint John:* San Juan de Puerto Rico.

Page 128. (1) *at our returne to visit . . . Virginia:* It seems highly probable that the original intention had been to winter with the colonists and return to the West Indies in the spring. Reversal of this procedure was practicable only with specialized knowledge of the Caribbean and some good fortune.

(2) *Master of the Moone-light:* John Bedford who had been in command since Captain Spicer's death.

(3) *Trynidad:* the choice of Trinidad is interesting. It had not yet been colonized by the Spaniards, nor was it frequented by the English. It was probably Cocke, from his experiences in South America and in the West Indies, who knew about its considerable possibilities as a winter base.

(4) *to meete with some English men of warre:* the plans for the converging of the English privateers on the Azores in September were known to the Spaniards.

(5) *lye atry:* holding the vessel hove to by means of sails set fore and aft.

(6) *a prize . . . taken by the John . . . in the Indies:* her prize crew was apparently drawn from both the *Little John* and from the *John Evangelist.* Her lading was wood and hides.

Page 129. (1) *the Captaines right arme strooken off:* Captain Christopher Newport lost his arm, or at least his hand. His lieutenant's name is not known. (See *Further English voyages*, pp. 247–9, 262; *RV*, II, 690–2.)

(2) *the other Spanish shippe . . . got away:* the first ship was that commanded by Juan de Borde (or Diego de Bode); the other was the *Nuestra Señora del Rosario*, Miguel de Acosta master (*Further English voyages*, pp. 247–9, 262).

(3) *Gallies . . . comming from Havana:* Cristobal de Pantoxa did leave Havana with the *San Agustín* and *Brava* galleys at about the right time and about 27 July/6 August picked up the crew of the stranded ship near where they had put ashore (ibid. pp. lxxviii, 250).

(4) *the Mary Rose:* the *Mary Rose* (600–800 tons) was the largest of the older ships in the Queen's fleet. J. A. Williamson, *Age of Drake* (1946), p. 379, mentions that Hawkins moved out to the Azores when Frobisher's squadron ran out of supplies.

(5) *the Hope . . . the Foresight:* the *Hope*, the *Nonpareil* (middle-sized ships, of 450–600 tons), the *Swiftsure* and the *Foresight* (smaller ships, under 400

tons) were all old vessels. The *Rainbow* was built in 1587, and was of about 400 tons (cp. Williamson, *Hawkins of Plymouth*, (1949), pp. 258, 260, 279).

(6) *Edward Bonaventure . . . Dainty*: the *Edward Bonaventure* of London, 250 tons, James Lancaster captain (Thomas Cordell owner); the *Merchant Royal* of London, 350 tons, Samuel Foxcroft captain (Thomas Cordell owner); the *Amity* of London, 100 tons, Walter Crunnelowe captain (Henry Colthurst and partners owners); the *Eagle* of London (tonnage not known; in 1589 her captain had been Henry White, and her owners Henry Colthurst and partners); the *Dainty*, galleon, was later to be taken by the Spaniards in the Pacific. Details will be found in K. R. Andrews, *Elizabethan privateering* (1964).

(7) *the king of Spaines fleete*: Pedro Menéndez Marqués had reached Spain with the treasure, unknown to the blockading forces, on 4/14 September, while on 31 July/9 August the decision had been taken in Havana to hold the fleets there until 1591 (*Further English voyages*, pp. lxxviii–lxxix).

Page 130. (1) *the coasts of Spaine and Portugal*: the decision to put back towards the Spanish coast probably meant that the English ships picked up a few extra prizes, but they did not stay long in Spanish waters, being home by the end of October.

(2) *Antony*: the *Anthony* may be the Earl of Cumberland's ship of that name, though she has not been heard of before 1593 (*Pilgrimes*, XVI, 18).

(3) *Sunday the 24. we came . . . to an anker at Plymmouth*: proceedings in the High Court of Admiralty as to the *Buen Jesus* had been set in motion by 11 October, and Captain Cocke and his master, Robert Hutton, were examined on 10 November, by which time it is probable that the *Hopewell* had been brought round to London.

Index of Subjects

178

Tulip tree, *Liriodendron tulipfera*, 155

Turkey, *Meleagris galloparvo*, 63, 84

turtles, 64, 94, 155; (land), Box, *Terrapene carolina carolina*; Chicken, *Dierochelys reticularia*; Mud, *Kinosternon subrubrum*; Musk, *Sternotherus odoratus*; Snapping, *Chelydra serpentina*; (sea), Loggerhead, Atlantic, *Caretta caretta caretta*; Kemp's, *C. kempi*; Green, *Chelonia mydas*; Leather-back, *Dermochelys coricea*

uppówoc, 58; *see* tobacco

Walnut trees, 7, 25, 51–2, 60, 64; Black walnut, *Juglans nigra*; *see also* Hickory

wapeih, 51; *see* Lemnian earth

wasebur, 53; *see* Pocone; Pokeweed

wassador, 31; *see* copper

wickonzówr, 55; *see* beans

Wild Potato Vine, *Ipomea pandurata*, 153

Willow trees, 65; Black, *Salix nigra* and *S. longpipes*; Harbison's, *S. Harbisonii*

winauk, 51; *see* sassafras

wine, 23, 89

Winter's Bark, *Cortex winteranus*, 133

Witch-hazel, *Hammamelis virginiana*, 65, 67

woad, 54, 89

Yaupon, *Ilex vomitoria*, 65; *see* holly

Yucca filamentosa, 150

Index of Persons and Places

Ooanoke or Blind town, Indian village, 26
Opossians, Indian tribe, 25
Oratina *see* Utina
Organes, Sierra de los, Cuba, 121, 129
Orista, Indian chief, 82, 83
Ortelius, Abraham, *Theatrum orbis terrarum*, 91
Osocan, Indian chief, 37, 41
Ottorasko *see* Hatarask
Oxenham John, expedition 1575, 17

Pamlico Sound, N. Car., xxi, 135
Pantoxa, Cristobal de, of Havana, 174
Paquype *see* Mattamuskeet
Pardo, Juan, captain expedition 1566–7, 158
Parmenius, Stephen, Hungarian poet, x
Parre, Thomas, 1585 colonist, 20
Pattenson, Hugh, 1587 colonist, 107
Payne, Henry, 1587 colonist, 108
Payne, Rose, 1587 colonist, 108
Peckham, Sir George, x
Pedro, a mulatto, 118
Pee Dee River, S. Car., 159
Pemisapan, Indian chief, 24, 29, 34–42; *see also* Wingina
Pena, Pierre, botanist, x
Petman, Nicholas, 1584 voyage, 12
Phevens, Thomas, 1587 colonist, 108
Philip II of Spain, 96
Philippes, William, 1585 colonist, 21
Phillippes, Thomas, 1585 colonist, 20
Pico, Azores Is., 130
Piemacum, Indian chief, 10
Pierce, Jane, 1587 colonist, 108

Pinos, I. of, Cuba, 121
Plat, James, assistant 1587, 166
Plymouth, xxi, xxiii, xxiv, xxv, 13, 19, 93, 130
Polyson, Michael, 1585 colonist, 20
Pomarie, Steven, 1585 colonist, 21
Pomeiooc, Indian village, 9, 18, 99, 101
Pomouik, Indian tribe, 10
Pooneno, Indian chief, 9
Poore, Richard, 1585 colonist, 20
Port Ferdinando, Carolina Banks, xx, xxi, xxii, xxiii, xxv, 133, 140; *see* Hatarask
Portocarrero, Lope de Vega, governor Hispaniola, 169
Port Royal river *see* Broad River
Portsmouth, 45, 81, 93, 106
Portugal, xvii, 14, 91, 92; bay of, 93, 98
Potano, Timacua tribe, 82, 83, 84
Potanon, Indian chief, 83
Potassi, Indian chief, 84
Potkin, Henry, 1585 colonist, 21
Powell, Anthony, sergeant major with Drake (1586), 79
Powell, Edward, 1587 colonist, 107
Powell, Wenefrid, 1587 colonist, 108
Powhatan, Indian chief, 137
Prat, John, 1587 child colonist, 108
Prat, Roger, 1587 colonist, 107
Prideaux,——, 1585 colonist, 20, 39
Privy council, xxiv, 167
Puercos, Rio de, Cuba, 121
Puerto de Plata, Hispaniola, 15, 139
Puerto Rico I., xxi, xxiii, 13–15, 95–6, 118, 132; town *see* San Juan de Puerto Rico
Purchas, Samuel, *Pilgrimes* (1625), xvii–xviii
Pysshokonnok, Indian village, 25

Supplemental Index to Preface

For a list of additional publications
write to
Historical Publications Section
Division of Archives and History
Department of Cultural Resources
109 East Jones Street
Raleigh, North Carolina 27611